The Victorian Home

The Victorian Home

*

JENNI CALDER

B. T. BATSFORD LTD
LONDON

To D.P.

and all those who sail in her

FIRST PUBLISHED 1977
© JENNI CALDER 1977
ISBN 0 7134 0817 0

SET IN 11/13 PT MONOPHOTO PLANTIN LIGHT
BY TRADESPOOLS, LTD., FROME
PRINTED IN GREAT BRITAIN BY
THE ANCHOR PRESS LTD., TIPTREE, ESSEX
FOR THE PUBLISHERS
B. T. BATSFORD LTD.,
4 FITZHARDINGE STREET, LONDON W1H 0AH

Contents

List of Illustrations

Acknowledgements

The Author and Publishers would like to thank the following for their kind permission to use illustrations from their collections:

The Radio Times Hulton Picture Library 1, 2, 6, 8, 13, 17, 20, 21, 28, 29, 32–34, 36, 37, 44, 51–54, 61, 62, 67, 76, 77, 80, 81, 85, 86, 93, 95; The Mansell Collection 7, 12, 15, 19, 30, 35, 58, 89, 99, 105; National Trust 10; Courtault Institute of Art 14; Victoria and Albert Museum 22, 49, 50, 73, 96; Museum of London 27; Mary Evans Picture Library 39, 42, 46, 57, 63; Science Museum, London 40, 43, 47, 100, 101, 104; Trustees of the Tate Gallery 60, 69, 72; National Portrait Gallery, London 82, 91, 97; Glasgow Art Gallery 70; Aberdeen Art Gallery 71; Weidenfeld and Nicolson Ltd 78; Society of Antiquaries of London 83.

The remainder are from the Publisher's collection.

The Place of Peace

In many of Dickens's novels, simultaneously comfortable and disturbing images of Victorianism, there is the quintessence of home. It is suggested by a young woman, cheerful and busy, managing an orderly household with housekeeping keys dangling from her waist, and work basket awaiting any leisure moments. Home is a place of comfort and refuge, but also of activity and responsibility. It represents a concentration of effort, good-natured effort, effort that benefits immeasurably the human beings the home contains. The home is a manageable unit of living, manageable by a woman; ideally a place from which friction can be abolished, where standards of behaviour and taste can be preserved, into which vulgarity and ugliness should not intrude. It is an environment that nurtures the expression of the best human qualities and encourages the most praiseworthy human activities.

This is how Dickens wanted to see the home, and on occasions represented it. The picture of the Victorian home in most of the fiction of the time, and many of us become first acquainted with Victorian England through its fiction, is essentially an environment maintained by women and controlled by men. The ideal of the home is most frequently enunciated by men: women concern themselves with how to create the ideal, and the practical problems were legion, men with the fact that the ideal should be created. Home and the female were inevitably intimately associated. Home without a woman in it lacked a crucial dimension. Even today, the word suggests the activities of the wife and mother, and the man who has a talent for home-making is accorded with virtues that are not only domestic but feminine.

Victorian attitudes to marriage reflect this understanding of the home as a place occupied by a woman who was, ideally, both decorative and useful. For a woman marriage meant the acquisition of an 'establishment', her own place, financed by her husband, but unless he was excessively tyrannical, like Mr Murdstone in *David Copperfield*, published in 1850, a place where she had at least some freedom of choice and activity, which she might not have had at all in the parental home. The man acquired a licit sex life (most middle-class Victorian men did not marry until they were 30 or so, and there were, tacitly, accepted means of avoiding celibacy), a situation where someone else was responsible for the provision of food and comforts, a decorative symbol of achievement and, perhaps most important, a solidity and a status which society approved, indeed deemed almost a necessity for the pursuit of a conventionally acceptable career, or occupation, or simply existence.

Marriage without a home was not so acceptable. Marriage in digs, or rented rooms, anywhere that the objects of permanency could not be set up, where the symbols of comfort and status could find no place, was bound to be dubious. In Dickens' *Our Mutual Friend* (1865), the dreadful Lammles, consumed by ambitions for wealth and social acceptance, live in rooms while keeping up a pretence that they are awaiting the 'doing up' of their own house. 'Their own house' does not exist, but it improves their status greatly if people think it does. Ownership did not matter so much, as rented houses were the rule rather than the exception throughout the Victorian period, but control did. Landladies were scarcely likely to be accessories to social success.

John Ruskin who, although his main concern was art commented on a great many things to do with taste and life-style, wrote this in 1865, about the home.

> This is the true nature of home—it is the place of Peace; the shelter, not only from all injury, but from all terror, doubt, and division. In so far as it is not this, it is not home; so far as the anxieties of the outer life penetrate into it, and the inconsistently-minded, unknown, unloved, or hostile society of the outer world is allowed by either husband or wife to cross the threshold, it ceases to be home; it is then only a part of that outer world which you have roofed over and lighted fire in.[1]

This is the home as refuge—its primary function, according to Ruskin. It cannot be separated from Ruskin's view of women—his main topic in *Sesame and Lilies*, from which this is taken, is women—for he considers it the woman's function to preside over this refuge. It is the woman who must ensure that the home remains 'a place of Peace'. The outside world, what we might think of as the 'real' world, is to be excluded. The home, and this means also marriage, is the salvation of modern man, because there he can forget the pressures and strains of the outside world, the commercial world, the competitive world, and relax, replenish his spirit, find comfort and solace. The modern woman, of course, was not to have any dealings with the real world. She could only preside over man's refuge, create man's refuge, if she were unsullied by the horrors that lay without. Inevitably, both the man who had no woman, mother, wife, sister, daughter, to create his home for him, and the woman who was without a man to create a home for, were, in a sense, homeless.

Countless pieces of Victorian writing, fiction and non-fiction, echo Ruskin's attitude. Home was a refuge, and women made it such. They could not make it such if they were allowed beyond its walls. It was used as a major anti-feminist argument. If women became involved in the same turmoil and frenzy that men wished to escape from when they entered their own front doors, how could they carry on their essential function as guardians of comfort and replenishment? And this function was essential, it was felt, not just for the individual, but to maintain the moral fabric of society. Ruskin's insistence on the home as a refuge was not just the need for a place of escape, but a belief in the moral necessity of peace.

We are by now not surprised at the Victorian attitude to women. What is equally striking is the attitude to work. Increasingly, since the Industrial Revolu-

1   Thomas Cubitt, the most famous and energetic of the Victorian speculative builders

tion, those who were not 'working class' had to work for a living. The leisure classes were getting proportionately smaller. The expanding middle class was the result of making money, and money-making, that devastating achievement of the Industrial Revolution, meant work. If making money had previously been the results of commerce and trade—it was merchants, above all, who bought their way into government power and up the social ladder—by the beginning of Victoria's reign it was increasingly manufacturers, industrialists, railway tycoons, and the bankers who were necessary to these, who were following those paths. Commerce had always been frowned on by gentility—look at Jane Austen's novels for a crisp expression of this. But if trade was unacceptable to the English upper classes, and even more so to the genteel middle class, who were that much more vulnerable, how much less acceptable was industry—until the wealth and power that industry could bring became undeniably obvious.

Work, then, was coloured by these attitudes. Commerce and industry were vulgar. They brought one into contact with coarse people and habits, their premises were inevitably dirty, often noisy; the demeaning and demoralizing effects of factory labour on the workers were only too clear to anyone who came close enough to see—which was something to be avoided, if possible. At the same time work was, in itself, good. Hard work was morally improving, and brought rewards (sometimes) that were both desirable and right. The 'work ethic' was a potent force. Hard work was good for the individual, good for production, good for trade, good for the country. The idle were condemned, but leisure was approved. Idleness was a sin, but leisure was the reward for those who proved they deserved it. The working class was encouraged to spend leisure hours, such as they were, in self-improvement, in attending night schools and libraries for instance. But the middle class tended to assume the right to less demanding pastimes, and leisure was a significant part of status aspiration. Hard work could buy status, but the more status one bought the less desirable it became to acknowledge what money-making involved.

Most of the middle class, especially in London and the south of England, were not involved directly in industry, but they very often were involved in professions whose livelihood depended on thriving production and trade, bankers, accountants, lawyers and the many, concentrated in London, who were involved in large scale merchant activities, the importers and exporters, highly respected and powerful, and their growing numbers of clerks, office boys and messengers who, if they were diligent and lucky, might rise and become themselves members of a secure and confident middle class. The traders, too, the shop-keepers, became increasingly conscious that money could purchase status, and inevitably, with the expansion of industry and overseas trade, and improvements in communications, shops grew, and by the second half of the nineteenth century the department store and chain store magnate took his place amongst Victorian successes.

But all this meant work, and it meant the earning of money, and the Victorians never did come to terms with their contradictory attitudes to these activities. Even when they saw the success and status that wealth could buy they could not get over the feeling that though hard work was righteous selling one's labour was not, and in

2   *Feminine activities in the Drawing Room, c. 1880*

some way adulterated life and involved one in a world that was dirty, impure, unfit for what was best in humanity. In order to preserve a moral and respectable view of oneself, there had to be an alternative, an alternative that preserved and emphasized the values that work seemed to destroy. That alternative was the home. From the perspective of the 1970s it might appear that the Victorians were only able to maintain this belief by ignoring, or distorting, the essential nature of family life. But for the Victorians family life was, had to be, moulded by this self-preserving attitude to the home. For the bread-winning father it was unlikely to be considered tolerable that, on his return from the competitive and adulterating day's work, he should be confronted by the challenge of an insubordinate son, or the discomfort of an inefficient wife. Both wife and child had to be a part of the maintenance of the refuge.

It is worth reflecting on what home had been, and still was sometimes in rural areas, where work and life were intimately bound and shared the same values—though this was decreasingly so, as Thomas Hardy's novels, written towards the end of the century, were to show. Home had been, before the Industrial Revolution, to a much greater extent the centre of life's activities. The urban experience, in which the division between home and work is characteristic, was not typical. Craftsmen worked in their homes. The leisured classes amused themselves in and around their homes. Only in London and one or two equivalent centres, Edinburgh for instance, was it customary for the men to seek their entertainment outside their own home or the homes of friends. The life of children was not dominated by school and education, and they were less likely to be excluded from adult activities. In the Middle Ages both the work and the play of adults and children were shared. There was little distinction between adults' games and children's games or, once a child was at all competent, between adults' work and children's work. As society and work became more complex, and activities inevitably more specialized, this was decreasingly the case. By the Victorian period middle- and upper-class children learned to be adults not by exposure to adult activity but by rigorous segregation and training. The governess only became necessary when mother, father and all the other adults who would have been present in the extended family of the medieval household, became remote.

In George Eliot's novel *Adam Bede* (1859) she describes the rural Midlands in the year 1790, drawing directly on her own experience of the locale and the way of life. In Poyser's farm we find just the unification of work and leisure which is disappearing in the next century. In and around the Poysers' kitchen all the essential activities of livelihood take place: brewing and butter-making, cooking and child-care, consultation and planning, eating and relaxation. The Poysers' kitchen is the hub of every aspect of life on the farm. The idea that when the men come in from the fields the door can be shut on their work is ludicrous. The idea that the women and children can be compartmentalized off into another area of life is equally ludicrous. Thirty years later Hardy would show that this kind of unity was fast disappearing, had already disappeared. But it had genuinely existed, for many centuries, as a deep-rooted feature of ordinary life. The Victorians on the whole had no interest in reviving a unity of life and work, though there were movements that tried to recapture something like it, particularly associated with William Morris. Yet the disunity tormented many Victorian thinkers and writers, some of them unconsciously. Dickens, for instance, did not at all like much of what he saw of the effects of cash and industry and commercial progress, but he, perhaps more than any other Victorian writer, fostered a sentimental image of the home as a place of cosiness and exclusion of the nasty world outside: a place of escape and not of confrontation, or even of reflection on the realities. Bright fires, closed doors, heavy curtains were all part of the protection against the cold commercial winds.

In *Dombey and Son* (1848) Dickens creates in the character of Mr Dombey a highly successful business man who cannot shed his business personality. He is a business man in the home as well as in the office, and blights the household. At the end of the book a reformed Dombey has learnt to relax in the home of his married daughter, enjoying his grandchildren, the world of business firmly excluded. In other words Dickens reinforced the disunity of life by insisting that to allow the world of finance inside the home was to destroy it. Dickens both exposed the fragmentation of Victorian life, and supported it. The sentimentalized image of home is very much a part of this fragmentation. Indeed, in some respects, life within the home was itself fragmented, and the cosy image was a way of suggesting a unifying symbol of life in the home. It is significant that Dickens tends to be at his most cosily sentimental when he is describing modest establishments—in which he himself did not live—where neither too much money, nor too much space, nor too much ostentation could interfere with a comfortable harmony.

But it was not only the contamination of money, the buying and selling of things and the buying and selling of labour, that it was desirable to shut out of the home. Society itself was ugly. The aspect of the urban world was not nice to look upon. There was dirt, there was noise, there was human excrement, there was starvation, there was crime, there was violence, all on the surface, all very close to the senses of all who ventured beyond their own front doors. To have an interior environment that enabled such things to be forgotten was a priority of middle-class aspiration.

The typical middle-class urban dwelling of the early Victorian period was likely to be a terrace house, and likely to be relatively new. Rapid urban expansion was a feature of late eighteenth- and early nineteenth-century Britain, and much of this expansion was for the accommodation of the middle classes. Edinburgh's New Town was abuilding in the 1820s, and although many of its first inhabitants were aristocrats, landowners and members of the prestigious legal profession, it became very much the residential area for the upper middle class, of merchants for instance, moving away from the port of Leith where their money was made, and of university professors. Thomas Cubitt, the great builder and planner, was building extensively in Bloomsbury and Belgravia in the 1820s, Bloomsbury less elevated in tone than Belgravia, slightly Bohemian. Thackeray's novels are an excellent indication of attitudes to the Bloomsbury and Tottenham Court Road area. In *Vanity Fair* (1847) Russell Square, an earlier development, is considered round

3   Benevolence and security exude from du Maurier's Punch *illustration, 1878*

about 1815 as not quite the appropriate residence for a successful business man. Cubitt wanted to put up houses for the socially elevated, but Belgravia was a much greater attraction for the status-conscious than Bloomsbury. The result was that many of his Bloomsbury houses remained empty for long periods. But a less aspiring family of more modest means, or an artistic one (Bloomsbury is studded with plaques to distinguished men and women domiciled there), might have chosen Bloomsbury in the earlier part of Victoria's reign, preferably one of Cubitt's developments, perhaps Gordon Square or Tavistock Square. Squares were preferable, as the suggestion of space and openness added grandeur to the terraces. Later Tottenham Court Road and the streets off it to the south became the scene of the working-class struggles depicted by George Gissing, seedy and run-down.

Belgravia dominates throughout the period as the fashionable environment for residence in the centre of London. Cubitt developed much of the Grosvenor estate, and the acceptability of his houses was due not so much to their design, which stuck largely to the by that time widely adopted neo-classical style with variations in detail and ornamentation, as the thoroughness of his planning and layout, and all-important attention to the amenities, not to say essentials, of drains, water supply, street lighting, and so on. Cubitt was a speculative builder in the great age of speculative builders, but he shared none of the vices that are usually attributed to these beings. While some new developments, put up fast to accommodate a rapidly growing urban population, disintegrated into slums, the distinction of Cubitt's solid building remains.

Bloomsbury then, and Belgravia, developments in Chelsea and Kensington, in Islington and Highbury and Kentish Town, and later south of the river as more bridges were built and omnibus routes were opened and the railways began to fan out southwards, this was where the building was going on in London, building, that is, for the upper and middle classes. Workmen's cottages were going up around the proliferating gas works and railway yards, and small semi-detached villas for the not so well-off began to snake out along the roads and railway lines leading out of the city, but for the respectable, not to say the ambitious, the areas of acceptability were clearly defined. 'Don't let him take you anywhere beyond Eccleston Square', a character in Trollope's *Small House at Allington* (1862) advises an about-to-be-married woman. The couple settle for a fictitious Princess Royal Crescent near Hyde Park, and this is how Trollope describes it.

> A residence had been taken for the couple in a very fashionable row of buildings abutting upon the Bayswater Road, called Princess Royal Crescent. The house was quite new, and the street being unfinished had about it a strong smell of mortar, and a general aspect of builders' poles and brickbats; but, nevertheless, it was acknowledged to be a quite correct locality. From one end of the crescent a corner of Hyde Park could be seen, and the other abutted on a very handsome terrace indeed, in which lived an ambassador,—from South America,—and a few bankers' senior clerks, and a peer of the realm. We know how vile is the sound of Baker Street, and how absolutely foul to the polite ear is the name of Fitzroy Square. The houses, however, in those purlieus are substantial, warm, and of good size. The house in Princess Royal Crescent was certainly not substantial, for in these days substantially-built houses do not pay. It could hardly have been warm, for, to speak the truth, it was even yet not finished throughout; and as for size, though the drawing room was a noble apartment, consisting of a section of the whole house, with a corner cut out for the staircase, it was very much cramped in its other parts, and was made like a cherub, in this respect, that it had no rear belonging to it. 'But if you have no private fortune of your own, you cannot have everything', as the countess observed when Crosbie objected to the house because a closet under the staircase was to be asigned to him as his own dressing-room.[2]

A 'correct locality' did not necessarily mean a comfortable house, yet Victorian snobbery was often such that the address meant more than the comfort. The experience of the Crosbies, moving into their cold, cramped, unfinished house with building still going on around them, would have been shared by many anxious to move into acceptable quarters.

The terrace house itself was not well suited to a modest style of life. To live comfortably in such a house servants were a necessity, for the structure of the living quarters was ill-suited to the convenience of the houseworker. Terrace housing varied in height, but a house of three main storeys, a basement and an attic was fairly typical. In the basement would be kitchen, pantry and store rooms, laundry rooms, and space for the servants to eat, and relax if they had sufficient

4 *'Family Prayers' by Samuel Butler, 1864*

leisure time. On the ground floor would be the dining room, usually to the front, with perhaps a library, or a morning room, a room that could be used as an informal sitting room, at the back. Entrance hall and stair well would take up considerable space. The first floor was the drawing-room floor, containing the most important and most imposing room in the house. Often, as in the case of the house in Princess Royal Crescent, the drawing room extended from the front to the back of the house. Sometimes it was L-shaped. Sometimes there were two separate drawing rooms connected by folding doors, so that there could be space for large-scale entertaining. The next floor would contain bedrooms, with a less grand and space-consuming staircase than that which connected ground and first floors, and in the attic the servants slept. More lavish premises, some of Cubitt's villas in Belgravia for instance, would have more space, especially space specifically designed for the leisure pursuits of the gentlemen, smoking rooms, a billiards room perhaps. Larger houses would have more space for children, a schoolroom (sometimes housed in the attic), day and night nurseries. There might also be a sewing room, or a music room. But there was not much scope for individual interpretation of the function of the rooms. Between the kitchen at the bottom and the children and servants at the top the gradations of use were careful, and almost always consistent.

In order to run a house like this a great deal of movement was necessary, in and out of rooms, up and down stairs. In the earlier part of the period there were no bathrooms (there were WCs in newer houses, but these were a luxury; in the well-to-do Edinburgh New Town household of Robert Louis Stevenson's parents an outside privy was in use in the 1860s—the alternatives were commodes and chamber pots, which the servants had to empty) and hot water for washing, cleaning or shaving had to be carried up from the kitchen. The same was true of fuel for heating. Although there was gas street lighting in the 1820s gas wasn't installed in private houses until the 1840s, and even then it was at first suitable only for lighting, not for heating or cooking. If the lady of the house wanted tea in the drawing room it had to come up two flights of stairs. Elaborate meals had to come up one flight, and be kept hot, which involved placing serving dishes in hot water. On the whole, neither husbands nor wives, nor architects, designers, visitors, no one at all involved in the design or control of the household, was concerned to make things any easier for the servants. Servants were readily available, and could usually be replaced without difficulty if they failed to meet the standards required. They made up for the deficiencies in common sense in house design and organization. It took some time before architects thought of designing kitchens near to dining rooms, and including amenities that eased life for those who did the housework, and even longer before such things became customary—longer in Britain than in the United States, where domestic staff was harder to come by.

It does not take very much imagination to see that entertaining in a Victorian house of any size required an immense amount of work. A dinner for 12, say, with a vast number of courses, ranging through soup, fish, fowls, joints of beef and mutton, game, side dishes, elaborate puddings and dessert, the ingredients all requiring to be fresh and therefore bought the same day, and preferably hand-picked, the food requiring to be hot and served in the proper fashion, could not be undertaken without a well-drilled troop of servants. And entertaining, even on a small scale, was almost always formal. Informality suggested impropriety, and the further up the status scale a family crept the less allowable it was. In Edinburgh, when the denizens of the squalid but bustling Old Town moved down into the elegant New, they felt constrained to abandon their old practice of informal supper parties where the food was modest and there were no pretensions, and entertain with a formality that seemed more suited to the loftiness of Georgian ceilings and the spaciousness of Georgian squares and crescents. As etiquette hardened into an expression of class morality rather than of practical good manners the style of entertaining became a crucial test of status. But the housewife did have aids, apart from her servants, for if she lived in a city much of her preparation and provisioning could be undertaken by tradesmen. The buying of food ready-made, puddings, tarts and pastries for instance, was as customary then as it is now.

In most middle-class households the life that went on within the home was essentially female, and the home was inevitably the expression of what were then the conventional female activities. As the Victorian period matured Victorian houses tended to become more and more crammed with bulky furniture and countless objects whose usefulness was limited or non-existent. In other words there became increasingly less space for activity. In the households that Jane Austen describes, in the early years of the century, a supper party could become a dance with no trouble at all. As Victorian houses became more cluttered any way

5   *The old and very young are powerfully linked in William Powell Frith's 'Many Happy Returns of the Day'*

of passing the time that involved action became less likely. Sedentary occupations were the general rule, once the housekeeping responsibilities had been attended to. Lack of occupation was frowned on. A variety of female pursuits evolved that could be undertaken without stirring from a chair.

Housekeeping in a fairly well-to-do household would probably consist of giving instructions, perhaps unlocking store cupboards (the Victorian mistress rarely trusted her servants) and measuring out the provisions of the day, ordering the meals, and possibly some direct supervision of a particular task. But this would normally only be necessary in the case of an inadequately trained servant, or perhaps preparations for a very special event. It was important that the housewife should *know* how to do all that was necessary in the running of the house, however rarely it was necessary for her to do it. Housekeeping manuals of the period were adamant that the mistress of the house should be closely involved in the running of the house. Training servants was one of her most important tasks, and she could not do that if she were not acquainted with the tasks they would have to perform. It was generally agreed that she should be able to do some cooking, preserving, pastry-making and so on; in fact around the middle of the century there was a distinct movement to get middle-class women to participate more in housekeeping, cooking and child-care than they had tended to previously.

But apart from housekeeping and instructing the servants, and in wealthier homes a housekeeper would be employed to take on all such responsibilities, the

6   *The family at tea in the 1860s*

7   *Victorian paternalism in the 1890s*

lives of middle and upper-class women were often inactive. They would visit, and they would go for drives, walks infrequently. They would go shopping, though to shop for food was an activity it was preferable to have done by someone else. Outside the cities there was an increasing number of pastimes women could enjoy, croquet, archery, and later tennis, as well as the traditional riding, but these required space and quite a lot of money. The indoor sedentary pastimes required considerably less of both. A major occupation was needlework, usually decorative rather than practical. Most women would have their clothes made by a dressmaker, the actual stitching done by the notoriously sweated labour that milliners employed, and mending would often be done by an itinerant sewing woman who would come to the house. The nurse would look after the children's mending. So the ladies of leisure would spend their time doing a variety of fancy needlework, netting purses, embroidering pen cases, or doing Berlin wool work. If they were charitably inclined they might spend their time plain sewing, running up shirts and shifts for the children of the poor. But on the whole we can partly attribute the growing clutter of things in the Victorian household to the fact that many women had little to do but make great numbers of things of limited use or value. A painted fire screen, for the protection of delicate skins from hot fires, had a function, but a proliferation of painted fire screens was clearly not necessary.

Certain other kinds of creative activity were acceptable in the home, but anything that suggested commercialism or professionalism was frowned on. Ladies were taught to draw and paint, sing and play the piano, but it was not desirable that they should do these things too well. It was important to preserve amateurishness in case there could be any idea that such accomplishments could become money-earning skills. Of course, a number of novels show how enterprising middle-class ladies fallen on hard times tried to make a shilling or two by selling their sketches, but only dire necessity would drive the well-bred to such a course. Yet one can guess that a number of women would have been quite willing to sell their talents. It was well into the second half of the century before it was openly acknowledged as a sad truth that sometimes middle-class women, however well brought up, had to earn their own living. There gradually emerged an opinion that women should perhaps prepare for such an eventuality. A main object of marriage was to avoid such a fate, and the middle-class home as the habitat of such marriages generally saw only the more genteel and non-commercial occupations.

I have suggested a typical picture, but there were many exceptions, and of course it was only a minority that could afford to think in terms of life as a matter of passing time rather than getting through essential labour. As always the exceptions throw light on the limitations of the rule. Elizabeth Gaskell, novelist and minister's wife, reveals in her letters the intense activity and liveliness of her household. She was active in a very constructive way as the wife of a Unitarian minister in Manchester; she was a mother much involved with her children, she did her share of housekeeping and cooking, and pursued her own career, writing fiction that reflects the scope of her involvements. Her household was no formally constructed pattern of sedentary living, but a home full of action and lively relationships. Outside London, perhaps, this was more likely to be the case, but Manchester 'society', as Mrs Gaskell's own novels suggest, imposed its particular kind of formality.

For the wife who could not afford to buy labour, or could only afford a single servant (which would still put her into the middle-class bracket) there would be little time for leisure. The servant might perform the hardest and dirtiest of household tasks, the cleaning of grates and the scrubbing of floors, but there would be enough work remaining in the care of house and children to keep her fully occupied. We tend to think of the loneliness and tedium of the housewife's life as a twentieth-century phenomenon. But it was there with the Victorians, particularly in the lower middle-class household in suburban developments, where the wife and mother had to work very hard, was cautious of acquaintance with her neighbours, and was remote from community feeling. The development of a strong and positive family feeling can be seen partly as a response to this kind of isolation.

Generally the Victorian home did not accommodate male activities, apart from the casual pursuits of smoking, reading and card-playing. For most men the serious business of life went on elsewhere, in the office, in the club, or at other more dubious places of entertainment. The home was for relaxation after work, but very often what it offered was not very tempting. It is significant that for the men the leisure activities within the home were even more limited than for the women. Men didn't do needlework. They sometimes sang, but much less often did they play an instrument. There was a distinct suggestion of femininity in playing the piano, or

8   *The cosy fun of this staged photograph is slightly jarred by an ominously stuffed-looking cat*

the harp, or the flute, unless, of course, one was a professional musician, in which case one was a member of the rather dubious artistic fraternity which was not altogether respectable. There was writing, but most male writers of the Victorian period considered themselves professionals; it was the women who were amateurs, filling up their leisure hours by writing novels, or verses, or letters to their friends. Victorian sneers about 'lady novelists', that 'singular anomaly' as W. S. Gilbert was to put it, arose from the fact that either they were considered frivolous amateurs, in which case they couldn't be taken seriously, or professionals, in which case they were improper. But on the whole men occupied their leisure time by smoking, drinking and talking, and reading the newspapers, all of which they frequently found more congenial at the club than in the home.

But I am talking here of wealthier families. The phrase 'Victorian family' often suggests a more homogeneous and united group of people, parents and children gathered in the parlour to read *The Old Curiosity Shop* or bowdlerized Shakespeare together. And it was this kind of image of home life that many Victorians tried sedulously to reinforce, the family close, united, sharing the same interests and the same activities, with father as the grand artificer and mother as the glue that held it all together. This image fits more readily into the smaller, more modest Victorian house than into the grander terraces, into the suburban semi-detached, with its bit of garden and touch of gothic ornamentation, and father travelling to the city every day on the newly opened suburban line. By the middle of the century countless city suburbs were developing acres of this kind of house, modest but decent, often jerry-built, but with the outward symbols of respectability. Unlike the four or five-storey terrace house, which demanded the spaciousness of wide streets, airy squares, elegant crescents, such two-storey villas could be thrown up in narrow streets, laid out to get the most into the smallest space. The pleasanter suburbs, hoping to attract a 'higher class' of resident, planted out trees and called their streets avenues, and made attractive use of existing park and common land—in Clapham, for instance, yet another area where Thomas Cubitt's skilled hand was at work. But even these were built with little attention paid to amenities other than visual. Suburbs were developed with the assumption that residents would find in the city centres their entertainment, their culture, even their shopping. Shops in residential areas were considered lowering, especially certain kinds of shops, such as butchers, that might be both messy and smelly. (Butchers often slaughtered on the premises, so there was the nuisance of both bleeding carcases and meat still on the hoof.) To live in close proximity to tradesmen was not considered desirable by the Victorian middle and upper classes, but as the century progressed practicalities, certainly for the less than very wealthy, became more important than pretensions, and tradesmen and shopkeepers themselves became more powerful as business grew. Expanding department stores, proliferating chain stores, grew where there were people to buy. More sophisticated methods of distribution, improvements in communications, were vital to this kind of expansion, and, typically in the Victorian period, progress overcame genteel resistance.

Suburban development meant that people had a greater choice of where to

9   *Almost an emblem-picture of content in Hunt's picture of life in a country vicarage.*
Family and servants are welded into a larger social group

live, and although various suburbs appeared to be much the same in character and
amenities, they all had their gradations in the social hierarchy. Some of these
seemed to be pretty arbitrary. Almost as soon as they went up many of the new
suburbs were being described as deserts empty of life and culture—the novelists
most strikingly reflected this kind of reaction. In the early years of the twentieth
century it is H. G. Wells who most extensively explores the wastelands of suburbia
that were amongst the many legacies of nineteenth-century progress. The suburban villa was home for increasing numbers of people, men who for the most part
were employed in a variety of not very exciting jobs and whose prospects were
limited, women who tried their best to make their homes decent, comfortable and
conformist, looking up to the example of those with more money, with the guidance
of women's magazines and manuals.

The middle-class example was the pre-eminent one. Middle-class taste and
morals, middle-class attitudes to the family, child-care and education, these were
proselytized with great energy throughout the Victorian period, but especially

mid-century, for then middle-class energy and achievement could be seen at its most triumphant. The respectable working classes were exhorted to imitate middle-class values, to construct their homes in modest imitation of middle-class taste, although always with a reminder of the necessity of humility and the dangers of pridefulness. And always the working wife was frowned on. It was the wife who made the home, who cared for her children within it, who brought her husband back to it when work was done, who provided the hot dinners and created the atmosphere of comfort and protection. It was in the nineteenth century that home-making became a major activity, an essential one for the preservation of the standards and values of the Victorians, and a justification for the existence of women who were denied activity beyond their protectively closed front doors.

Order, Harmony and Comfort

'When the father returns home . . . it ought to be a scene of order, harmony and comfort', wrote Sarah Stickney Ellis, a prolific commentator on the home and the family, in *The Mothers of England*. There were many who suggested that the domestic ideal involved the elimination of all signs of the hard work that was necessary to maintain it. For the home to remain a place of peace the great domestic struggle could not be allowed to impinge on the qualities of relaxation.

The Victorian family image would be impossible without servants. In many ways it is servants who define the all-important Victorian middle class, for no household without a servant could claim that status. At the very least a young girl, perhaps not yet in her teens, was necessary as skivvy, a maid-of-all-work to carry out the dirtiest and most unpleasant jobs—and the dirtiest jobs in the Victorian household were very dirty indeed. Very often the skivvy would not be resident because of lack of space, but would come in daily, or if she were resident would have scarcely adequate accommodation, a makeshift bed in the kitchen or under the stair.

An income of £300 a year is frequently mentioned as the magic figure, above which a decent, though modest household could be maintained. But Victorian fiction is full of hesitant aspiring bridegrooms who wonder if a married couple can really manage on, say, £400 a year, and Victorian domestic magazines are full of advice on the subject. Here, in Eliza Cook's popular poem 'Three hundred pounds a Year'—and she wrote more sentimentally on the subject of marriage elsewhere— we can get the general idea of what the expectations might involve.

> *Sweet girl! you know three hundred pounds*
> *Would prove a slender axis*
> *For household wheels to run their rounds*
> *In yearly rent and taxes.*
> *You see, dear, that our home* must be
> *Out West, about the squares,*
> *With good reception rooms—full three*
> *And servants' flight of stairs.*
> *You* must have 'soirées' now and then
> *(Though I can't see their use) ;*
> *And I* must often have some men
> *To dinner—'a la Russe'.*

I've asked my uncle for his aid;
Of course, he won't accord it;
And so our bliss must be delayed,
For means, love, won't afford it.
A housemaid, cook, and liveried boy
We must, at once engage;
One of the two we must employ—
A footman or a page.
I cannot well resign at 'Lord's',
And you, dear Flo, of course,
Must go to balls and make your calls
With decent brougham and horse.
I must keep up my name at 'White's'
Despite all uncle says;
You still must have your opera nights
And show on Chiswick days.
Now, if I had three thousand, dear,
You know I would not hoard it;
But on three hundred pounds a year!
I really can't afford it.[1]

Victorian husbands were expected to keep their wives not just in the style to which they were accustomed, but often in the style to which they aspired, which was a major reason why most middle and upper-class men married relatively late. They needed a good income before marriage was possible. It was considered to be not only risky to marry without a suitable income, but immoral. Young people were warned that love was not enough. For most people marriage did not suggest the consummation of a love match, but the setting up of an establishment.

But what were the realities of middle-class incomes? A teacher or a junior clerk might earn as little as £60 a year, but this did not mean that teachers and clerks did not marry and run homes and have children. It was possible to live decently on such a sum; even if it did mean one could not enter the servant-employing class, a profession of that kind placed one in the middle-class fringes. A reasonably successful tradesman, not so acceptably middle class, might earn around £150 a year and employ a servant, who might be paid £6 a year. The improvident Micawbers of Dickens's creation continued to employ a servant of sorts, as an aid to their pretensions to gentility, and the maid's absence was a sign that things were very bad indeed. The Micawbers' servant was their last weapon against the threat of poverty. The working classes did not employ servants, though working mothers would often pay a few shillings a week to a child-minder, usually an elderly and often incapable woman or a very young girl. Girls of nine or ten frequently cared for babies and young children. Working-class incomes were reckoned in shillings per week rather than pounds per year, and though servants' wages were incredibly low, in comparison with debilitating and health destroying mill work, for instance, an income of, say, £10 a year, with food and lodging, was not such a bad deal, in spite of long hours, very little free time, and virtually no protection against overweening employers. Factory work paid better, 12/6 a week perhaps, but the costs were also greater.

The vast distance between the price of middle-class respectability and working-class subsistence is obvious. The symbolic value of servants was that it made the great divide even wider. In the novels of George Gissing the immense importance of this, and he is writing about the last 20 years of the century when the phenomenon of the depressed middle class had become a more insistent reality, is one of his preoccupations. *New Grub Street* (1891) is an excellent example. There he details the stuggle to maintain the signs of respectability in the face of an inappropriate income.

But of course the employment of servants had much more than symbolic value. Household work was inevitably extensive and very hard, as we have already seen in the case of the vertical terrace house. Lighting by oil and heating by coal and inadequate street cleaning meant a great deal of dirt, and at the beginning of the period there were virtually no mechanical aids to housework. By 1900 there were washing machines and carpet sweepers, and the extensive use of gas and electricity reduced dirt considerably, but in 1840 gas was rare and electricity non-existent. There was not only dirt to be dealt with. There was fetching and carrying, shopping, cooking, the care of fires and lamps, the cleaning of silver and brass, washing and mending of clothes, bedmaking—an elaborate procedure if carried out properly, the care of children, all of which were basic tasks that had to be done in the most modest and unpretentious household. The housewife who had to perform all these tasks without aid clearly had to work extremely hard. But the mistress of a household amply supplied with servants could be, if she chose, a lady of leisure. Inevitably, though, there was a price more than the simply monetary that had to be paid for the privilege of servants, and this was that it was impossible for employers to escape sharing their lives with their servants. It was impossible to lead an entirely private life if there were servants involved in almost every aspect of it. Relationships between master and mistress and their servants, and between their children and their servants, were a characterizing feature of home life.

How much income was necessary before a life of leisure was a possibility? With an income of above £300 a year it was reckoned that two servants could be employed, a maid of all work and perhaps a nursemaid if there were children. With an income of £400 to £500 a year a cook could be employed as well. By the end of the century, when servants' wages had risen and there were reiterated complaints about how hard it was to find good servants, a revised edition of Mrs Beeton (which was first published in 1861) reckoned that an income of £1000 a year was necessary before three servants could be employed, but this depended on circumstances, on whether you lived in town or country, and whether you employed a man servant—needless to say, men were paid more than women and thus their status value was greater. To run an acceptably genteel household three servants were the minimum necessary, and in the earlier part of the period this would have cost a total of between £30 and £60 a year. By the end of the century it would have cost perhaps three times as much. A genteel household was one in which the mistress of the house could count on a fair number of leisure hours in which to pursue the approved activities and her social life. Social life of course depended on to which level of fashionable life one belonged, or aspired, but at the least it would involve a certain amount of visiting, which had to be done at the proper hours in the proper way. Morning visits were fairly informal and required less dressing up than afternoon visits. Cards were left if the person visited was not at home—which could mean that she was genuinely out, or that she was simply not available, and it was not polite to question which. There were different types of cards for different occasions, to express condolences for instance, or to say goodbye before a trip abroad. Anyone with middle-class pretensions would have a supply of cards—they were a kind of passport to acceptability.

This kind of semi-formal visiting was very much a female occupation, and was regarded more as a social obligation than as an amusement. It was not done to stay too long, and the conversation was hardly likely to be either intimate or relaxed[1] unless there was a juicy bit of scandal to be chewed over by friends who knew each other well. Of course, in a small town or village visiting was likely to be less rigidly organized than in the cities, where the very confusion on the streets seemed to suggest that the formalities must be clung to. But all the same the premium was on doing things properly, with the genteel aping the aristocratic, and the lower echelons of respectability doing their best to win their way into the ranks of the genteel.

Manners, in other words, and style of life, were less a matter of personal convenience and consideration for others as of following a certain set of, in many cases, meaningless rules. Often the demands of polite society were positively inconvenient to all concerned, and involved a degree of pretence and hypocrisy which the Victorians themselves were aware of and attacked. The battle against snobbery and hypocrisy was waged throughout the Victorian period, yet to little effect. When the anti-Victorian backlash came into effect it was hypocrisy above all that was the target, yet it had been hypocrisy that provided the most constant target for some of the century's greatest writers, Thackeray, Dickens, George Eliot, Meredith. To a greater extent than we are sometimes ready to acknowledge the Victorians were aware of the flaws in their society. But the fact that so many of these flaws were a part of middle-class confidence, middle-class self-awareness, and the inevitable obverse of these, middle-class vulnerability, explains a great deal. If the Victorian period was the great age of middle-class achievement, of middle-class energy and heroism, it was also the period when this aggravatingly undefinable class was trying hard, even desperately, to characterize and identify itself. Its only guides were those of the established upper classes. The major threat to its sense of security seemed to be a potentially violent working class. The middle class on the one hand longed for aristocracy—even the most hardened democrats were liable to have a weakness for blue-blood—and on the other it fended off the masses who swarmed below. The middle class had to be exclusive, in order to

10   The Cheyne Walk home of Thomas and Jane Carlyle painted by Robert Tait in 1857

define itself, and it had to be imitative in order to be acceptable to those above.

All this had a great effect on the way people lived. Of course the middle classes challenged the upper classes with their money and their increasing power, and the establishment of middle-class standards that came with this. They didn't challenge the class structure of British society, they connived at it, but they reweighted the balance of power. Their values, their way of living, their ideals of marriage and the home, their symbols, dominated society.

The home and the structure of life within it was at the centre of the middle-class view of life. It has frequently been pointed out that never before had 'things' been so important. Objects became symbols of standards and life style: the two were inseparable. Gentility and morality became one and the same. Aristocrats could afford to be eccentric, or lead irregular lives, because blood was blood and even if cash and reputation were lost a title was still worth a great deal. But the middle class could not afford, or thought it could not afford, to be eccentric or risk reputations. In spite of this the Victorian Age is crowded with notable eccentrics, many of them private and inward looking people, or outwardly and energetically obsessive, which is itself a reflection of the pressures of the period.

So the objects that one's house contained were immensely important. Things cluttered one's drawing room not because they were beautiful but because they were symbols of one's standards. Objects could be reassuring if life refused to fit into the approved patterns. Taste had connotations of standards and morality; 'good' taste was less a question of artistic sensitivity, more a question of understanding what was proper. It is worth reflecting on the extent to which this is still the case: we have not yet outgrown the tendency to judge people on the ostensible symbols of their lives and to talk of taste as if it implied a moral criterion. Modern homes are still full of the equivalents of aspidistras. It is still important for people to represent themselves in terms of displayed objects, whether these are for show only, or for practical purposes—a washing machine, a record player, even books, can be as important for their display value as for their usefulness or the pleasure they give.

In the early part of the Victorian period the interior of the home was still relatively light and unburdened. Georgian taste had manifested itself in light colours and clearly defined shapes, in elegant furniture that was not necessarily comfortable, in spaciousness and openness. The Victorian interior became increasingly burdened and enclosed. Thick carpets and heavy curtains were in dark colours, net curtains and leafy plants at the windows obscured the light, dark wood was preferred, mahogany in particular, and furniture became heavier, more solid, more ornamented, and sometimes, but not always, more comfortable. Comfort was certainly a priority, as the world outside became increasingly un-comfortable, or rather as an awareness of the world outside inevitably grew. Wallpaper, a rarity in the Georgian period as it was so expensive, became more widespread as paper-making techniques developed, and it was again dark of colour and heavy of texture. Wood that was naturally light was stained dark—many Victorian houses still contain dark stained wood panelling. A completely satis-factory explanation of this tendency to darkness is hard to find, although some suggestions can be made. Clearly it helped obscure the dirt. In the age of coal fires heavy curtains were an aid to draught exclusion—and sunlight can be a cruel exposer of defects in order and cleanliness. But it is hard not to see the darkness as part of the womb-like tendency of the Victorian home, to see thick carpets and curtains as a significant element of sanctuary, and solid furniture as representative of solid virtues. The clutter that would have been typical of a middle-class Victorian interior of, say, the 1860s, added to the overburdened atmosphere. Objects could protect as well as enhance and reassure. And a lack of clutter was considered to be in bad taste. Manuals on home improvement specifically instructed readers not only to drape their fireplaces but to provide the maximum amount of space for 'things', blue-and-white china, Wally dogs, glass domes of wax fruit, silver and brass, engraved and coloured glass and, increasingly, objects of interest from distant parts of the Empire.

Inevitably there was a reaction. By the 1880s interiors were becoming lighter again, dark red was giving way to light green, orientalism became fashionable, furniture made out of bamboo, Japanese vases, light materials instead of heavy velvet were more widely used. But earlier than this there began a more interesting reaction, interesting because it was taking advantage of Victorian taste at the same time as improving it, and that was the movement towards more intimate craftsman-ship at the centre of which was William Morris. It was the crudities of mass production that offended Morris. His own colours tend to be dark, his furniture

11 'The daughters of England suitably employed during an evening at home.' From a moralizing series of illustrations in The Daughters of England by Sarah Stickney Ellis, 1845

12 Below Stairs.
A servants' eye-view of a pauper child. An illustration from Frances Trollope's Michael Armstrong, 1840

heavily and ornately carved and in a sense very much in tune with current Victorian taste. For one of the most significant features of Victorian art and interests was medievalism, and Morris and his associates the Pre-Raphaelites encouraged, even exploited this. What is quite certain is that they did not create this interest, as is sometimes suggested. We have to go further back and look at literature and architecture, the Gothic novel and the Gothic cathedral, and, pre-eminently, the historical novels of Sir Walter Scott, imitated throughout the century, for the beginnings of the medieval revival. But this will receive much more attention later, as it is of major importance in the whole discussion of Victorian taste.

Most of the clutter was concentrated in the public rooms, in drawing room or more modest parlour, and dining room. Bedrooms tended to be more sparse, although bedroom furniture, beds, wardrobes, chests and so on, was bulky. Apart from the basic furniture, including a marble topped wash stand with jug and basin, bedrooms normally contained little else. (Our contemporary emphasis on lavish bedrooms is a fairly modern development, obviously reflecting an inclination to create a luxurious environment for sex.) Kitchens could be cluttered, certainly if the full range of kitchen equipment recommended by Mrs Beeton was acquired, but the emphasis is utilitarian rather than decorative. Mrs Beeton does modify her specifications according to class of household—her categories are mansion, good class house, middle-class house, and very small house—but even for her middle-class house she lists over 130 items as necessary for cooking, the preparation of food, and cleaning in the kitchen, and this doesn't include the implements required for serving and eating the food. But although to our eyes now certain pieces of Victorian kitchen equipment have an attraction that our own plastic and chrome lack, the overriding concern in the kitchen was practicality. Some of the items were highly ingenious and reflected a fundamental concern with the culinary arts. The preparation and presentation of food, for all the dubious reputation of British cooking, was of the greatest importance to the Victorian household, and most Victorian cookbooks contain instructions on how a dish should be arranged and served as well as how it should be cooked.

For the consumption of food good silver and china were necessities, and even quite humble homes, however ordinary their everyday crockery, would have superior sets for visitors. The best china might exist more for show than for use, but it was important for it to be there, to be brought out, perhaps, for a wedding or a christening. In a wealthier household the scale of entertaining might be such that in terms of sheer quantity the basic necessities outdid anything we would now expect. Dinner plates and tea cups were reckoned in dozens rather than half dozens. The growth of the pottery industry was a response to the enormous demand for all qualities of product.

The preparation and consumption of food was a centre of Victorian life. It is, along with its associated theme entertaining, a major topic in Victorian fiction. What people eat, where they eat, how they eat, at what hour they eat, are highly significant reflections of style of life, and in the hands of some writers a reflection of morality also. There is something risqué about lobster salad and champagne, associated as it so often is with the entertainment of gay ladies, but shrimps and bread and butter are thoroughly respectable. Food, of course, becomes more elaborate according to size of income, a plain dinner of boiled mutton and pudding for the not very well-off, a more complex meal of several courses, fish, fowl and cutlets, pudding and dessert, for the modestly wealthy, and a greater array of courses including game and elaborate side dishes for the really well-off. Menus and recipes in women's magazines reflect this. What one ate was expected to reflect one's status and income, and it was almost obligatory to grow more elaborate as one's circumstances improved. Recipes in magazines usually contained the estimated price of the meals suggested, and it is worthy of note that differences in price between what we would now consider expensive food—veal fillet, for instance—and the less expensive—breast of veal—was vastly less than it is now. So that, given the fact that the poor could scarcely afford to eat meat at all, apart from bacon which was distinctly cheaper than fresh meat, standards of living were reflected more in how elaborate and diverse was the food one ate rather than in the basic ingredients. Economy is frequently emphasized in Victorian recipes—the myth that Victorian cookery is lavish with dozens of eggs and pints of cream is misleading, since these items were genuinely cheap and there is an overriding impression of economy-mindedness in instructions about food. The cost of ingredients was usually carefully estimated. Extravagance and wastage was condemned. Some manuals pointed out that it was not in fact necessary to eat meat every day, and carefully detailed how, say, a joint of mutton could be stretched to provide main meals for several days. The Victorians practised that rather necessary habit of eating left-overs, although the snobbish looked down on it. The frequent mention of hashes and curries as well as the simpler cuts off cold joints and slices of cold meat pies, and the occurrences of menus that particularly include as one of the courses a dish that utilizes the dinner of the day before bear witness to this. The reason is obvious. It was difficult to keep food for any length of time. The choice was between throwing it away, or eating it up rapidly.

Another striking feature of Victorian eating is the immense variety of food contained in recipes and menus. The range of cuts of meat, of game, of kinds of fish and varieties of fruit and vegetables is vast, in spite of the evident disadvantages of unreliable communications and lack of methods of preserving. Even when remembering that it was necessary to keep to what was in season, the variety is striking. However, it may be somewhat misleading, as the food actually specified in novels and journalistic writing tends to be more limited, with mutton, roast, boiled or as cutlets, top of the charts, fowls frequent, oysters and lobster for treats, steaks occasional, veal cutlets more favoured, and roast beef oddly rare. Often the most detailed and memorable meals in Victorian fiction are the most modest, the dinner of steak and kidney pudding prepared by Ruth Pinch for her brother Tom in that rather repulsively coy scene in *Martin Chuzzlewit* (1844)—the recipe is preserved in Eliza Acton's famous cookery book—or the meal prepared by the Barton family in Elizabeth Gaskell's *Mary Barton* (1848) of ham and eggs, with fresh bread and butter brought home in a cabbage leaf.

Food is a vivid focus of Victorian activity and of housewifely responsibility. The failures of poor Dora in *David Copperfield* are demonstrated by her inability to produce an edible meal. Cooking was a vulnerable process when fires could so easily go out and oven temperatures could not be readily controlled. It is no accident that the vast bulk of Mrs Beeton's *Book of Household Management* deals with food and the technicalities of cooking. The provision of a substantial hot meal for the man of the house was a pivot of the day's activities, and that this should be done with grace, punctuality and due regard for his taste and convenience was a major part of the wife's duties. The time at which this meal was provided tended to vary according to the circumstances and requirements of the family concerned

13 The Housekeeper

as well as according to status—in general, the higher the class the later the dinner hour. Men who were at work all day would need to dine in the evening, and the hour would depend on when they returned from work. Mid-century the evening meal in an average middle-class household would have been eaten between five and six, with perhaps a late supper at the end of the evening. In fashionable society after-dinner entertainment often began at about nine, with a supper, which might be cold but was not necessarily simple, served late. Suppers after the theatre or opera were usual, and were a favourite way for young men to entertain the actresses and opera girls who were easy prey for the smart fellows, or for the restless middle-aged, with cash and time to spend. By the end of the century the dinner hour for polite society could be as late as seven or eight, and clearly the later the hour of the evening meal the more necessary was a midday meal of some kind. In the early years of the century lunch scarcely existed, for there would be a large meal eaten in the middle of the afternoon. As the dinner hour crept onward lunch emerged, often as a buffet, with cold dishes set out on the sideboard from which people could help themselves if and when they felt inclined. For the working middle class a mid-Victorian lunch might be a chop with greens and potatoes in one of the proliferating restaurants that were taking over the function of the eighteenth-century coffee house and catering for office workers. For factory workers it was a bite of bread and cheese, or whatever could be conveniently carried to work. For the agricultural labourer also the midday meal often had to be something portable, to which has been attributed the development of the Cornish pasty and the Forfar bridie. Restaurants and tea shops became more numerous as the century progressed, with the first Lyons tea shop opening in 1890, and they became also places where ladies could properly dine unescorted. Restaurants opened in department stores were a great help in this respect. But the necessity of women eating out in a respectable fashion did not really arise until there was a significant female middle-class work force.

On the whole ladies dined in their own homes or in the homes of others like themselves. Children did not as a rule dine with their parents, but had a nursery lunch in the middle of the day, when good, plain and indescribably boring food was served. Anything at all rich or highly flavoured was deemed pernicious to both digestion and character. Sarah Stickney Ellis recommended that mothers should be present at the children's midday meals as the acquiring of proper manners and habits could not safely be left to the example of servants. Family tea times became more frequent as tea became a meal between lunch and dinner rather than a refreshment after dinner. Mrs Beeton recommends the provision of thin bread and butter, sandwiches, cakes and biscuits for afternoon visitors, in which we recognize the polite institution of afternoon tea—another problem for the servants, as afternoon visitors might arrive at any time over a period of perhaps two hours, and fresh tea and edibles had to be provided on demand. As lunch and tea grew in status and substance breakfast diminished. In the early nineteenth century breakfast was often a stupendous meal, particularly in the country when the partakers might well have had several hours of outdoor activity before sitting down to it. A

14 Frith's 'Five o'clock Tea'

late breakfast and an early dinner, both of large dimensions, were generally the only meals. But breakfast would be a substantial, protein-filled meal, with a range of hot and cold dishes which might include cold game pie or devilled kidneys, ham, steaks, eggs, a variety of bread and rolls. As the hasty departure for the commuting train became normality breakfast inevitably became a less elaborate affair. By the end of the century Kellogg had invented his corn flakes and the fully fledged breakfast was a thing of the past except in the country houses of the very rich. The vestiges linger in eggs and bacon.

The business of the day began considerably before breakfast for the responsibly minded mistress of a household. First, she must have reliable servants who would be up betimes, five or six o'clock, to prepare the fires, clean and light the kitchen range so that hot water and hot food could be provided by breakfast time, dust and arrange the dining room before the family assembled, and generally have all in readiness. This is the way Mrs Beeton outlines the initial activities of the wife and mother.

> Having risen early and attended to the toilet, see that the children receive proper care, and are clean and comfortable. The first meal of the day, breakfast, will then be served, at which all the family should be punctually present. . . . After breakfast is over, the mistress should make a round of the kitchen and other offices, to see that all is in order, and that the early morning's work has been properly performed by the various domestics. The orders for the day should then be given; and any questions which the domestics may ask should be answered, and any articles they require given out. . . .
>
> Prompt notice should be taken of the first appearance of slackness, neglect, or any faults in domestic work, so that the servant may know that the mistress is quick to detect the least disorder, and will not pass unsatisfactory work. Small faults allowed to pass unreproved quickly increase. A failing easily cured if promptly dealt with, is almost hopeless when it has been allowed to develop into a habit.[2]

The mistress's duties are largely supervisory, but that means a proper concern for correctness and efficiency. This is the theme that is echoed throughout the century. The mistress of the household must be responsible. She may not have to scrub and clean and cook herself, but she has the weighty duties of seeing that others do these things properly. Manuals of advice to women emphasize this continually, and condemn frivolity and time wasting. On the other hand vast quantities of fiction read by young women of all classes were absorbed with a life of fashionable leisure to which it was often assumed that all females aspired. Very often this fiction appeared in the same magazines that solemnly advised them to prepare for the responsibilities of household management and the care of a family. The fact that the Victorian home contrived to contain and tame these contradictions, as it managed to disguise or ignore a number of others, is of great significance.

Once the domestic wheels had been set in motion the climax towards which all tended was the moment when husband and father sat down to his main meal of the

15 Upper-class ennui

day and wife and mother concentrated on maintaining the comfortable harmony
which her day's responsibilities ought to have created. The structure of the Victorian family was solidly patriarchal. A man's wife had minimal status or rights, and
her only identity lay in the man whose wife she was and in her domestic role.
Whatever she did could only be done in his name. A married woman's property
and earnings, if she had any, belonged to her husband until 1873 when there were
modifications in the law. Thus, legally and economically, she had no basis on
which any kind of authority could be established. The home and everything in it
belonged to her husband. The money she spent was her husband's. Her husband
was legal guardian of her children. So her very existence was by courtesy of the
man she married, and needless to say that was a situation that was frequently
abused.

If it is true to say that most women accepted this, indeed acceptance was written
into the education and training they received and into the nature of home life and
the standards it purveyed, it is also true that throughout the Victorian period there
was an undercurrent of questioning and challenge. The feminist movement did

16   The resplendent formality of Mrs Beeton's supper table. From the 1895 edition

not really pick up speed until the 1870s, when social and economic realities as well as political ones were increasingly acknowledged as a part of the world women had to cope with. But we can find the questioning in fiction much earlier. Women novelists were multiplying, and wrote, as well as a great deal of rubbish, some of the greatest and most interesting and revealing novels of the century. In the novels of Charlotte Brontë, in the 1840s and '50s, and of George Eliot, in the 1860s and '70s, for instance, we find young women challenging the patriarchal bias, directly and indirectly. In such novels there is an illuminating dimension to add to what can be said about the Victorian home. We can see that there were women for whom the home was a prison—and men too, but they had various means of escape, and if they resorted to them it was generally considered the woman's fault. It was part of the wife's business to see that her husband was so comfortable, well-fed and amused at home that he would have no inclination to seek diversion elsewhere. If women were so inclined they were expected to repress it.

It was assumed that wife and children would conform to a man's expectation to return to a home after his day's work, or other activities, that was a well-ordered refuge from the world of friction and fear. If children were present, and very often they were neither seen nor heard as far as their parents were concerned but were left entirely to the care of nurses and nannies, they were expected to refrain from intruding their personalities on the parental harmony. In fact, one of the most striking features of Victorian attitudes to children is a distinct unease at the idea that children have, or should have, individual personalities. It was not just the question of the demand that children should submit to parental, particularly paternal, authority. There was a reluctance to accept, as there was with women, and in so many respects Victorian society treated women as children, that children might have identities of their own and creative energies that were irrelevant or hostile to the activities of adults. Again, the theme of the relationship between parents and children was one that absorbed many Victorian writers. They were aware of the anomalies but on the whole could not cope with them. Only at the end of the century, when writers like Samuel Butler burst out against the crippling effects of paternal authority, was there open revolt against a system whose tendency was to repress the individuality of children.

One problem that engaged the minds of many who were concerned to instruct the inexperienced was that of how a mother was to cope with her children, particularly her sons, when she was denied the authority that so obviously attached to the father. Family harmony might depend on this. The mother clearly had to be seen to have some authority otherwise her children would not respect her, and respect was essential. She could instruct her daughters in her own skills, and thus demonstrate her superiority and experience, but what about her sons? It was widely taken for granted that boys were, by nature, difficult. (The continuing assumption that boys are intrinsically wilder, more violent, more rebellious and so on than girls seems to me odd.) Mothers had to cope, although they could always use the ultimate weapon of threatening the vengeance of papa. The ubiquitous Mrs Ellis attempts to tackle the problem. She suggests that sons will only learn to respect their mothers—and they must learn this, otherwise they are likely to have no respect for women in general—if she can demonstrate her 'right-mindedness', her moral consistency, and her, if she has it, cultivated intellect. Mrs Ellis is all for the education of women, partly for this reason, but she insists that it should be within the appropriate limits. Aping male achievements would not be proper. A woman, she advises, should teach by example rather than by force (which played a conspicuous part in education) and therefore her moral persuasiveness has to be powerful. Further, she points out how much more satisfactory it is to husbands to have the kind of wife that boys will respect.

There are many good women extremely anxious to have a good dinner placed before their sons and husbands on their returning home, and very properly so; but why are they not equally anxious to set before them an intellectual refreshment! The answer is an obvious one—that they would not relish it so well. Yet again I would ask, may not this be because it is not dressed and arranged with half the skill and care bestowed upon a favourite dish? I appeal not to those who are deficient in education, and certainly not to those who are deficient in natural talent. They must do the best they can, and endeavour to please in some other way; but I do appeal to intellectual and cultivated women, when I implore them to spend a little more time, a little more thought, and a little more pains, in studying how to be intellectually agreeable in their own families, in order that they may exercise a lasting and beneficial influence over their sons, for without this, I am convinced, although they may be loved as mothers, they will never be esteemed as friends, and still less looked up to as counsellors, whose advice may be appealed to in every season of difficulty or trial.[3]

It is of note that Mrs Ellis suggests that the object is to be 'agreeable', and that these talents should be developed for the edification of husbands and sons. There is no mention of the woman's own satisfaction or pleasure except that to be gained from an awareness that she is doing it all for the men of the family. This is typical. What is also typical is the emphasis on, as it were, packaging. As she packages the dinner to please her husband, 'with skill and care', as she packages herself, so she should package her intellect.

Many manuals indeed specifically warn women against being too clever in the company of men. Men don't like clever, opinionated women, it is pointed out; it is to a woman's detriment to appear so. Again, women are constantly advised to package their intellects in such a way as to smooth male egos rather than challenge them. Women were told they should not be stupid, but also told that the purposes of their intelligence were limited by the expectations of men. So husbands did not bring their problems home with them to be discussed with their wives, but wives, nevertheless, with gentle intuition, were to understand that these problems existed and do all they could to mitigate them.

The Victorian home could not have existed without women. This was the essential female contribution to Victorian society, and should never be underestimated. The home, ruled by men, worked at by women, is one of the most representative images of the period. Its legacy, especially in terms of our continuing expectations about family life and home-making, has been powerful. Its celebration in its own time was continuing. The rest of this book will be chiefly concerned with what constituted that home, the life within it, and what it meant as the century progressed.

In the Country and the Provinces

The hierarchical structure of life was strong outside the cities too. Money went further, and life was less ostentatious, less concerned with the novel, more old-fashioned perhaps, and less hurried. But standards were just as important, and so were the fine differentiations that stratified society. In most rural areas society was organized in a manner that was still distinctly feudal. There is a very clear impression of this in Elizabeth Gaskell's novel *Wives and Daughters* (1866) which describes society in the little country town of Hollingford. The period is before the 1832 Reform Bill, so it is pre-Victorian, but the established structure of life in the country changed slowly. There are the 'great folk' at the Hall, Lord Cumnor with his land and his influence; there is the squire with much less land and much less influence; there are the respectable local residents, the vicar, the doctor, a sprinkling of genteel ladies; and there are the tradesmen and tenant farmers, and the servants and hired hands. The structure is simple but distinct at every level, and although the levels mingle it is only on the understanding that everyone remembers his place. Lady Cumnor can be friendly to the doctor's daughter without either thinking they are equals.

Tradition maintains the hierarchy and tends to affect life in a more intimate fashion than the city allows. Habits and customs are long established, adjusted to rhythms and demands of life that did not change quickly. They are more important than fashion. When in *Wives and Daughters* the doctor's second wife introduces newfangled ideas about the way the house should be decorated and life within it ordered the rhythm of the household is deeply disturbed. The doctor's quick bite of bread and cheese in the middle of a busy working day is considered boorish by his wife. She wants to improve his status while he is quite content to accept things the way they have always been. And as status is dependent on the verdict of those at the Hall the goal to be aimed for is the achievement of intimate terms with the great folk.

Social and economic life inevitably centred on the local big family. The owners of the land were the arbiters of local life. They had rights and privileges that no one else had (although sometimes they did not have much cash) and powers that could affect the well-being of anyone within their domain. As the chief employers and the biggest spenders they were the major source of economic security: the welfare of the community often depended on them. They expected a considerable degree of feudal loyalty, and in return the more conscientious were prepared to accept a degree of feudal responsibility, although this varied considerably. The responsibilities might include keeping the homes of tenants and workers in good order, caring for the sick and helpless, assisting with local schooling, donating money for local causes. That the great folk should influence life to a considerable extent in rural homes and communities was generally accepted, and strongly advocated by many. The upper classes had of old been the purveyors of standards, and there were some Victorians who did not like to see the middle classes taking over as guardians of morality, and felt that the special privileges and responsibilities of the traditional landowners were essential features of a well-ordered society. This attitude is reflected by Gilbert Scott, the great Victorian architect, in his *Secular and Domestic Architecture* (1857).

> Providence has ordained the different orders and gradations into which the human family is divided, and it is right and necessary that it should be maintained. . . . The position of a landed proprietor, be he squire or nobleman, is one of dignity. Wealth must always bring its responsibilities, but a landed proprietor is especially in a responsible position. He is the natural head of his parish or district—in which he should be looked up to as the bond of union between the classes. To him the poor man should look up for protection; those in doubt or difficulty for advice; the ill disposed for reproof or punishment; the deserving, of all classes, for consideration and hospitality; and *all* for a dignified, honourable and Christian example. . . . He has been blessed with wealth, and he need not shrink from using it in its proper degree. He has been placed by Providence in a position of authority and dignity, and no false modesty should deter him from expressing this, quietly and gravely, in the character of his house.[1]

Of course there was liable to be a considerable amount of self-interest involved in this kind of rationalization of the class structure, but there were many, Disraeli and the Young Englanders for instance, who saw the responsible enactment of such a system as the country's only salvation.

In the larger communities, in the market towns and growing provincial centres that had sources of economic dependence other than the land, the influence of the landed proprietor was inevitably less. In George Eliot's Middlemarch for instance, a small town with a growing sense of its own importance, the local landowners, squires rather than noblemen, contend for influence with the local men of wealth and standing within the town. These latter were likely to have made their name out of trade or manufacture, origins of cash which were not quite respectable (only inherited wealth was really respectable) but their power was undeniable. In the larger communities, where life could not be dominated by a single titled landowner the newly rich middle classes had more scope for influence. They may have imitated in their social life the outward symbols of the old rich, but their influence in local government, in running local institutions, in initiating local symbols of success—town halls and so on—and in determining standards was crucial. In the great industrial towns, Leeds, Manchester, Birmingham, we can see the operation

17   Upper-class drawing room, c. 1840

of money and uninherited power even more vividly.

It can safely be generalized that life in the rural communities and smaller towns was more informal in many ways than in the cities, and the pace more relaxed. Speed, toil and crowdedness were the words increasingly used in descriptions of cities, and although the agricultural worker had to work painfully hard at times, those who were not in an economically precarious position had a less stressful life than city dwellers. Households tended to be less rigidly divided, the kitchen more the centre of life (although as a family moved up the social scale the tendency was to move the kitchen further and further away from the living quarters), the servants more a part of family life, the children less confined to nursery and schoolroom and freer in their outdoor activities. The old established rural middle class, Tullivers and related families in George Eliot's *Mill on the Floss* (1861) are a good example, held dear certain symbols of their respectability but suggested at the same time a way of life that was more open than that of their confined, and perhaps more threatened, urban counterparts. The symbols were of the greatest importance, for they represented the quality of life, not just status. For the Tullivers, the dinner service, the table linen, the best sheets reserved for the purpose of burial, are such symbols, and their importance is involved in a continuity of family life and an acknowledgement of tradition which seems to belong peculiarly to the country.

The more intimate society of the provinces brought greater pressure to conform. Odd or anti-social behaviour could not be swallowed up in a seething mass

of humanity, as could happen in the city. This was not just the result of curiosity
about the doings of neighbours, but of a feeling that it was important for the community as a whole to know what individuals were doing. A rural community was,
in fact, more communal, and thus more vulnerable to hostile influences. It was
partly the pressure of feudal custom, and partly distance and poor communications
that were responsible. Communities had a more specific sense of identity and a
self-defensive attitude in protecting it. Life was far less formal, but the outlandish
or over-adventurous or scandalous were less tolerated, for anti-social behaviour
could be more seriously damaging in a small community, a bad reputation harder
to disguise. Newcomers and intruders were spotted at once, and often resented
unless they demonstrated a willingness to conform to the local ambience. But
increasingly as the century progressed there *were* newcomers in rural communities,
and very often newcomers whose status was considered to be dubious. There were
those who had made money from trade or manufacture who wanted to buy rural
comfort and quiet. From the first stages of the Industrial Revolution the inclination was to move away from the places where the money was made, because they
were unsightly, dirty, contaminating. Cities boomed in suburban building. The
merchants of Liverpool and the industrialists of Manchester built themselves
spacious houses in healthful Southport. Yorkshire millowners built country houses
on carefully chosen sites which avoided a view of their source of income. There
were those who wanted to buy themselves the status of country gentlemen, as
Disraeli did, believing that his political ambitions were unrealizable without a
house and land of some dimensions. As the possibilities of commuting developed
there were more and more who chose a country life just out of reach of the suburbs.
By the 1870s there was a boom in country-house building which represented the
summit of the movement from urban money-making to rural repose.

Many newcomers specifically wanted a niche, as high as possible, in the local
hierarchy, and felt that this could be acquired with a new house and a demonstra-
tion of economic status. They became employers of local labour, servants, garden-
ers, stablemen, went to church regularly, attended local events, and took their
share of the responsibilities of the gentry. But often they seemed to the old
established to be brash and vulgar. They brought with them new ideas, city ideas,
and were more receptive to the newest in fashion, in novels, in household gadgets,
or in curtains, than their long-term neighbours. Inevitably quite introverted
communities became exposed to new ways and untraditional influences. A growth
in mechanization on the farms contributed to this. Rural life was changing at its
most basic level, in its farming methods and its treatment of the land, and this
affected the way in which agricultural labourers both lived and worked, often to
their detriment. Men of enterprise were entering the rural communities, farm
managers with unorthodox ideas, men like Farfrae in Thomas Hardy's *The Mayor
of Casterbridge* (1886)—or like Dr Lydgate in *Middlemarch*, not an agricultural
man but, like Farfrae, a man of energy and fresh outlook.

The wave of building that was going on within and outside the cities in the
post-Napoleonic and early Victorian period was reflected in the publication of

18   *Interior of Scottish cottage, c. 1880*

19   *The rewards of virtue. A Lancashire working-class family enjoying a relaxed evening*

20   *A cottage interior, 1872*

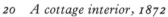

books of house designs. The most famous of these was J. C. Loudon's *Encyclopaedia of Cottage, Farm and Villa Architecture*, first printed in 1833, reprinted several times in the subsequent 20 years or so, and used extensively for at least 50 years. Loudon presented a great range of designs for suburban, town and country houses, executed in various styles, to suit a wide variety of taste, appropriateness and expense. He was not himself an architect, but a gardener, who published a vast quantity of gardening manuals, but applied himself to the subject with an eclectic imagination and some commonsense, and was a great success. C. J. Richardson's *The Englishman's House* (1871) was a similar manual (less extensive) for the latter part of the century, and included designs for a selection of non-urban housing from a gardener's cottage (three rooms plus scullery and larder) to a 'country residence for a lady of rank' with a 25 by 18-foot drawing room. In between were park lodges, a 'picturesque cottage' for a 'peasant', a country rectory, and a small country house of 'a superior gentlemanly character'.

Traditionally provincial building had conformed to local styles, determined to a great extent by local materials and needs, which had changed little over the years. The interest in architecture and in improvement, which was very much present in the Georgian period and which we see so interestingly reflected in Jane Austen's novels, was mostly confined to the wealthy. And although of course money from trade and industry increasingly financed new building the elegant Georgian squares and crescents were still mostly occupied by the titled and the traditionally rich. New building outside the cities was still very much a question of local builders putting up what they had always put up. But the new pattern books broadened the horizons of prospective houseowners. Here was a range of styles and amenities to choose from, carefully tailored to the existing class and economic structure of society. The great 'battle of the styles' between Gothic and Neo-classical meant for most people not a rigid choice of a distinct type of design but a proliferating eclecticism from which anything could be selected. Tudor beams, or Swiss chalet balconies, or castellation for the new country home? It was all there.

In the country there was more scope for design because there was more space. There was no need for crowding living space into tall terraces or making the most of expensive urban land. But a signal feature emerges from a study of Victorian design books, and that is that variations in design were very much a question of external characteristics. Picturesque cottages were designed for peasants, but the amenities within conformed to a rigid opinion of class requirements. Gothic frills on the outside might be considered uplifting to the humblest soul, but there was not much concern for alleviating the life within. Cramped rooms, a cold water scullery, dark, narrow staircases, did not allow for much practical improvement in the quality of life. The internal requirements of housing were totally geared to class and status, not to use or size of family. C. J. Richardson's design for a small country house is for an 'eminent provincial solicitor'. He is a man well known in his locality, and therefore his house must be respected as well as himself. But he is no more than a provincial solicitor, so the modest grandeur of the 'country residence for a lady of rank' cannot be permitted. The rooms are smaller, the accommodation for servants less extensive, the cellars less commodious, and the external aspect of the house is similar to the country rectory that appears on a previous page. Of course if there was money enough grandeur could be demanded, but grandeur without the dignity of status was considered offensive.

By the 1850s, Mark Girouard says in his book *The Victorian Country House* (1971), the amenities and standards of a gentleman's house generally conformed to a widely accepted view, and did not change considerably for the rest of the period. He writes:

> A gentleman's house should be substantial, serious and preferably in a style associated with the traditions of English country life. It should be dignified, as was suitable for the rank of its owner, but not ostentatious; designed for family life and the entertainment of friends rather than for show. It should provide decent quarters for servants. It should protect the womanliness of women and encourage the manliness of men. It should be comfortable but not luxurious.[2]

Robert Kerr, who published his *The Gentleman's House* in 1864, considered that the essentials were comfort for the family, convenience for the servants, and elegance 'without ostentation'. Kerr, like so many others, adopted a tone of absolute authority when he discussed what was required. 'However small and compact the house may be,' he said, 'the family must have privacy and the servants commodiousness; and the whole dwelling must display an unassuming grace. If, on the other hand, the circumstances of the owner and his tastes are such that magnitude and refinement ought to expand into state, even grandeur must not be pretentious, or wealth ostentatious, and the attributes of an agreeable English home must never be sacrificed.'[3] The strictures against ostentation are significant. At all costs anything suggestive of vulgarity should be avoided. This book was clearly written partly to inform the new rich how to adopt the ways of the old rich and how to refrain from brash vulgarity into which their new status might otherwise tempt them. Kerr has a great deal to say on the subject.

> . . . elegance unassuming and unelaborated, touching in no way the essentials of home comfort, never suggesting affectation and pride, moderated by unimpassioned refinement, and subdued even to modesty, will be almost invariably acceptable. Even where extreme wealth and exalted rank render it incumbent upon a family to surround itself with the most cherished products of industry and genius, it will be rarity and cost, perfection of workmanship and pure or piquant excellence of design, rather than splendour or luxurious richness or imposing grandeur, which will be esteemed; simplicity still, and subdued power—the greater the power the stronger the subduing hand—will be cherished even in magnificence, and the glare of pomp despised.[4]

It is a condemnation of comfort and refinement that is to be aimed for, and all Kerr's suggestions, or rules, for the ways rooms should be arranged and used have this in mind. The over-elaborate, the over-ornate, the conspicuous display of wealth, are all condemned. The emphasis on 'subdued power' is highly revealing—the powerful, of course, can afford, in more ways than one, to be subdued.

With such clear guidance on how to live as a gentleman an expanding upper middle class took its place quite readily within the established communities. The grosser and more offensive errors could be avoided—although they were not always. The virtually authoritarian attitude towards the way homes should be arranged and organized is reflected in almost everything that was said on the subject of how these things should be done. The sensitivity about taste was partly the result of the fact that the structure of society was changing, that more and more people could afford to imitate the upper classes. It was considered important that this should be done properly, that the bounds of propriety should not be over-stepped and that the traditional class structure should, as far as possible, be respected. So that it was very important that the country solicitor should not aspire to the magnificence of the titled landowner, even if he could afford to, and that the artisan should not begin to think in terms of drawing rooms rather than parlours. House design was very much geared to what a controlling class considered the others *ought* to have. Designs were for lawyers, or vicars, or engine drivers or farm labourers, not for young married couples, or large families.

Arnold Bennett in his novel *Clayhanger* (1910) describes how the hero's father, a printer, earns his way out of the house above the printing shop to the house on the hill away from the central squalor of the town. This is in the Potteries, one of the many areas where pleasant living space, fresh air, and an outlook inoffensive to the eye were increasingly at a premium. The period is the 1880s, but the need to get away from not only the industrial centres but also a ravaged countryside existed long before. The rural life described by Elizabeth Gaskell and other novelists of the period who were interested in the interplay between the traditional rhythms of life and new people with new ideas was only part of the story. Hardy gives us another, in his descriptions of the unrelenting hardness of agricultural life, and Ruskin emphasizes another, when he draws attention, as he does with dedication and commitment, to what modern industrial society was doing to the countryside.

> Just outside the town I came upon an old English cottage . . . left in unregarded havoc of ruin; the garden gate still swung loose in its latch; the garden, blighted utterly into a field of ashes, not even a weed taking root there; the roof turned into shapeless rents; the shutters hanging about the windows in rags of rotten wood; before its gate, the stream which gladdened it now soaking slowly by, black as ebony and thick with curdling scum; the bank above it trodden into unctuous, sooty slime: far in front of it, between it and the old hills, the furnaces of the city foaming forth perpetual plague of sulphurous darkness; the volumes of their storm clouds coiling low over a waste of grassland fields, fenced from each other, not by hedges, but by slabs of square stone, like gravestones, riveted together with iron.[5]

This was the rural landscape damaged by industry, something which disturbed Ruskin profoundly, but which few others took much notice of in those terms. That he should focus his outrage on what had once been a home is significant, for it was the quality of life, family life, life in the home, that this damage was affecting. Amidst such ugliness how could people be expected to live good lives? Although numbers of social reformers were anxious to improve housing, in the cities and the country, and wanted also to improve the quality of life of the underprivileged, Ruskin was one of the few who saw the stark and intimate relationship between industrial blight and ordinary life.

But it was not only industrial blight that produced gruesome scenes such as the one Ruskin describes. There was agricultural blight also. The kind of well-ordered society that Gilbert Scott suggested, with the aristocracy taking both their privileges and their responsibilities seriously, did not necessarily work satisfactorily for those at the bottom of the heap. Disraeli was one of those who felt that the answer to England's ills lay in the titled and the powerful shouldering these responsibilities with greater enthusiasm and commitment. In *Sybil, or the Two Nations* (1841), one of the novels in which his political ideas appeared, he describes what he might have called the results of feudal neglect. This is a cottage interior in a small rural town.

> With the water streaming down the walls, the light distinguished through the roof, with no hearth even in winter, the virtuous mother in the sacred pangs of childbirth gives forth another victim to our thoughtless civilization; surrounded by three generations whose inevitable presence is more painful than her sufferings in that hour of travail; while the father of her coming child, in another corner of the sordid chamber, lies stricken with that typhus which his contaminating dwelling has breathed into his veins, and for whose next prey is perhaps destined his new-born child. These swarming walls had neither windows nor doors sufficient to keep out the weather, or admit the sun, or supply the means of ventilation; the humid and putrid roof of thatch exhaling malaria like all other decaying vegetable matter. The dwelling-rooms were neither boarded or paved; and whether it were that some were situate in low and damp places occasionally flooded by the river, and usually much below the level of the road; or that the springs, as was often the case, would burst through the mud floor; the ground was at no time better than so much clay, while sometimes you might see little channels cut from the centre under the doorways to carry off the water, the door itself removed from its hinges, a resting place for infancy in its deluged home.[6]

As this indicates a rural slum could be every bit as devastating as an urban slum, and the mere fact of being beyond the contamination of industrial activity did not automatically improve life. As one clergyman of the time put it, 'It is idle to suppose that the mere fresh air of the country is all-powerful to prevent epidemics in villages, and to remedy the defects of a confined locality.'[7] This is part of a plea for sanitation reform. Even where the primitive was rather more picturesque than Disraeli's description it was not necessarily more healthful.

There had been specific interest in the improvement of housing for the agri-

21   Manchester cotton operative's home, 1862

22   The frugal though 'homely' cottage painted by F. D. Hardy, c. 1850

cultural labourer, as there had for the industrial labourer, for some time before Disraeli wrote *Sybil*. There had been plans and schemes for model housing, and enlightened landowners had sometimes ventured into them in a practical way. Some of the new rural housing in the early part of the century was in fact the result of the need to house workers in certain growth industries. The mill villages of Yorkshire and Lancashire were sometimes designed as a package deal financed by the millowners. The sites of new mills, which depended on water power, were frequently rural initially, although sometimes urban expansion engulfed them. At Egerton, near Bolton, for example, which is still pleasantly rural, a tiny community was transformed by the neatly laid out model cottages which housed the workers at the new mill in the valley. Order and uniformity were what characterized such schemes, many of which, like Egerton with its Cobden Street and Bright Street reflecting current concerns, have a neat attractiveness.

For both mill worker and farm labourer it was not considered necessary to provide much space, and sanitation, in the 1830s and '40s, was still in its infancy. The denser the housing the more drastic the effects of bad, or in some cases virtually non-existent, drainage were likely to be. As there was a tendency to put up terraced rows of farm-workers cottages, which we often think of as being characteristic of industrial housing, the rural community was sometimes as densely housed and no better off than the urban. The main consideration of the model cottage designers (many of whom were amateurs, like Dorothea Brook in *Middlemarch*) was the provision of clean, decent living space. In 1862 the Yorkshire Agricultural Society published plans for labourers' cottages which were typical of the kind of thing being produced at that stage. These are for separate dwellings, whereas perhaps earlier a row of joined cottages would have been more common. Most of the designs, some of which have some slight Gothic ornamentation, include living room, scullery and pantry on the ground floor, and three small bedrooms upstairs. One has an outside privy which is entered through the coal house, which reveals a singular lack of imagination. The cost of putting up such a cottage would be between £100 and £200. The cost of putting up a fairly modest house for a rural gentleman might be something like £2000.

Life within such a cottage might well have been fairly comfortable, especially if the landlord was decent and undertook the kinds of responsibilities that Disraeli would have liked to see. The landlord in an agricultural community was almost certainly the employer as well, so life could be much dependent on his goodwill— how dependent a number of Hardy's novels reveal. The quality and comfort of home life in a farm labourer's cottage also depended greatly on the skill and industry of the housewife. For, if the middle-class Victorian home presented a cleaning problem exacerbated by size and clutter and stairs, it was no easy matter to keep a family and its environment clean when space was confined and water perhaps had to be fetched from a pump. Often a family occupied considerably less space than was available in newly designed cottages. In *Lark Rise to Candleford* (1945) Flora Thompson describes an Oxfordshire village in the 1880s, and there most of the cottages had a single room downstairs where all the cooking, cleaning, washing and living went on, and at the most two bedrooms upstairs, one for the adults and the other for the children—who were often numerous. In that community hard work was the watchword, not only in keeping clean, but in providing the family with food, for much of what was eaten were vegetables the family grew themselves, and the pig that was raised and slaughtered each year. The standard farm labourer's wage of ten shillings a week could not bring in much extra: even dairy produce was a treat. Here Flora Thompson describes a mealtime.

> When the men came home from work they would find the table spread with a clean whitey-brown cloth, upon which would be knives and two-pronged steel forks with buckthorn handles. The vegetables would then be turned out into big round yellow crockery dishes and the bacon cut into dice, with much the largest cube upon Feyther's plate, and the whole family would sit down to the chief meal of the day. True, it was seldom that all could find places at the central table; but some of the smaller children could sit upon stools with the seat of a chair for a table, or on the doorstep with their plates on their laps.[8]

Flora Thompson describes Oxfordshire rural life with affection, and radiates a sense of the moral worth of the sparseness, the unending hard work, the communal cooperation. But there were slums, and disease, and desperate poverty, and the agricultural slump at the end of the 70s, which so greatly affected Hardy's attitudes to Wessex life, accentuated the deficiencies. Engels had studied the condition of the agricultural labourer as early as the 1830s (his *Condition of the Working Class in England* wasn't published in English until 1892) and had found poverty and the misery that went with it endemic. Things had not changed greatly by the end of the century, for although some of those who controlled the fate of the agricultural worker were more enlightened, he was still within that control, and had generally less opportunity for improving himself than the urban worker—and any kind of labour organization or trade union development was more difficult, although it did come. The kind of rural wretchedness that Hardy's novels reveal is rather different from the clean, industrious, sparse but decent home life that Flora Thompson describes.

Life changed less for the farm labourer through the century than it did for most other country residents. His home life, his diet, his activities remained much the same—though sometimes conditions deteriorated. While improved communications and distribution brought some of the benefits of mass production into the homes of those who could afford them, these didn't have much effect on the labourer's way of life, although he was probably earning more and eating better at the end of Victoria's reign than in the 1880s described by Flora Thompson. The eye of the reformers and improvers was focused more on the cities than the country, for there it was harder to escape the slums and insanitary conditions whose proliferation legislators, however good their intentions, had not been able to control. Although there were some who were genuinely concerned with improving life in the villages as well as in the towns their achievement was not generally significant. One such was S. H. Brooks who, earlier though less dramatically than Ruskin,

23 and 24   Designs for a 'Small country Villa' and a 'Picturesque Cottage' from Richardson's The Englishman's House, *1870*

expressed his concern for preserving the amenities of the countryside. His *City, Town and Country Architecture* (1847) concentrates on designs for the railway age, revealing an energetic sense of progress mingled with an appreciative understanding of the picturesque.

'In travelling through many parts of this country,' Brooks writes in his introduction, 'we have frequently been surprised at the incongruity occasioned by the many inapplicable erections in some of the most beautiful and picturesque parts of it, and equally as much at the inappropriate application of their intended purposes.'[9] He sets out to contribute towards remedying the situation. His designs are very much of the age in their practical functions, though perhaps in advance of their time in their quick reaction to the new realities. He includes a terrace of houses above shopfronts, railway buildings tastefully laid out and including housing for the railwaymen and their families, and what he calls a 'domestic club house', a plan unusual at the time for apartment housing for the middle class, 'a handsome and commodious building . . . suitable for chambers for married people; each suite of rooms to be complete in itself, and to contain—say, two handsome drawing rooms, communicating with folding doors, a best bedroom, and dressing room, kitchen, and servant's offices.'[10] He points out a system of this kind would mean cheaper rents. Flats for the middle classes did not in fact appear in the south until much later in the century, although there had for some time been a northern tradition of flat dwelling. A significant proportion of Edinburgh's New Town was built as flats, conceived on a spacious scale.

The 'domestic club house' was an urban requirement. In rural terms Brooks was concerned with accommodating progress without damaging the picturesque, a concern that was rare at the time, and his opinions on such basic amenities as drainage and water supply were in advance of what was generally considered acceptable—although of course Thomas Cubitt had built his reputation partly on the attention he had given to these requirements. Although Brooks was all for the picturesque he was no romantic. He knew well that often lurking behind the pretty were the unhealthy and the insanitary. His architectural ideal was one that combined space, uniformity, efficiency, uncontaminated water and good air. His use of the word 'picturesque' is an extension of the eighteenth-century idea: nature must be tamed, but not just to make it pleasanter for human senses. It needed taming for the sake of health also.

Brooks was concerned with the quality of life, but like most Victorian designers he was ruled by class stratification of how life should be lived. Although he was concerned with the moral condition of the working classes he was also happy designing rest houses, 'casinos' as he called them, to be built on the extensive estates of aristocratic landowners. He did not question the appropriateness of such structures, where parties of the leisured could take their ease as they moved about the estate, to the lives of the privileged, nor did he find it irreconcilable with his concern for the less well off. But he also quotes with approval the Reverend E. Feilde who argued that as the economic conditions in the country improved the lower classes ought to get a share of the general benefits. However, Brooks' vision

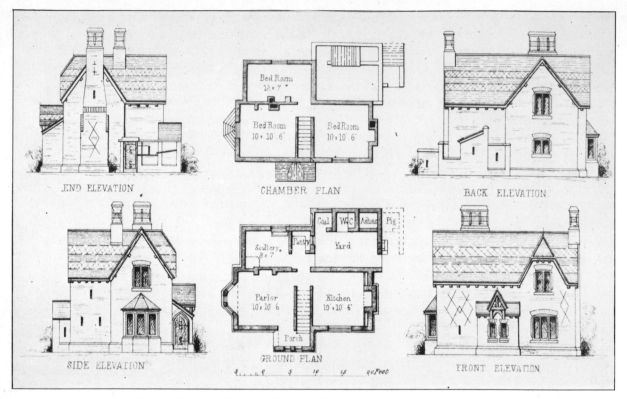

END ELEVATION   CHAMBER PLAN   BACK ELEVATION

SIDE ELEVATION   GROUND PLAN   FRONT ELEVATION

25   *Prize-winning plans for labourers' cottages, 1862*

of what constituted improvement might seem a little deficient. He saw no reason why two rooms, rather than one, should not be the accepted standard for working-class housing: although such a hundred percent expansion would clearly alleviate considerably the situation of a cramped family, the suggestion that it was as much as a family *ought* to have seems unduly limiting. Especially as Brooks himself considered that the lower classes had little opportunity of improving themselves morally and intellectually if they were forced to live in crowded, confined and dirty conditions, and in an age of progress and enlightenment he felt it ought to be possible to abolish slums and improve the working class. 'A dingy and barbarous cottage may suit a dark and barbarous age, but in the present days of improved knowledge, a wider diffusion of domestic comfort, something a little beyond bare walls and perforated earth floors, and patched windows, may reasonably be looked for at the hands of those who can afford the indulgence.'[11]

New houses of the right design could improve the quality and the moral worth of life within the home—the Reverend Feilde envisages an environment for a new, reading proletariat—and in the community as a whole. The choice of style and the character of the dwelling was very important, for it was more than a matter of suiting individual requirements or tastes—in fact, individual, as opposed to class, requirements did not seem to play a very great part in house design. The battle of the styles was not argued in terms of structure or beauty or durability, but in terms of moral aesthetics. For Ruskin, and for many others who were less articulate, the home was the crucial moral environment, and a deficiency in taste could reflect a deficiency in life. The moral tone of a worker's cottage, and by implication of a worker's existence, could be raised by the addition of a few Gothic embellishments on the outside structure—the Gothic without, it seemed, making up for the lack of space and piped water within. For Ruskin and many of the great Victorian architects, who were responsible for transforming the profession, the Gothic was a direct reflection of a superior religious and moral sense. Clearly the scope for Gothic expression was much greater in vast public buildings, but the home was not beyond its range of influence.

But in fact there could be no absolute ideal for home life for just as class determined the amenities of housing the domestic ideal was cannily adjusted to class demands. The lower classes were encouraged to imitate the upper only to a certain extent. Robert Kerr's strictures against ostentation reflect a deep-seated fear that the upward moving lower middle class, for instance, might outdo its

26 *Disraeli's study at Hughenden Manor*

traditional superiors, might disrupt the established order of things by demonstrating unavoidably and shamefully that wealth could challenge and take over older
forms of power. Power must be subdued; the more vulgar its source, the more
necessary was its subduing. The line between the middle classes and the aristocracy had to be preserved (although the aristocracy increasingly kept itself going
by marrying middle-class money) and constant vigilance for signs of nouveau
riche lack of dignity was maintained. The model for the lower classes was a middle-
class one, but a line had to be drawn there too. Imitation was flattery, but it could
not be allowed to assume the proportions of rivalry. The knowing of one's place
was the essential item of the class catechism.

In the provinces we can see this process much more clearly than in London and
the larger cities. It is the novels and the memoirs of country and provincial life that
illuminate with most clarity the relationship between the quality of home life and
class. The feudal structure remained clearly defined into the Edwardian era, and
incomers, except in those cases where rural areas were totally transformed by the
kind of population explosion that industrialization inevitably brought, largely
found their place within it. In many cases it was a question of plumping out a scant
professional class, and in the long run it resulted in the kind of genteel semi-rural
life that is present in so much Edwardian fiction, the homes with large gardens and
tennis courts that we find in E. M. Forster, a spacious if not gracious way of life
still maintained by servants. By that time a non-landowning style of country life
was established, typified by a 'country rectory' style of house, a favourite design of
such Victorian architects as Street and widely imitated and adopted throughout
the century. These were roomy houses, not too rigid in structure, more open and
relaxed than most urban housing could afford to be, although the style is present
in the more wealthy suburbs. They would have a spacious lawn, a kitchen garden,
perhaps a tennis court and stabling for a pony or two. Such a residence suggested
a head of the household who was a professional man, a home counties orientation,
a life that was leisurely, values that were middle class but reasonably flexible and
not too concerned about money, vegetables fresh from the garden to accompany
meat and wine of good quality, a young man in cricket flannels, a young girl taking
tea on the lawn with her tennis racket beside her. We are familiar with the images.
They are highly suggestive of a quality of life we characterize as the quintessence
of the golden years before the First World War. It was a kind of life that emerged,
for the privileged middle class, through the Victorian period. But it was only for
the few, and for most it was brief. And the thought that the masses might strive
towards such a life, or attempt to imitate it, seemed no less extraordinary at the end
of the century than at the beginning.

Working Class Homes

Slums were a widespread feature of Victorian existence. In most parts of the country it was impossible to avoid the presence of poverty and squalid living conditions. It was not just age and deterioration that created the slum, but over-crowding, inadequate drainage, lack of access to water. In slum conditions it was impossible to keep dirt and disease at bay. A slum was an environment in which a human being was lucky to survive: the phrase 'home life' could not begin to conjure up any of the suggestions of comfort or harmony that it contained for the better off.

There were damp mud floors, unmended roofs, lack of sanitation in every part of the country, but the most obvious concentrations of slums were in the cities, and many of them were relatively new, dating as they often did from the period of rapid expansion immediately before Victoria's reign. There were the slums that had ripened out of decaying old housing in the centre of Manchester, in Glasgow, in London's East End, but there were also the new slums, like the terraces put up for cotton operatives in Preston, with an open sewer flowing between them at the back. Each house had an earth closet in the backyard which emptied into the sewage ditch, and twice a year the landlord sold the contents. Dust heaps in the streets were a common feature of the urban landscape, and they were a saleable commodity. In some places night-soil carts made the rounds daily and collected the accumulated excrement of the previous 24 hours: an unwholesome job, but a profitable one. Life must have been dominated by smell. The impossibility of separating human waste from water supply meant that infection and disease could spread like lightning. There were frequent epidemics, and it was a long time before their causes were understood.

In *Mary Barton* Elizabeth Gaskell described the life of the Manchester poor, and amongst her many striking pictures—and they came from direct experience—there is this one, of a slum street and a cellar home.

It was unpaved; and down the middle a gutter forced its way, every now and then forming pools in the holes with which the street abounded . . . As they passed, women from their doors tossed household slops of *every* description into the gutter; they ran into the next pool, which overflowed and stagnated. heaps of ashes were the stepping-stones, on which the passer-by, who cared in the least for cleanliness, took care not to put his foot. Our friends were not dainty, but even they picked their way till they got to some steps leading down

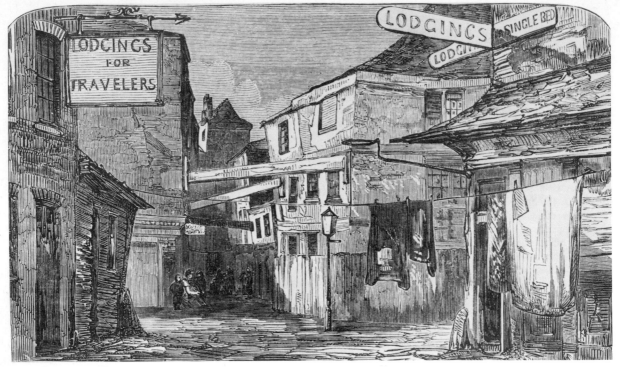

27   *Duke Street, Southwark, c. 1860*

28   *No 4 Thornton Court, Tickle Street, Manchester, 1862 shows the desperate poverty of the cotton operative*

into a small area, where a person standing would have his head about one foot below the level of the street, and might at the same time, without the least motion of his body, touch the window of the cellar and the damp muddy wall right opposite. You went down one step even from the foul area into the cellar in which a family of human beings lived. It was very dark inside. The window-panes were many of them broken and stuffed with rags, which was reason enough for the dusky light that pervaded the place even at mid-day. After the account I have given of the state of the street, no one can be surprised that on going into the cellar inhabited by Davenport the smell was so foetid as almost to knock the two men down. Quickly recovering themselves, as those inured to such things do, they began to penetrate the thick darkness of the place, and to see three or four little children rolling on the damp, nay wet, brick floor, through which the stagnant, filthy moisture of the street oozed up; the fire-place was empty and black; the wife sat on her husband's chair, and cried in the dank loneliness.[1]

Between 40,000 and 50,000 families lived in similar Manchester cellars, many of them Irish, the most exploited labour of the period. The husband of the family described above is sick and unemployed. Soon he will be dead. There is no money and no means of relief apart from that provided by the neighbours, two of whom are visiting the cellar in this passage. The homes of the employed when times are good make a striking contrast, Mary Barton's own, for instance, where that heart-warming tea was enjoyed. Mary's home is frugal, but it is neat and clean and supplied with fire and food. In bad times though, when wages could be reduced and men laid off, or when the operatives were on strike, life deteriorated rapidly. A subsistence wage could provide necessities, less than that meant suffering. Lack of food and lack of warmth brought inevitable demoralization, and a demoralized human being, starving and cold, cared less and less about the domestic virtues of order and cleanliness.

The Manchester cellars and the 'rookeries' of London, which Dickens and Gissing and social commentators of the last quarter of the century describe so unforgettably, were amongst the most notorious of Victorian slums. But millions of families all over the country lived on a borderline between poverty and squalor, and it took so little to send the poor into the depths of destitution. There was bound to be a point beneath which it seemed hopeless even to try to maintain a plausible existence. Ill-health, an accident at work, a strike, an epidemic, sacking, all could deprive a family of the major breadwinner, and although the wife, and after 1833 children over the age of nine, might also be wage earners, they could not earn as much as a man. A woman, perhaps at the mill for a 12-hour stint or longer (before the Ten Hours Bill of 1847), still had domestic chores and very likely younger children to care for before and after work. Those children who were old enough were often expected to work all their waking hours. Life for the working class was, indeed, filled up with work—for those who were in employment. For many, especially for the young and the women, there was scarcely any other feature of life for six days of the week. There was no way of disguising the realities of its demands. Work was the only weapon against disease, filth and squalor, all of which could destroy human beings with frightening rapidity, but very often the work itself involved the risk of dirt and disease, of deformed or maimed limbs, or contaminated lungs. For most of the working class the environment of home was preferable to the environment of work, but nevertheless there was not the time or space or opportunity for many positive qualities.

Home life has its suggestion of the occupation of leisure time. There was little of that, particularly for women, although the Ten Hours Act stipulated maximum working hours in the cotton industry. What leisure time the men had was often spent in the pub, one of the few places where they could congregate and relax. Gradually working men's clubs and improvement associations grew, and opportunities for attending evening classes came into being. But self-improvement took the men away from the family circle, and although there are some cosy pictures of the artisan's family life to be found they do not dispel the persistent impression that the city and the demands of work were both hostile to the home and the family, unless there was enough money to keep this hostility at bay. For an impression of this hostility I borrow the words of Geoffrey Best, from his book on *Shaftesbury* (1964).

> . . . the early Victorian city was extraordinarily hostile to the poor. For it was trying all the time to tip them over the edge of ordinary poverty into the abyss of hopeless, helpless poverty. Ordinary poverty was bad enough for at any rate the unskilled workers. It meant long hours and small pay for every member of the family who could earn anything. A miner might send his children down the mine, a weaver might send his to the factory, to help pay for gambling and beer or to purchase the trimmings of social ascent, but for poor unskilled people in the city, where rents and food costs were both high, every penny was a matter of survival or sinking—until or unless you gave up the struggle to survive. Rents were high because city ground was so valuable; ground and rents were cheaper on the outskirts, of course, but normally you could not live there because you had to live within quick walking distance of the chance of work. Because rents were high, you could not afford much room to live in. Even well-paid skilled men, before the era of workmen's trains, might find it hard to live 'respectably', with their boy children and girl children in different bedrooms. The artisans at Maudslay and Fields in Lambeth, making the best marine steam-engines in the world, were living in the sort of narrow cramped little cottages that passed as slums in Lancashire. Yet they were among the *élite* of the labouring class, much nearer the lesser white-collar workers and tradespeople than they were to 'the poor'. The London poor lived in much worse places. . . . They lived in older, squalider rows of cottages that had once been just suburban, or in the flimsy houses that had been more recently crammed into the still vacant spaces of such areas, turning them into thickets of courts and alleys. They lived in tenements run up in gardens and backyards of once prosperous properties

that had now run down. They lived in 'rookeries': big old houses converted into warrens of one-room and two-room dwellings; rickety, unsanitated noisy firetraps, hideous in daylight and stygian at night. . . . They lived in shacks and cabins in the shanty-towns that had their brief inglorious existences on the less eligible low-lying suburban lands until values reached a point that made it worth some developer's while to drain it.[2]

The effect of such housing conditions, fostered by the city, was to degrade humanity, to destroy human dignity. It was amazing that in spite of everything there were those who clung to every vestige of 'home' that they could, who wore themselves out to maintain some kind of decency. Of course, it was just this that the more privileged members of society encouraged them to do, to keep themselves clean and refrain from strong liquor, and not to over-indulge in the consolations of the marriage bed. The lower orders were to be discouraged from breeding. The middle classes saw the dirt and drunkenness and the destitute children, and produced advice that seemed simply common sense. Only the greatest of the Victorian reformers could see things as effect rather than cause.

It was not only the absence of the men that made a stable family life a luxury for the underprivileged. It was also often the absence of the wives and mothers. Particularly in certain areas large numbers of women were employed, in Lancashire and the Potteries, for instance, and many employers preferred women and children—because they were cheaper. In 1857 it was calculated that 30 per cent of married women in the cotton districts were employed, two thirds of whom were textile workers. The figures were similar in the Potteries. Here are the comments of a factory inspector of the time. 'A vast majority of the persons employed at night and for long periods during the day are females; their labour is cheaper and they are more easily induced to undergo severe bodily fatigue than men.'[3] The kind of life that a married female operative led can be imagined. The inspector goes on:

> Half an hour to dress and suckle her infant and carry it out to nurse; one hour for household duties before leaving home; half an hour for actually travelling to the mill; twelve hours' actual labour; one and a half hours for meals; half an hour for returning home at night; one and a half hours for household duties and preparing for bed, leaving six and a half hours for recreation, seeing and visiting friends and sleep; and in winter when it is dark, half an hour extra time on the road to the mill and half an hour extra on the road home from the mill.[4]

As is suggested here, the younger children would be left in the care of minders, who were often old women or young girls. It wasn't unusual for a nine year old to be left in charge of a baby, and she could well be more competent than the old and infirm who might be the only alternative. The first nurseries were set up as charitable institutions in the 1850s, and there were very few of them.

The employment of women was widely condemned. It was seen as an offence to feminine decency, as a threat to the family and as leading directly to immorality. Many saw the factories as dens of vice and factory workers as, anyway, people of

29   A London slum-cellar near St Giles, c. 1840

30   Robert Owen housing experiment at New Lanark was the precursor of many later paternalistic schemes

inferior morals. There were those who felt that the heat and discomfort of factory conditions heightened sexuality (middle-class decency was always liable to associate squalor and sex). The fact that men and women mingled freely in their work was highly improper and bound to lead to all kinds of dubious activities, many felt. The fact that sheer exhaustion must have done more to curb the rising population than anything else, both in discouraging sexuality and increasing the risk of miscarriage, does not seem to have occurred to middle-class observers.

Shaftesbury was one of many who condemned the working woman.

... the evil is spreading rapidly and extensively, desolating like a torrent the peace, the economy, and the virtue of the mighty masses of the manufacturing districts. Domestic life and domestic discipline must soon be at an end; society will consist of individuals no longer grouped into families; so early is the separation of husband and wife, of parents and children.[5]

The woman was seen, by the middle and upper classes, as the keystone of home life, and even in cases where the employment of women was not in itself offensive, in the traditional female occupations such as millinery, the duty of the married woman was to be at home. She should be caring for her children, rather than putting them out to nurse, keeping her home clean, and cooking a hot dinner for her weary husband's refreshment on his return from work. The logic of such advice, that the male breadwinner should be paid a decent wage so that wives would not need to work, escaped most commentators.

Working women were seen as the cause of a great deal that was wrong with working-class life, for the home was inevitably a focal point of improvement. In 1904 August Bebel published *Woman Under Socialism*, an innovatory work, but which still insisted that family life was crucial (in spite of the attacks of Marx and Engels on the family as essentially a bourgeois and conservative institution) and that women at home were the essential supports of family life. He wrote, 'with the extension of female labour, the family life of the working class goes even more to pieces, the dissolution of marriage and the family is the natural result, and immorality, demoralization, degeneration, diseases of all natures and child mortality increase at a shocking pace.'[6] Bebel's concern was to stop the exploitation of women, which he rightly saw in their employment as cheap labour and the general attitude of society, at all levels, towards them. It is interesting that he continued to see the family as at the heart of a fulfilled life and as an essential unit in a socialist society, for this view was, in Europe, thoroughly bourgeois. (The Jewish attitude to the family might be an exception, for in the diaspora the strength and unity of working-class family life was of the greatest significance.)

Certainly in Britain the voices raised against working women were uniformly of the privileged classes, and were part of a message that insisted that only a woman at home, making it clean and comfortable, would keep a man from seeking less desirable haunts.

The man who goes home on a Saturday only to find his house in disorder, with every article of furniture out of its place, the floor unwashed or sloppy from uncompleted washing, his wife slovenly, his children untidy, his dinner not yet ready, or spoilt in the cooking, is much more likely to 'go on the spree' than the man who finds his house in order, the furniture glistening from the recent polishing, the burnished steel fire-irons looking doubly resplendent from the bright glow of the cheerful fire, his well-cooked dinner laid on a snowy cloth, and his wife and children tidy and cheerful. If the man whose household work is neglected or mismanaged is of a meek character and has been unfortunate enough to get for a wife one who is a termagant as well as a sloven, he will have to devote his Saturday afternoon to assisting in the woman's work of his own house. But when the husband is not of the requisite meekness of spirit, he hastens from the disorderly scene, and roams about in a frame of mind that predisposes him to seek the questionable comforts of the public-house, or to enter into some other form of dissipation . . .[7]

That domestic work was woman's work was so obvious that it did not need to be stated: only a 'meek' man would descend to doing the chores 'in his own house'. That a man's time outside paid employment was his own was equally taken for granted. It was up to the wife to make home as enticing as possible; if her man sought other forms of amusement she had only herself to blame. This was a direct reflection of the middle-class ethic; the middle-class wife was told much the same—that if she did not undertake the responsibility of making home attractive she could not blame her husband for spending his evenings at the club, or seeking more dubious forms of entertainment.

The message to the working woman was repeated continually. In *The British Workwoman*, a journal begun in the 1860s to convey a middle-class voice to the working woman, one of the major themes is (in spite of the title), don't go out to work. 'Wife of the labouring man! Take warning in time. Try to make your home happy to your husband and children. Remember your first earthly duty, and, whatever be the temptations to go out to work, STAY AT HOME!'[8] The middle class felt that fostering an orderly family life amongst the labouring classes was a means of controlling potential chaos which would be a serious threat to themselves. Another of *The British Workwoman*'s messages is that women 'should learn to esteem and value those for whom they work',[9] in other words to accept the status quo of the class structure. All the middle-class feelings of vulnerability, and sensitivity about status, can be detected in these attitudes for, after all, mid-century around 75 per cent of the population was working class. Although we think of the Victorian period as being the age of the rising middle class, its dimensions were still comparatively small. A great deal of the political power was still in the hands of the landed aristocracy, while below them was the mass of underprivileged, to which it was so hard to give shape and form. It could only be to middle-class advantage to foster orderly and decent habits amongst the poor, to try to identify them in terms of their own requirements. A woman at home, it was felt, might make all the difference between a rioting striker and a hard-working labouring man.

O. R. McGregor, whose book on *Divorce in England* (1957) is a key work in the

31   *Working-class model housing. Peabody Square, Islington, 1866*

32   *Working-class planned estate of Shaftesbury Park, Battersea, c. 1872*

33   A London working-class home. Golden Lane, 1872. Ornaments and cheap framed prints attempt to maintain 'respectability'

understanding of the family as an institution, suggests that the whole idea of working-class family life, with an identifiable culture which we now tend to look back on with nostalgia and which in reality only existed for some and in the last quarter of the nineteenth century, is in part at least a middle-class creation. The middle class encouraged the working class to imitate their version of the home on a vastly smaller scale, and to a great extent inspired and engineered the social reforms which made the imitation possible. The middle-class acceptance of social obligation provided, McGregor says, 'the framework within which a working-class family unit appropriate to the conditions of industrialism became established.'

> Working-class people could not themselves perform the familial duties prescribed by the middle-class family code. The very bases of this conception—a clean and decent home and the leisure to pursue family life within it, the health and education of children, the protection of dependents—were only secured by collective action and public provision . . . the working-class family became a going concern only with the protective shelter of expanding social services.[10]

And in a sense the working class had to pay for such provision by showing itself willing to accept and abide by whatever the social obligation of the better off was prepared to grant. It was an unequal bargain, but better than nothing. There was some improvement for some, though at the end of the century the poverty and squalor and conditions militating against home life in Britain's cities, Glasgow's Gorbals, London's East End, were as appalling as ever, as a great deal of documentation verifies.

Much of the improvement was general, and not particularly aimed at the labouring classes. Sanitation, for example. By the 1850s many cities were making some attempt to control the problem of human waste. Covered drains were built to replace open sewers (though many of these continued to empty into the rivers: the Thames remained a sludge of disease-carrying filth) and more care was taken to provide an uncontaminated water supply. But disease was still rife. Cholera, typhus, smallpox, diphtheria and lung diseases were the major killers, and the slowness in bringing them under control was partly due to a reluctance to believe that a contaminated water supply was the means of contagion. The miasmic theory of disease, which held that infection was carried by bad air, predominated in the nineteenth century, even when the connection between cholera, for instance, and contaminated water, was patently demonstrated. In 1849 William Fair first suggested a correlation between water, elevation and the spread of cholera, and by 1866 all doubts concerning the murderous role of contaminated water had been removed. But bad air was a concept the Victorians were reluctant to part with. There was, though, in the 1840s, an increasing concern about public health and a growing commitment to action, and Edwin Chadwick, determined sanitation reformer, had a great deal to do with this. In 1848 there was a Public Health Act which set up a General Board of Health and Local Boards of Health, which was a first step towards cleaning up the towns. But even this was six years after the publication of Chadwick's report on *The Sanitary Conditions of the Labouring Classes* which

34   'A Court for King Cholera' by John Leech, 1852

had established in detail the intimate connection between disease and bad sanitation.

Work on improving sewage systems and water supply was slow and variable. The middle classes, who were of course most likely to be benefitting from such facilities as did exist, did not take kindly to the idea of paying rates to provide improvements that would most radically affect the lives of others. The fundamental facts of sewage were so much in evidence in early Victorian life that perhaps to a certain extent they were accepted as part of the landscape. That there might be ways of disposing of excrement efficiently, and removing the smells and the disease and the filth underfoot, came slowly to some. And sanitary improvements alone could not transform the lives of those whose need was greatest.

Concern for the housing of the poor had grown initially out of the need to provide housing in the rapidly growing industrial areas. Most of what was put up, in mill villages, in towns, anywhere it was necessary to house large numbers of factory workers within reach of the factory gates, was jerry-built, cramped, destined to lapse in some cases almost instantly into slum conditions. Primitive sanitary arrangements were often responsible. With the infamous back-to-back terraces the sharing of privies and water supply often meant that these essential amenities were some considerable distance from the home. Water was precious if every drop had to be carried, and not likely to be used lavishly in the interests of keeping clean. The temptation not to make use of the privy, which was probably stinking and filthy, was great. In Sunderland there was an average of one privy to

76 people, in parts of Manchester over 7000 shared 33. On the landlords' part there was a reluctance to spend money, reflecting a general assumption that the factory operative was barely more than an animal, that his needs were not those of a civilized human being, and that for the purposes of work he could be treated with less care than a (considerably more valuable) machine. It was hardly surprising that workers sometimes took their revenge on these machines.

There were enlightened men, though, who thought in terms of providing not just reasonably decent housing but model communities for their workers. As early as 1800 Robert Owen had set up New Lanark, a community of workers for his mill on the banks of the upper Clyde. He built flats, and provided a school and other facilities, and allowed the children who worked in his mill time for their schooling. The tall, dark buildings, in the Scottish tenement tradition, still rise out of the narrow glen with a certain sombre dignity. They reflect, in their precision and uniformity, the need that was felt to impose some kind of organization on the lives of the workers. The same kind of reflection can be seen in Saltaire, the much later brain-child of Titus Salt, Bradford woollen manufacturer. Saltaire was on a larger scale than New Lanark, with over 4000 inhabitants by 1871, and was the result of a noble intention. Salt wanted to provide a healthy and moral environment for his workers and their families. He wanted order, and he wanted to provide them with the means of improvement. There was a school, chapels, an infirmary, almshouses, a library and reading rooms, and facilities for physical recreation—a gym and Saltaire park. In 50 years ideas about what could legitimately benefit the workers had progressed. But of course those who were housed in Saltaire could only make use of these products of enlightenment on the master's terms, and these were ultimately terms of employment. This was paternalism in practice, the provision of a standard of living far beyond the experience of most industrial workers in return for good behaviour, obedience and conformity, in the home and on the factory floor. And of course the standards were set by the employer: for anyone to ask for more or to criticize would have been seen as a direct challenge to the system itself.

What was considered the proper standard for housing the urban worker? There were a few cooperative housing associations which enabled better-off workers to set their own. In mid-century Edinburgh a housing cooperative built terraced flats (on the maisonette principle) which were so successful they were imitated by other groups in other parts of the city. The houses have considerable charm to the twentieth-century eye, and are now regarded as desirable residences. And they do indeed have several attractive and sensible features which have made them superior housing. They are built in orderly rows on the fringe of Edinburgh's New Town beside the Water of Leith, which admittedly then carried, besides sewage, the refuse from numerous mills and tanneries further up river; the site was damp and unhealthily low-lying. But the development shared its general location with middle-class housing. There is an open aspect, and gardens and trees, with both a public park and the Botanic Gardens nearby, and only a few minutes away from one of the New Town's most elegant squares. The

35   Lord Shaftesbury   *36   Titus Salt, founder of Saltaire*

houses themselves are not tall, a ground floor and two low-ceilinged upper storeys, possibly because it was felt that anything higher would be too intrusive on the New Town skyline, and each flat has a front garden. Each unit contains two flats facing different ways, with an outside stair to the upper flat, which makes the individual gardens possible—in other words, the terraces were not back-to-back, but constructed in such a way as to show both economy and imagination. The rooms are very small, and the provision of space is little better than that for the agricultural labourer, but there is no doubt that these were, for their times, superior dwellings of a distinctive character.

This was privileged housing for the privileged worker, and contrary to the usual practice of placing lower-class housing out of site of middle-class eyes. Lower-class housing wasn't meant to be nice to look at, although, as we have seen, sometimes a little decorative embellishment was regarded as appropriate, and neatness was an approved feature. It was preferable for lower-class living to be clean and orderly, but not desirable, except to a handful of progressive individuals, that the environment for such living should be pleasing. In most cases the attitude to working-class housing remained severely functional, for there were profits to be considered, and most of those who put up new housing for the workers were local employers and builders. Their aim was to provide low-cost housing, and as land was expensive space cost money. So new housing did not, for the most part, help to cure the ills of overcrowding, and the chronically poor and the unemployable had no chance of new housing anyway.

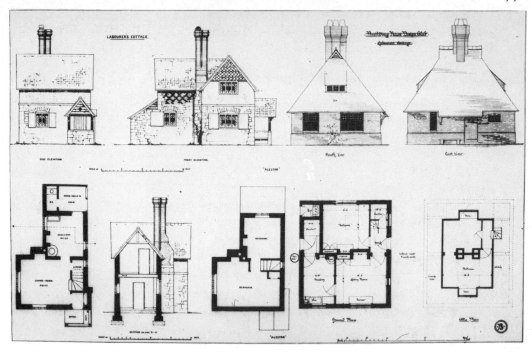

37   *Designs for labourers' cottages,* The Building News, *1877*

In good times the working-class interior could be pleasant enough. With the man of the house and perhaps a son or daughter in employment, when the mills and factories were booming and wages were relatively high, when there was money enough to pay for some comforts and a woman at home to work at them, the working-class home could be a place of positive qualities. Here, from *Mary Barton* again, is Elizabeth Gaskell's description of a Manchester millworker's home when times were good.

The room was tolerably large, and possessed many conveniences. On the right of the door, as you entered, was a longish window, with a broad ledge. On each side of this hung blue-and-white check curtains, which were now drawn, to shut in the friends met to enjoy themselves. Two geraniums, unpruned and leafy, which stood on the sill, formed a further defence from outdoor pryers. In the corner between the window and the fireside was a cupboard, apparently full of plates and dishes, cups and saucers, and some more non-descript articles . . . it was evident that Mrs Barton was proud of her crockery and glass, for she left her cupboard door open, with a glance round of satisfaction and pleasure. On the opposite side to the door and window was the staircase, and two doors; one of which (the nearest to the fire), led into a sort of little back kitchen, where dirty work, such as washing up dishes, might be done, and whose shelves served as a larder, and pantry, and storeroom, and all. The other door, which was considerably lower, opened into the coal-hole—the slanting closet under the stairs; from which, to the fireplace, there was a gay-coloured piece of oil-cloth laid. The place seemed almost crammed with furniture (sure sign of good times among the mills). Beneath the window was a dresser with three deep drawers. Opposite the fireplace was a table, which I should call a Pembroke, only that it was made of deal, and I cannot tell how far such a name be applied to such humble material. On it, resting against the wall, was a bright green japanned tea-tray, having a couple of scarlet lovers embracing in the middle. The fire-light danced merrily on this, and really . . . it gave a richness of colouring to that side of the room. It was in some measure propped up by a crimson tea-caddy, also of japan ware. A round table on one branching leg ready for use, stood in the corresponding corner to the cupboard; and if you can picture all this with a washy, but clean stencilled pattern on the walls, you can form some idea of John Barton's home.[11]

This is an extremely detailed picture, carefully put together from Mrs Gaskell's own observation—she visited many working-class homes. When the strike comes, John Barton's home gradually becomes bare, as articles are sold or put into pawn in order to buy food. And such comfort is small consolation for the death in child-birth of his wife.

Later in this scene the Barton family and their friends sit down to the convivial tea I have already described. The food and the firelight suggest just the cosiness that we tend to consider typically Victorian. This room, like the middle-class home, is a refuge, and the streets outside have been described for us, so we know fairly precisely what is being shut out when the door is closed. The curtains are drawn, the geraniums, 'a further defence from outside pryers', act as shields, and reinforce the impression that the aim of the Bartons is to create in their home a haven of comfort beyond the influence of the outside world and outsiders. Mrs Gaskell of course also succumbs to the middle-class ideal, but her feeling for the positive qualities of this ideal is strong. But if for the middle-class family the ideals were a possibility, for the working-class family they scarcely were, for the workers were too near the sources of their security, and too vulnerable to influences and conditions beyond their control. It might be said that every working-class family with an eye to improvement was striving for that supreme moment when a closed door could *really* signify the shutting out of a hostile world.

Improvement was much in the minds of some of the better off of the working classes (the lower one was in the world, the more of a mockery such an idea seemed) but it was even more in the minds of the philanthropic middle class. The general view was that it took character, morality and hard work to move up in the world, and that too much assistance was a bad thing. Certainly in the 1840s it was felt that the poor were not victims, but bad managers, or feckless. They brought it on themselves. They did not work hard and fear God. They squandered what money they had on drink. They were liable to take advantage of any offer of help. This attitude is reflected most strongly in the 1834 Poor Law, which kept poor relief below the rate of the minimum wage level, which was often itself below

38 'Cold, misery and want destroy their youngest child'

subsistence level, and refused it outside the workhouse. The workhouse accommodation was never remotely sufficient for all those who might have qualified, but in fact many feared the workhouse to such an extent that they would work for lower wages rather than enter its doors. In the workhouse families were separated, men and women housed in different quarters, and the inmates were poorly fed and put to work at what were often revolting and virtually useless jobs—bone-crushing, for instance. There was outraged criticism of the Poor Law, particularly in the north, for it was seen as an instrument of the employers, a way of keeping wages low. With the workhouse as an alternative men and women would work for a pittance rather than face its harshness. And of course it also disrupted family life. It was not a means of social support so much as a punishment for being poor.

The Poor Law improved nothing. It threatened families, while middle-class evangelicalism, particularly in the midlands and the north of England, was another voice, in some cases the same voice, raised against the moral deterioration of the working class. Self-discipline was the watchword, at a time when bread and work would have been more apt. The middle-class attitude was a combination of the desire to improve with the desire to control. They were haunted by the threat of the mob, drunk most likely, dispossessed and violent. They feared the destruction of their property. The mob had to be tamed but only the deserving were to be rewarded. The workers must be educated, but not too much. They were to be encouraged to spend their leisure hours with improving pastimes, but it would be dangerous if they acquired too sharp an awareness of their position. So the wife was encouraged to stay at home and create domestic security, and the husband to make use of the gym and reading rooms.

There were some who had quite ambitious ideas on the subject of working-class improvement. Here the architect S. H. Brooks defends his own suggestions as to the amenities he considered ought to be available for the self-improvement of the underprivileged.

> Place within the reach of all the means of harmless and cheerful recreation. . . . They consist of reading rooms, popular lectures, books, concerts, public parks, and salubrious and comfortable houses. Fastidious persons, who find fault with everything, are alarmed, lest such aids as these should advance the intellectual, without improving the moral qualities of the people. Let them remain quite at their ease in this respect. The principle object to be served by reading rooms, lectures and so forth, is the substitution of harmless for pernicious recreations.[12]

Brooks wanted to defuse the problem of improvement by emphasizing 'harmless' activities. The fear was of an educated working class that would use its education as a weapon. Brooks almost seems to be suggesting that the 'harmless' would not, in fact, provide intellectual improvement, not that intellectual improvement was harmless. It was a problem that exercised thinking Victorians greatly, how to tame the working class and at the same time to avoid the principle of equality.

There were those who were anxious to believe the best of even the least promising examples of human nature. Strong drink was a useful scapegoat, and the public house an object of great suspicion. It was suggested that if reading rooms and parks were placed temptingly before the eyes of the working man he would eschew the beer in their favour. Although middle-class benevolence was constantly encouraged, and it was in the Victorian period that there was established a strong tradition of social concern, a belief that a straightforward increase in wages might go a substantial way towards working-class improvement in health and cleanliness and nourishment was not favoured. That the working class should have more money to spend than was absolutely necessary to keep body and soul together was considered not only dangerous but 'against the economic law', until socialist ideas developed more strongly towards the end of the century.

Even William Cobbett, who worked so hard to expose rural conditions in the 1830s, and condemned so feelingly the iniquities and squalor of 'the great Wen', urged care and good management and hard work as the salvation of the labouring classes in much the same way as the middle-class benevolent paternalists, although he was admittedly a little before his time in his convictions and his message. In his *Cottage Economy* (1850) Cobbett says 'economy means *management*, and nothing more' and proceeds to illustrate how good management can be achieved. He does

39   Warmth and plenty—the fruits of industry and moderation

insist that a 'competence' is necessary, that a family must be beyond 'pinching poverty' before a useful and happy life can be led. But his version of the family chimes with that of the Victorian middle-class ideal. The father is the source of authority and responsible for the welfare of his dependants. It is his 'very first duty' to provide a good living. He must rule by love, not fear, but nevertheless he must rule. An urge towards self-discipline and industry again lies behind most of what he says. There seemed to be no other way to cope with the fearsome imbalance of the class structure.

Domestic economy became an increasingly important subject. The ignorance of the poor of how to make the most of what they had appalled many commentators. Girls often never learned to clean or cook or sew because they were out to work at such an early age, or their mothers were out to work and had no time or opportunity to instruct them. Although working-class girls were expected to do their share of adult work when they were very young and often had little opportunity to discover the meaning of play or to enjoy the immunity from responsibility which it is usually assumed children are at least partially allowed, they often had very little understanding of what came to be called 'domestic economy'. By 1876 'domestic economy' was a compulsory subject for girls at board schools; it was realized that there was little point in trying to keep working-class girls at home if they did not know how to cope domestically. The lessons of Mrs Beeton were adjusted to suit more frugal households, for her message above all concerned the responsibility of the housewife, with servants or without, to provide food, cleanliness and comfort in a well-regulated manner.

A stable well-run home was of the greatest importance to Victorian society and to Victorian confidence. A great deal of the reaction to the worst of urban infestation, to the appalling filth and the smells and the degradation of humanity, was composed of fear rather than pity. It was the possibility of disorder and disease that caused many of even the greatest and most disinterested reformers to turn their attentions to the lives of the other three-quarters of the population. The homes and the lives of the working class had to be ordered, and for the most part the middle class provided the aims and the means for doing so. Unstable homes could threaten society. Well-ordered homes were instruments of control, a means of taming the exploited. Give people a degree of satisfaction and comfort within their own four walls and they would be less likely to make rash demands, or to embark on actions that might prejudice the safety of what they already had. For the most part, the working class, especially the better-off and more successful, readily imitated the picture of domesticity that the middle class held out before them, and it was largely this imitation that created that brief period of flourishing working-class identity and culture that existed at the end of the century. But there were voices raised against the whole idea of the home and family. There were those who condemned it. Communists saw it as a means of repressing the proletariat, feminists (some of them) as a means of repressing women. Here is a fictional voice, from Disraeli's *Sybil*, echoing first the concern that the working-class home was disintegrating, but arguing that this was not only inevitable, but good.

> You lament the expiring idea of Home. It would not be expiring if it were worth retaining. The domestic principle has fulfilled its purpose. The irresistable law of progress demands that another should be developed. It will come; you may advance or retard, but you cannot prevent it. It will work out like the development of organic nature. In the present state of civilization, and with the scientific means of happiness at our command, the notion of home should be obsolete. Home is a barbarous idea; the method of a rude age; home is isolation; therefore anti-social. What we want is community.[13]

This is spoken with such conviction and clarity that one suspects that Disraeli must have had some real sympathy for this view of the home as a crude and repressive institution.

Inside the Home

The Victorian interior suggests to us now bulk and darkness, bulk perhaps ornately decorated, darkness illuminated by fire and candle or gas light—but those are the insistent characteristics. These tendencies had a number of causes, some of which I have tried to indicate, but there was one particularly important motivation. The Victorians were highly conscious of themselves as Victorians; they wished to define themselves in cultural and structural terms. They were interested in the symbols of their worth and achievement. And they wanted to create, in art of all kinds, a style that was specifically, definitely and expressively of the progressive and achieving nineteenth century.

Although when we think 'Victorian' to ourselves we almost certainly think 'Gothic', in many ways the Victorians failed to find that style, for eclecticism is the most striking feature of Victorian architecture, and to a great extent that eclecticism is reflected inside the home also. The Victorians ranged widely for their inspiration, to the east, to the middle ages, to literature. They were greedy for influences and for variety. Decoration was a key word in the Victorian attitude towards what should go into the home. 'Find out what will make you comfortable, build that in the strongest and boldest way, and then set your fancy free in the decoration of it', Ruskin said in one of his *Lectures on Architecture and Painting*.[1] 'Fancy' suggests giving free rein to individual taste, but this did not seem to happen often. For it was generally felt that through decoration a family expressed its proper understanding of life and beauty, and the understanding of beauty was deemed a moral quality. With this kind of thinking conformity, even an anxious conformity, was bound to be to the fore.

In discussing Victorian decoration one should never speak of the *merely* decorative, for decoration was regarded as an essential, and good taste in the choosing of decoration a highly significant quality. Many Victorians saw themselves as arbiters of good taste, as moral guides to the appreciation of beauty, Ruskin chief amongst them. When he speaks of building boldly 'what will make you comfortable' he is not meaning to suggest that all styles of building are equally suitable or acceptable. Many Victorians, if asked to set their fancy free, would have felt totally lost. But by the second half of the century there were numerous books and aids to the art of decorating the home, covering every aspect from carpets and wallpapers to the selection of furniture and ornamentation of all kinds. One such writer, Christopher Dresser, himself a designer and much concerned with educating public taste, wrote, 'Art can lend to an apartment not only beauty, but such refinement as will cause it to have an elevating influence on those who dwell in it', and went on to describe in detail how this 'elevating influence' could be obtained.[2] But this was in 1879, when there was a widespread feeling that the education of taste would improve the quality of life. In the earlier part of Victoria's reign there were few words spoken on the subject, and when we think of Victorian vulgarity, overstuffed armchairs and wax fruit, it mostly has its origins before 1860.

The vulgarity was partly the consequence of a growing middle class that had money to spend and no tradition to follow in the spending of it. These were the people who could afford to pay for comfort and security, and who cast around for adequate symbols of their status. We have seen how the Victorians invigorated the powerful expressiveness of things, the idols of the home. At the same time the vulnerability of the middle class made it unlikely that they would be adventurous in their taste, so that in the first part of the century there tends to be a growing exaggeration of accepted ideas, in furniture for instance, and very little that is new. To assert one's bourgeois status it was not at first wise to be novel or different. Later the middle class became more daring, and to be the first to have some new gadget or the latest in curtain fabrics brought some kudos. (There was, of course, an increasing variety of things to choose from.) Novelty became an end in itself.

Inventiveness had reduced the housewife's occupation, if she could afford to benefit from it, and to have servants. She no longer brewed her own beer and baked her own bread, or made soap and candles, and she did not need to make her children's clothes. More and more could be bought readymade, and more and more services could be bought. Yet anything that could be seen as an aid to the smooth running of the household was clearly desirable. The range of these by the end of the century was impressive. In the kitchen alone there were ingenious varieties of graters, mincers, slicers and beaters—the *principle* of all that we use now was there. Aids to cleaning were also developing—carpet sweepers for instance. But mid-century one of the first rules of good management had to be that everything had its place, and that place was where it should be if not in use. The provision of stands and shelves designed to house specific objects—shelves above the mantelpiece for porcelain, stands for plant pots—proliferated. There was a great deal of furniture that was of little use except as a surface on which to place things—but these surfaces were necessary. Dressers and sideboards were designed with numerous little shelves on which vases or statuettes could be placed. There were little drawers and compartments for objects that were better out of sight. Without a degree of regimentation chaos would have ensued.

There were a number of general improvements which made life easier for those who did the hard work of the house and life more comfortable for those who enjoyed its results. Heating and ventilation exercised the minds of a number of people who were concerned with house design. Ventilation was considered especially important, because of the fear of stale air and a belief that it could breed disease. Open windows were important, but to allow fresh air in without the dirt was a problem. For some, the necessity for fresh air, which of course in the larger

40   *The Bathroom, c. 1880. Ornamentation and functionality, a common theme in Victorian design*

cities was unlikely to be very fresh, entailed wide-open windows in the dead of winter. And even with the windows closed, draughts tended to be more of a problem in large Victorian houses than stuffiness. Coal fires and gas lighting increased the difficulty of maintaining clean air, and they were problems that were never adequately solved. If the air without was smelly or smoggy one could not do very much about the stale air within. But it exercised much thought, particularly in the later part of the century.

Experiments in heating were more successful, though central heating never caught on. Various forms of central heating were being experimented with in the early years of the nineteenth century—Walter Scott installed steam heating in Abbotsford in 1823—but most people stuck to the open fires that heated only a fraction of the area of their large rooms, and depended on servants for the carrying of fuel. Some considered central heating to be unsafe, or unhealthy. But the main reason for the lack of popularity of central heating (which American visitors considered barbaric—their own rapid development of central heating, like so much of American domestic progress, can be seen as a response to the servant problem) was the complacent acceptance of the way things had always been. Even in the best society it was assumed that those near the fire scorched and had to protect their

41   In contrast to the previous illustration, the stand-pipe in Frying-pan Alley, Clerkenwell

skins with fire screens, while those at a distance froze. This was a fact of life. This, plus the deep-rooted superstition that it was healthier to be cold, accounted for a great deal.

In humble households the single source of heat in the kitchen, which in working-class homes would also be the only sitting room, provided hot food, hot water and general warmth, and was economical in both fuel and effort. Heat in larger houses was a major and time-consuming responsibility of the servants. The tending of the fires was a basic duty, and those barely on the middle-class rung would have a skivvy whose main task this would be. The cleaning and stoking of the kitchen range, in particular, was the most menial of duties, and reserved for the lowest of the low in the servant hierarchy. (I had an acquaintance, who died recently in her 70s, who talked of her first job at the age of 13, up at five in the morning to light the ranges of a high-class hotel before the First World War. Slowly she worked her way up to chamber maid.) The kitchen range or open fire were the only methods of cooking during the first half of the century, though the range could be quite sophisticated and elaborate. There were gas cookers on show in the Great Exhibition, but these did not come into general use until later. Like so much of what was in the Great Exhibition they did not reflect anything remotely close to general usage. By the end of the century there were not only electric cookers, but also electric hotplates, kettles, frying pans and so on. But most Victorians through most of the period would have eaten meals cooked on a kitchen range, and many of them were ingeniously designed and functioned with great efficiency. For a household in which there was considerable baking and where large joints of meat were regularly roasted a kitchen range, with its spacious ovens and continuous heat (so long as the fire was maintained) was appropriate. But it did need work. Fuel would be brought in from the coal hole, which in a terrace house would be a cavern off the area under the street. The last task of the evening, perhaps late, when the last guest had gone home and the tea and coffee things and the glasses had been cleared away, again for the lowest of the servant hierarchy, would be the cleaning of the range.

Mrs Beeton and others laid great stress on the cleanliness of the kitchen—and a dirty fire meant a dirty kitchen, as did mice, even rats, and other forms of wild life. Cockroaches were common denizens of kitchen quarters. Not all kitchen workers were as scrupulous as might have been desired, but there was no lack of products available for the battle against dirt, though the battle against unwelcome residents was trickier. There was a varied selection of polishes and soaps, mops and brushes, burnishers and scrubbers. Mrs Beeton recommends a tiled kitchen, but a distempered one would have been more usual, and certainly more economical. Tiles were preferable because they could be wiped down: distemper could only be renewed. (My grandmother remembers cooking on a kitchen range in pre-war Sunderland, which had the inside of the oven whitewashed. The whitewash had to be renewed weekly.) But in spite of an increasing variety of branded cleaners on the market, the amount of time needed to keep a kitchen clean was immense, and there was no way of avoiding the basic hands-and-knees scrubbing. Floors,

42　*Design for an ice-box, 1872*　　　　44　*Hand-operated tub washing machine, 1890*

43　*Flavel's Kitcheners shown at the Great Exhibition of 1851*

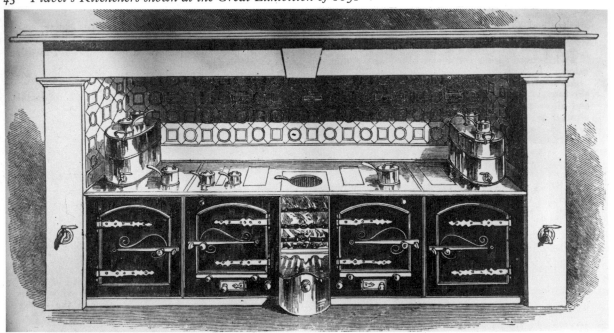

surfaces—mostly wood, some marble—and walls all collected coal dust and grease. Varnished wallpapers became quite widely used, especially for kitchens that doubled as sitting rooms. They were easy to clean, and allowed a range of colour. Mrs Beeton has a lot to say on the subject of floor coverings. The usual kitchen floor was either scrubbed wood or, in different parts of the country, flagstones or tiles. In large houses concrete was considered a suitable flooring material, but in the later editions of the *Book of Household Management* (by which time Mrs Beeton herself was dead) linoleum is being firmly recommended. Linoleum was patented in 1860, and by the end of the century it was a favourite material, not only in kitchens, but anywhere that practicality was the foremost consideration.

Kitchens in spacious houses had to be large if only to accommodate the man-power needed to run them. But room had to be found also for the quantity of gear that cooking on a large scale required. Not only was there a great variety of kitchen implements and utensils, but many of them had to be of large dimensions. Pots and pans, fish kettles and baking trays, bains maries and mixing bowls, had to be chosen with cooking for ten or twelve in mind. Ingenious inventions came on the market, such as mayonnaise mixers, freezing machines, bread slicing machines, coffee roasters and knife cleaners. But, although a wealthy household's kitchen might include all these and more, such lists do not give us an adequate picture of a normal working kitchen just as today's glossy magazines do not convey the kitchens that most of the population inhabit. Here is the kitchen of a provincial lower middle-class household, shopkeepers and very respectable, in the 1860s.

> Forget-me-knots on a brown field ornamented the walls of the kitchen. Its ceiling was irregular and grimy, and a beam ran across it. . . . A large range stood out from the wall between the stairs and the window. The rest of the furniture comprised a table—against the wall opposite the range—a cupboard, and two Windsor chairs. Opposite the foot of the steps was a doorway, without a door, leading to two larders, dimmer even than the kitchen, vague retreats made visible by whitewash, where bowls of milk, dishes of cold bones, and remainders of fruit-pies, reposed on stillages; in the corner nearest the kitchen was a great steen in which the bread was kept.[3]

This is a cellar kitchen, as many Victorian kitchens were, with inadequate lighting and a general atmosphere of gloom. The basement kitchen of a town terrace house would have direct access to an area, with coal holes and other storage space under the pavement, and steps used by tradesmen in their deliveries. The kitchen would probably have a scullery in which washing-up was done, possibly a laundry room, pantry and larder and wine cellar. These would have stone slab shelves, which were an asset in keeping things cool. But they were also dark and hard to clean, a play-ground for mice and beetles.

Gas lighting helped to improve subterranean quarters, although initially it was messy, smelly and noisy. Gas mains were being laid in the 1820s, though it was some time before gas was of a good enough quality to be used inside the house. By 1834 there were over 600 miles of gas mains in London, but it was not until 1842

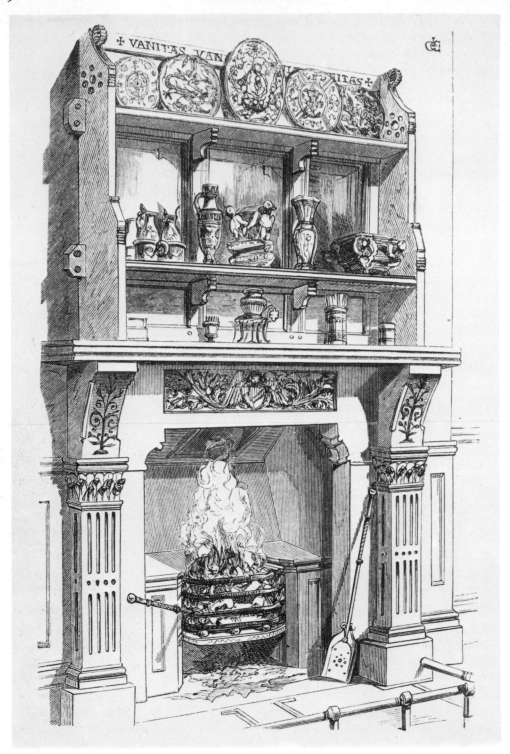

45 *Architecture-in-the-home. A mantelpiece by Charles Eastlake, 1872*

that there were the first installations in private homes, although Scott, along with his central heating, had gas lighting specially installed at Abbotsford in the 1820s. He had personal connections with the local gas company—one of the first. By the 1860s gas lighting in middle-class homes was widespread. In 1868 there were gas geysers for heating water. Cooking and heating by gas came later.

All of this improved life in the kitchen as elsewhere in the house. Candles or the more primitive forms of oil lamps (paraffin lamps did not come into use until the 1850s) were scarcely adequate for most kitchen tasks. In the drawing room gasoliers replaced chandeliers, often elaborate and glittering with glass. But candlelight continued to be important, as the large quantities of candlesticks and candelabra in the Great Exhibition suggest, for gas remained largely the privilege of the urban areas. For many households it was not until electricity began to supplant gas, in the 1880s, that the old ways of candles and oil lamps could be left behind, for electricity was more easily transportable than gas. As we have noticed, electricity brought not only lighting, and later fires and cookers, but electrified kitchen utensils of an amazing variety. As far as the kitchen was concerned electricity marked the transition from Victorian to modern.

Around 1850 there were a number of significant changes and improvements which had long-term effects on the interiors of houses, and also on their construction. The abolition of the brick tax in 1850 and of the window tax in 1851 made a vital material and a vital amenity cheaper, and improvements in the making of plate glass also contributed to more and bigger windows. By 1850 there were also revolutionary printing methods being employed which made, for instance, wallpaper much cheaper. Before then, wallpaper was a rarity and even in quite well-off homes would be reserved for a single special room. In the latter half of the century the use of wallpaper became standard, and with its increase in use came a greater interest in its design. Wallpaper became a focus of design concern in the 1870s, and its patterns and colours became increasingly dominant in the general conception of a room. In 1853 the advertisement tax was abolished, and in 1855 the duty on newspapers, and this opened the gates to widespread advertising which in its turn affected the sale of commodities of all kinds. What was happening, in fact, was the gradual development of a consumer oriented society. What went into one's house became no longer a question of what could be seen in other people's houses or in the shops, but of what was increasingly displayed in other ways. Buying for the home, which at one time was mainly something that was done when an establishment was set up at the time of marriage, became something that went on all the time. It wasn't a case of obsolescence so much as of novelty. There were always new designs, new styles, new fashions, which made the old less acceptable. Newspapers and magazines were always tantalizingly reminding one of what was available.

The period was one of rapid change. But taste did not change so quickly as to make the dominant impression of Victorian taste, the bulk and clutter, irrelevant, and the fact that this particular phase of nineteenth-century taste was confirmed and celebrated by the Great Exhibition makes it inescapable. In furniture, until well past mid-century, the curve was king, and cabinet-makers were content to imitate, or elaborate, accepted designs. Some of the pieces in the Great Exhibition were grotesque, and impossible to imagine in an ordinary home—and it was unlikely that they would ever be found there. There were pianos, swollen and curled and carved, dressers elaborately covered in vines and bunches of grapes, wreaths of flowers and fruit and animals abounded on chair legs and drawers and cupboard doors, anywhere where the carving did not actually interfere with the article's function—and sometimes where it did. The more the better, as if the major principle was that practicality should be heavily disguised. Candlesticks, vases, lamps, fire grates, salt sellars, mirrors, picture-frames, clock stands, cutlery were frequently densely scrolled in curved shapes. Ornament was, in itself good, and what is reflected in the Great Exhibition is a parting of the ways between ornament and utility. Utility indicated nothing, except perhaps worthiness. Ornament indicated good taste, financial status and moral awareness. The self-esteem that characterized the Great Exhibition was a product of the grotesqueries that it contained. But in terms of actual progress in design the International Exhibition held 11 years later was much more significant.

Along with the curve went comfort, and comfort was, partly at least, responsible for the decline in taste. I quote from John Gloag's book on *Victorian Comfort* (1961).

> In time, the love of comfort debilitated the critical faculties, and the decline of taste in the 1820s and '30s coincided with the rise of an insensitive plutocracy whose leaders unconsciously cultivated a philosophy of comfort, which was adopted by the middle classes, expounded in its material aspects by Dickens . . . and embraced by everybody who enjoyed modest, easy or affluent circumstances. . . . The decline of educated taste and appreciation of good design began in the 1820s, sinking lower and lower until the Great Exhibition of 1851, when Victorian comfort and Victorian taste were stabilized respectively at high and low levels, which remained, with minor exceptions and variations, generally acceptable to all classes for the rest of the nineteenth century.[4]

It was assumed that taste was something that status automatically endowed one with, but gradually a belief emerged that taste had to be educated, and that this was an important part of a general education. If, as Gloag suggests, for the majority the actualities of home comfort did not greatly change later in the century, there was amongst a significant minority a considerable alertness to the possibilities of design.

Comfort was experienced directly. It was quickly realized that early Georgian furniture was rather too sparse, upright and unpadded for those whose aim it was to purchase a comfortable life with new wealth. The bulk was partly the result of padding, but also a reflection of substance. Thick carpeting and heavy draperies contributed to the cosiness, to the atmosphere of comfort. But there were contradictions. Elaborate carving was more likely to interfere with the ease of living than contribute to it. Heavy furniture that was difficult to move about made cleaning more difficult, and dirt could undermine comfort. Even accepting that the wealth bought servants as well as furniture it is hard to reconcile the impracticality of much Victorian furnishing with a dominating influence of comfort. It seems clear that for many the symbolic value of ornamentation was as significant as the need for comfortable surroundings. Improving techniques and the excitement of experimenting with new materials combined with readily available cash to produce objects for enhancing the middle-class home. They were often neither useful nor comfortable, but they were important.

Here are some of the objects illustrated in the Great Exhibition catalogue whose elaborate decoration all but disguises their practical function, or which have no practical function at all: caskets, inkstands, a thermometer bracket, vases of artificial flowers, ornamental chimneypieces, pedestals on which to put vases or statuettes, goblets, carved still lives. These were made from a variety of materials with which there was experimentation at the time, iron for instance, glass, pottery, silver. In some cases real leaves and foliage were electro-plated. The ready money, the need for symbols and the desire for comfort all combined to the detriment of taste, and as they combined there grew a way of thinking that rationalized what was happening. The lofty ideas of the great Gothic architects could be borrowed to suggest that ornamentation was not only good, but to the glory of God. Comfort was a proper reward for hard work. The synthesis of ornament and comfort was a highly appropriate expression of a middle class who used religion and morality as weapons of self-protection. From this grew a belief that taste itself was an expres-

46   *Electric floor-polisher, 1894*

sion of morality, and that it was highly desirable that taste should be regularized and controlled.

Charles Eastlake wrote one of the first books specifically on taste within the home, although women's magazines had been offering advice earlier in the Victorian period. His *Hints on Household Taste* was published in 1868, considerably after the Great Exhibition but before the more interesting and exciting influences had taken hold of design. We can take him as a mid-Victorian voice on the subject. In the early pages of his book he writes,

> The faculty of distinguishing good from bad design in the familiar objects of domestic life is a faculty which most educated people—and women especially—conceive they possess. How it has been acquired, few would be able to explain. The general impression seems to be that it is the peculiar inheritance of gentle blood, and independent of all training; that while a young lady is devoting at school, or under a governess, so many hours a day to music, so many to language, and so many to general science, she is all this time unconsciously forming that sense of the beautiful, which we call taste—that this sense, once developed, will enable her, unassisted by special study or experience, not only to appreciate the charms of nature in every aspect, but to form a correct estimate of the merits of art-manufacture.[5]

We can read this as an articulate middle-class challenge to the belief that good taste was an inherited quality in the possession of the upper classes. Like anything else, taste could be learned, and whether or not we ourselves coincide with any aspect of Victorian taste is not as important as the fact that Victorians took the whole business with increasing seriousness. There remained of course vast tracts of complacency, but the voices of such as Eastlake, Ruskin, Christopher Dresser and William Morris made a considerable impression.

Eastlake echoed the call for a national style of architecture, with which many architects were preoccupied but without producing anything convincingly and specifically mid-Victorian. Rather than borrowing features from past ages and other counties, Eastlake says, 'We want in England a less refined and more nervous expression of architectural beauty—bold and sturdy features, which will hold their own against wind and rain and defy the smoke and traffic of our busy coal-burning towns.'[6] Although he approves of the recognition of 'old English traditions' and 'Border chivalry' (and acknowledges the debt to Scott) that fostered Gothic architecture it is clear that he is troubled by the lack of contemporary inspiration. He is looking for something more expressive of mid-Victorian energy. He wants directness, simplicity, condemns the phoney, and sorrows over the effects of mass production. He dismisses the fruit and the flowers, the hares and the hounds, and states firmly, 'Every article of manufacture which is capable of decorative treatment should indicate, by its general design, the purpose to which it will be applied, and should never be allowed to convey a false notion of that purpose.'[7] In the 1860s we can see emerging a vigorous application to the problem of the divergence of the *dolce* and the *utile*.

47 and 48   The impressive machinery of the Victorian kitchen

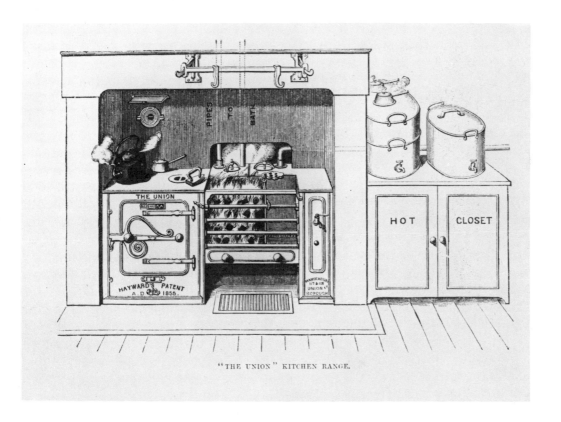

"THE UNION" KITCHEN RANGE.

Eastlake's principles and beliefs were those that William Morris and his company of craftsmen and designers were already putting into practice. But the most significant aspect of Eastlake's writing is that he sees taste not as a matter of good and bad, but of right and wrong, and what he puts forward as the appropriate ways to treat the interior of a house are not suggestions, or advice, but rules. 'Paper-hangings should in no case be allowed to cover the whole space of a wall from skirting to ceiling,' is one of many.[8] It was a reaction not just to a lack of taste, but a lack of order, a lack of principle, in early Victorian interiors. And it was the beginning of the attempt to lighten the heaviness of the Victorian home, to introduce gayer and lighter colours, more lively patterns, and more delicate furnishings. Energy, movement and light gradually found their way in through the protective layers of the Victorian home, through an insistence on the morality of design.

We have to visualize a characteristic interior, a living room—though it would be called a parlour or a drawing room. The walls are a dark colour, dark red perhaps. They might be covered with an embossed wallpaper. The woodwork is stained a dark brown. There is a patterned carpet on the floor, which perhaps has a bold, bright colour on a darker background. There are heavy curtains at the window, with white lace curtains, impossible to keep clean, and plants on the window sill carefully arranged to interrupt any possible glare from outside. There are a sofa and two armchairs, and again their colour is probably dark, brown or dark green perhaps. There is a dresser, a 'cottage' (small, upright) piano, occasional tables, all in dark wood and with some carved decoration. There is a coal fire, a mantelpiece, a mirror above it with an ornamental frame, brass fender and coal scuttle, or perhaps cast-iron, a fire screen. There is a writing desk, with all kinds of little drawers and compartments, and a treasured silver inkstand. There are stands for vases, porcelain, glass and silver on the dresser and mantelpiece. There is a gate-legged table which can be used for family tea-time by the fire. If it is a modest home without a library there are bookshelves containing the family reading. The more activities went on in such a room the more clutter there would be, sewing baskets, newspapers, magazines, implements for writing and drawing, and there would be suitable racks or stands or boxes for storage. There are more chairs, a chair for the writing desk, a piano stool. And on the walls there are pictures: engravings, prints once the technique had been developed—copies of Old Masters were favourites, photographs, pieces of tapestry worked by the ladies of the household, water-colours possibly also done in the home, pictures made out of shells or dried flowers, carvings designed as wall hangings. The suggestion of drapery is very much present. There are table cloths and runners, antimacassars and cushions. If it is summer the empty grate might well be draped, or in some way disguised—pleated paper was a traditional method. If it is the best parlour, or a drawing room that is only used when there are guests, there may be dust covers, or covers for everyday use, which can be removed when there are visitors.

A room of this kind could have been found anywhere at any time in the nineteenth century, and even in the twentieth. I have been inside Scottish provincial and rural homes which in the 1950s still retained a distinct Victorian flavour, a

49   Collard and Collard's rococo piano-fortes, 1851

flavour that comes not with the collection of antiques, but with the long residence of Victorian artefacts undisturbed in the same room. But there were changes within the Victorian period, not necessarily as the result of changing attitudes in design, but often in response to more prosaic needs. Much of the newer housing was built on a smaller scale. The suburban parlour had not the space for a vast sideboard, the suburban bedroom could not take a huge four-poster. The latter gave way to smaller half-canopy beds, and then to brass and cast-iron beds, though the iron bedsteads were mainly for children and servants. But many of the beds in the Great Exhibition were still enormous, and the wardrobes and dressing tables were likely to be of corresponding size. Decoration in the bedroom tended to be minimal. The furniture might be carved or inlaid, the bed canopied, the washstand prettily set with tiles or marble, but there were few decorative additions to the basic bedroom necessities, few objects apart from, perhaps, silver backed brushes and enamelled containers on the dressing table. The fact that ornamentation was crowded into the public rooms emphasizes its symbolic value. Bedrooms, like kitchens, were utilitarian.

Furnishing and decoration had a further function than the provision of comfort and status. Part of its job, although it was never put quite like this, was to accentuate

50   *Gothic wall-paper, 1851*

the difference between the world outside the front door and the world inside. The white lace curtains and the plants at the window were not just there to keep out light, but to keep out intrusion, like Mary Barton's geranium. They were another feature of the barrier against threat and chaos. The solidity of Victorian furnishing suggests the need for security, a need for the home to represent that security in every way possible. The belief that women in particular needed protection, and should not even be aware of the dimensions of the threat outside, encouraged the filling of the rooms in which their activities were centred with beautiful objects that would suggest aspects of art and nature, but not of industry and economics. The industrial world was barred from the domestic world, but the industrial world had of course provided many of the improvements that the Victorian home enjoyed. But although the ingenuity and inventiveness of Victorian industry and engineering manifested itself so significantly in the home, and so dramatically on a large scale outside the home, with railways, bridges, tunnels and steamships excitingly demonstrating the genius of the heroic engineers, the everyday world on the doorstep of the Victorian home was late to benefit from all this energy.

The streets remained dirty. While adventurous railway projects proceeded with speed, ten years of wrangling over the best system of disposing of sewage and over who should be responsible lapsed between the time the need for extensive sewage systems was governmentally acknowledged and work was actually begun. Inside homes that boasted sophisticated kitchen equipment and the best of expensive taste in furnishings sanitary arrangements remained primitive. It was not just the vexed question of the disposal of human waste that was at issue, but the radical problem of water supply. The concept of a continuously and generally available uncontaminated water supply was of revolutionary dimensions.

In the 1840s London's water supply was in the hands of eight joint-stock companies, which were both inefficient and unscrupulous. Even those lucky few who had water supplied direct to their homes could not expect it to be always available. This is how S. E. Finer, the biographer of Edwin Chadwick, describes the situation in London.

Only the richer areas were adequately served and over 17,000 houses had no water whatsoever, but relied on the 'poison wells', thick with scum and oozing with sewage; 70,000 out of London's 270,000 houses were supplied in groups of twenty or thirty by stand-pipes running an hour per day, three days per week. The evil was exaggerated by the companies' system of intermittent supply, which necessitated the use of storage receptacles. This was no hardship to those who could afford capacious lead cisterns, but to the poor with their winepipes or butter-tubs it was quite another matter. Sometimes the stand-pipe was out of order, or the water cut off because the landlord had not paid his water-rates: sometimes the housewife missed her place in the queue. Whatever the cause, it meant going without water for two days. In all cases the wretched women, their men being at work, had to lug the heavy load to the top of the tenements. The poor therefore were niggardly in their use of water. Children went unwashed.

Water in which clothes had been washed was used over and over again. Vegetables went into the pot uncleaned. The drinking-water, standing for days in half-rotten tubs and uncovered butts carpeted with dust and soot was nauseous to the taste and flocculent with dirt and sediment. Very often the condition in which it arrived at the stand-pipes was no better.[9]

As always the poor got the worst of it. Water was a commodity, like any other, and had to be paid for, and the poor were in no position to complain about the product they got. (It is not surprising they preferred to drink other kinds of liquid.) But even in the case of the rich it is hard to reconcile the great emphasis on the virtues of the Victorian home, its comfort, its morality and its well-ordered life with the slowness in coming to terms with problems of sewage, dirt and scant water.

The fact that to some extent such problems could be shut out obviously did not hasten their solution. The pleasing distractions for the eye that the middle-class home provided were a camouflage not only for the competitive world of masculine work but for the sights and smells that lay outside the front door. The fact that it was considered morally improving to feast one's eyes on beauty rather than on poverty, on the imitation of nature rather than on natural squalor was a significant part of the conspiracy against improvement. We can see it now as a rationalization. We can see the whole idea of the home as refuge as a rationalization of escapism, making a positive virtue out of turning one's back on the ferocious facts on the other side of the front door. What is important to remember is that it was the Victorians who first experienced the need to rationalize. They required positive values, difficult in a time of disparate and conflicting fact, and they had to shape what was available.

But of course for thousands of households it was a quite unconscious shaping. It was a response to the necessary adapting of tradition and convention to modern needs. Basic elements of human comfort had always been treasured, modest conviviality before a blazing fire, self-generated entertainment, the relief of a dry roof and a hot meal after a day of rough weather. These are the root, the instinctive needs, and they are incorporated into the Victorian interior, stabilized, judged, and fixed. The fact that life was speeding up, that events were developing so fast, that steam power and machines drove human beings at a rate that had been unimaginable, that inventive energies burned and produced so quickly, all this surge of power that was responsible for so much of what characterized Victorian life, these things themselves constituted threat. The home was a fixture, a permanency, it *shouldn't* change, it should be not only stable but static. With such beliefs it was wholly appropriate that the insides of Victorian houses should be weighed down and filled up and that anything that suggested the ephemeral, quick movement, light should be inadmissable. Taste, in other words, was intimately related to social fact and reaction.

Yet the impression of the Victorian interior I have tried to convey need not be typical. It is at best a convenient way of establishing a partial truth. It discounts the effect of human life and individuality on things, for I have presented it more in terms of the effect of things on human life. It discounts personality, individual pressures and influences, atmosphere that can only be generated by the pulse of living people. At the same time it is surely the case that a great deal of what constituted the Victorian interior scene mitigated against vitality: the qualities of protection tended to be the qualities of sterility. The result was not always complacent comfort; it was often tension. What conflicts, what passions, what repressions, what extremes of human behaviour do we find in the pages of Dickens at the same time as he fondly portrays the contented domestic scene. We read of cruelty and destruction in that same context of candelabra and florally wrought sideboards that nourished domestic security. Neither furniture nor wallpaper nor wax fruit dead beneath a glass dome can be an adequate reflection, or even an adequate symbol, of human life.

It is from the novelists that we get the vivid hints of life. Here, to conclude the chapter on an appropriately homely note, is a short paragraph from the opening chapter of Anne Brontë's *The Tenant of Wildfell Hall* (1848), a novel of dramatic incident and mystery, but with a core of observation of the way people lived. It is a quiet interior provincial scene, pleasingly suggestive of rewarding activity and modest comfort.

On entering the parlour, we found that honoured lady [the hero's mother] seated in her arm-chair at the fireside, working away at her knitting, according to her usual custom, when she had nothing else to do. She had swept the hearth, and made a bright blazing fire for our reception; the servant had just brought in the tea-tray; and Rose was producing the sugar-basin and tea-caddy, from the cupboard in the black, oak sideboard, that shone like polished ebony, in the cheerful parlour twilight.[10]

Home-making

By the middle of the nineteenth century it was generally agreed that the skills of home-making were a vital accomplishment of the married woman. Yet, as this was being warmly asserted, by novelists, by social commentators, by journalists, it became clear that it was a function for which most women were extraordinarily ill-equipped. There was little in a woman's education to prepare her for the realities of housekeeping, the demands of domestic economy, the management of servants, the care of children, the cultivation of taste. Behind most ideas about the education of women lay the assumption that a life of leisure was all she needed to be equipped for, that it was, in fact, rather vulgar to think in any other terms. But all these tasks were a part of home-making, and a part of what made women important. This was their role, this was what made their lives morally positive. Deprived of these essential functions, and deprived as they were of most other activities, women could be little more than symbols of sexuality and saintliness.

Home-making, of which housekeeping was only one aspect, tended to come on the young middle-class wife out of nowhere. The working-class wife might have acquired a degree of practical experience if she had not had to go out to work at an early age. The daughter of an artisan would probably have taken on domestic responsibilities as a little girl. She might have had to mind the younger children, wash them and dress them, cook a hot dinner for a father returning from work, sweep and tidy, or even, like Charlie in Dickens' *Bleak House* (1853) assume sole responsibility for the family at a tender age. The adolescent Charlie is breadwinner, housekeeper and mother. The middle class was wary of allowing responsibility to their children, and the better manager the wife and mother was, the less opportunity for the daughter to acquire some of her skills. (It is interesting that Dickens' middle-class 'good housekeepers', Agnes Wickfield and Esther Summerson, are motherless daughters.) For many young middle-class girls marriage was a doubly alarming event, for it could mean not only the hinted-at horrors of the marriage bed but the assumption of an entirely new kind of responsibility. For many it meant learning how to handle money for the first time, perhaps having to manage on a limited income after being used to plenty. The job of making and maintaining a home could be an overwhelming prospect.

There was a growing tendency throughout the century to emphasize the practical usefulness of women, and this was linked, not with the increasing strength of feminism, but with a defence against some women's demands to have more

experience of the male world of work and competition. To assert women's usefulness within the home was to keep her more firmly out of the big world. The image
of femininity became less fragile, but no less confined for, it was said repeatedly,
those women who wanted to take a more active part in life outside the home could
only do so at the expense of neglecting their domestic duties, and domestic duties
were paramount. If there was neglect husband, children and the family itself
would suffer. The attack was two-pronged, against the women of fashion, who
consigned their homes and their children to the care of others so that they could
enjoy the social whirl, and against the feminists, who seemed to be disparaging the
traditional functions of women for their own selfish ends. For feminism was
frequently represented as selfish, as well as more seriously a threat to the family,
and thus to the social structure, and thus to the state itself. Feminist aims seemed
radically disruptive in a way many Victorians could not stomach.

I have suggested that for most Victorians the idea of marriage and the family
could not be separated from the idea of home. This did not often mean home
ownership, for renting was far more common than buying, so that the modern
implications of having a home of one's own, suggesting as it does the superiority of
proprietorship, did not apply so widely. The houses that Cubitt put up in Bloomsbury and Belgravia were most often rented—it was through rents that many
speculative builders made their profits. The villa in Holloway in the Grossmiths'
Diary of a Nobody (1892) is rented—with £2 off the rent because of the railway at
the bottom of the garden. The flats and houses of Edinburgh's New Town were
rented. The most likely occasion of ownership outside the landed gentry would be
in the case of a manufacturer who had a house built on the fringe of an industrial
town, as Darius Clayhanger does. But ownership was not widely aspired to, and
was not significant in the idea of the home. What was important was the quality of
the home, the quality of the taste it displayed, its organization, and the moral
qualities these things reflected. Quality was the aim of home-making.

The making of a home was not only woman's work but work that should be
hard and dedicated. It was full of rewards, or was represented as such, and no
middle-class woman of the period could have been unaware of the satisfaction she
was meant to derive from knowing that she herself had created that special atmosphere, those special comforts, that neatness and orderliness, that responsible
expression of good taste. She knew not only that she was useful, but that she was
essential to the comfort and well-being of all who dwelt in her home, and that this
home reflected, was the *only* reflection of, her achievement and her importance.
Home-making was not only a duty, it was a right. Frances Power Cobbe, a progressive commentator on women's roles, said in her book *The Duties of Women* (1881),

> The making of a true home is really our peculiar and inalienable right,—a right
> which no man can take from us; for a man can no more make a home than a
> drone can make a hive. . . . It is a woman, and only a woman,—and a woman all
> by herself, if she likes, and without any man to help her,—who can turn a house
> into a home.[1]

51   A late Victorian drawing room with every surface covered

She sees home-making, in fact, as an assertion of female independence, with which she is considerably concerned. It is something that men *can't* do, which makes it even more special as a female activity. She goes on to say that the essential aim of home-making is the creation of a 'moral atmosphere'; 'nobody must be morally the worse for living under her roof'. That is woman's responsibility, and a heavy one it is, for the creation of such a home was a contribution towards the improvement of society.

The Victorians were highly sensitive about interference with an individual's rights and privacy, and tended to hesitate to place restrictions on the individual even where those restrictions were plainly for the general good. For instance, W. Cooke Taylor, who concerned himself with the conditions of millworkers in Lancashire, vehemently opposed the registration of child-minders, a proposal that aimed at reducing infant mortality, and the limitation of the working hours of children, on the grounds that such legislation would invade the privacy of the family, come between the mother and her child, and interfere with the parents' right to make their own decisions concerning their own children. 'Better by far that many another infant should perish in its innocence and unconsciousness than to be a victim of such a state of things', he insisted.[2] On the other hand there was a great eagerness to instruct and advise. Evangelicalism, rather than legislation, was felt to be the way to do things. Persuasion, rather than the law. Hence the growth of a vast body of literature in the Victorian period that was designed to inform, instruct and propagandize. The art of home-making did not escape. Every level of society was addressed on the subject of the necessity of a 'moral atmosphere' in the home, and informed how it could be achieved.

Frances Power Cobbe ardently supported a degree of emancipation for women. She felt they ought to have the vote and the opportunity to enter into public life, for she considered women well equipped to contribute positively 'to the virtue and happiness of mankind' inside or outside the home—but this should be as well as, not instead of, 'the making of a true home'. An increase of public responsibility on the part of women could in fact enhance the quality of their private responsibilities. Both were considered by such as Frances Power Cobbe (who was, of course, far from typical) to be a part of women's social, religious and personal duty. This emphasis on the importance of home-making, this discussion of the home as a unit of society, was clearly partly the result of a psychological need to make women's activities appear more significant. The cause and effect of the cult of the home are hard to disentangle, and they are inseparable from attitudes to women. Did the cult of the home emerge as a context for the idealization and repression of women, or did the idealization and repression generate the cult of the home? Clearly, both were happening simultaneously, and encouraged each other.

Home-making was both a practical and a moral function, and thus represented exactly the ideal of womanhood. But its objects and results had, in the kind of emphasis home-making was given, nothing to do with the expression of personality, or individualized taste, or particular interests and special activities. It was a generalized quality of comfort and good taste that was aimed at, and it was this that numerous books and magazines concerned themselves with. The home was not a context for a woman's personality, not an area of freedom for her, but an environment that tested her qualities. Taste seemed to have nothing to do with personal likes and dislikes, and everything to do with what was considered acceptable by its arbiters. (Interestingly, this has now become much less the case.) We have seen how taste became increasingly important. If, earlier in the period, the housewifely qualities of neatness, order, and attention to detail seemed all-important, later taste was to become the significant criterion. Taste could be reflected in every aspect of the way the home looked, the things within it, and the way it was run. Taste and etiquette mingle. There is confusion—for instance, is it bad *taste* to serve a meal in a certain way, or faulty *etiquette*? Is it bad taste to wear two particular colours together, or simply unfashionable? Although men like Christopher Dresser and William Morris knew what they meant by taste, and felt they understood the morality involved, the word came to be increasingly and confusingly used by many who had little idea of what it could mean. For the home-maker on the receiving end of multitudinous advice this kind of confusion scarcely made it easier for her to learn to exercise her own judgment. Inevitably she was drawn to rely on rules.

Frances Power Cobbe emphasizes the creation of a moral environment. But the learning of languages and music with a smattering of general science was hardly likely to help the potential home-maker practically or morally. As late as

NO. 1. DECORATION OF A MANTELPIECE.

52   Decoration of a mantelpiece, 1889

2. HOW TO DRAPE A PIANO.
By Mrs Talbot Coke.

53   How to drape a piano—the legs,
let it be noted, are exposed

1897 Mrs Haweis was complaining in the *Lady's Realm* of November of that year that girls 'are taught to be nothing but the playthings of their parents—over-dressed, under-trained, even for marriage'.[3] In 1917 Mrs Menzies published her *Memories Discreet and Indiscreet by a Woman of no Importance*, and this describes her marriage in the 1870s and the more serious implications of ignorance, clearly in this case both sexual and domestic.

> I was shot into the realities of life after the manner of those days, in a condition of absolute black ignorance of practically every fact of life that would be almost unbelievable to girls of that age today—happily for them. The fact that I had not the faintest idea of what I was doing was a matter of legitimate self-congratulation to my parents as proof of the success of the upbringing they had bestowed on their child. It seems a little incongruous that a man who, say, for instance, murdered an aged aunt, should be regarded as such a naughty fellow and probably hanged, while the people who launched their daughter into life before they knew what they were about should be adjudged quite praiseworthy. The gentleman who murdered his aunt had only shortened an old life, while the others had done their best to ruin a young one.[4]

That such ignorance must have been the cause of many private agonies doesn't require much guesswork. Practically there was, as we have noticed, a growing body of literature designed to fill in the blanks that parents in some cases deliberately left. Sexually, although there were manuals of advice, they continued reticent and were often more concerned with equipping women to endure than to enjoy. It is more problematic to guess at the possible connections between private difficulties of this kind and the emphasis on a moral atmosphere in the home. The home was meant to be an environment of warmth and love: efficiency should not deaden the affection. It is tempting to see the cult of the home as partly a compensation for what must have been often a lack of warmth and spontaneity in more intimate relations. In the home there could be created an atmosphere of calm and certainty which could as much counteract the uncertainties within as the threats of the great world without.

Criticism of the facts of sexual ignorance arose slowly and hesitantly. Criticism of widespread domestic ignorance was open and frequent. In a novel of 1857, called *Below the Surface*, the author shakes her head over the motives for marriage.

> The prospect of marriage is to a young girl full of vague excitements and pleasure. To be mistress of her own house, of her own time; to enter into society; to be released from all restraint save from one whom she believes to be blindly and madly devoted to her. . . . Thoughts like these agreeably agitate her mind. She looks little into the stern and prosaic realities of the matter. Freedom, power, pleasure seem to be just within her grasp.[5]

Thirteen years later in another novel the complaint is in essence the same. Women have a completely false notion of what marriage is, or should be, about. The later author writes, 'The longer men live in this world, the better they comprehend how seldom a wife proves in any sense a helpmeet to her husband.'[6] In most women, these writers felt, an understanding of the practicalities involved was lacking. It is clear that the home-making role was a very important aspect of man's view of woman. It incorporated all the ways in which she was expected to assist him, and it is not surprising that the male voice is loud amongst the volumes of advice to females. In 1845 the Reverend Joel Hawes was lecturing ladies in America who were undergoing the more academic forms of education at the Mount Holyoke Seminary, and warning them that 'The husband is ruined who does not find his house a respectable, social, neat and happy home; and such a home he will never find if his wife is a slattern or is indolent and unskilled in domestic affairs.'[7] A proper home was considered to be essential for the moral functioning of men as well as women, though they were not expected to gain from contributing to its creation. The assumption is that domestic tasks are demeaning for a man, and if left to him a reflection of the inadequacy of his wife. And home means the environment of the married couple. The bachelor is often considered dubious because he is without what could be considered a proper home, and the spinster to be unfortunate and unfulfilled. But it is not sexual fulfilment that is lacking, rather the moral fulfilment to be gained from caring for others and making life comfortable for them.

Education was the major problem. How were women to be taught to create a moral environment, especially when it was not desirable for them to know what immorality consisted of? The problem was partly solved by defining morality in readily comprehensible terms of economy, good management, a sense of duty, and by characterizing good taste as the expression of a moral sense rather than aesthetic —or rather, by emphasizing the desirability of the morality of aesthetics. It was easier to understand what was beautiful if it could be seen in terms of what was good, and vice versa. Books with a practical bias were coming out fairly early in the century: there was Mrs Parkes' *Domestic Duties, or Instructions to Young Married Ladies* in 1825, James Luckcock's *Hints for Practical Economy in the Management of Household Affairs* in 1834, *The English Wife, a Manual of Home Duties* in 1843. After about 1850 they began to proliferate. Mrs Beeton's is the best known, but there were many others. In the 1880s Mrs Eliza Warren produced a number of volumes particularly designed for those with lower incomes. Her *A Young Wife's Perplexities* instructs on how to manage on £150 a year; another volume is entitled *Cookery for an Income of £200 a Year*, (1886 and 1887 respectively), and so on. In all her books she goes into great, and sometimes tedious, detail.

In *A Young Wife's Perplexities* Eliza Warren briskly states the necessity for domestic education.

> Talk about girl graduates and having successfully passed a Cambridge examination—what for, I should like to know? Why, even a governess would be all the better, more valuable in her position, if she were well up in domestic lore. I would have girls educated sufficiently to be companionable, and to earn their bread if need be; but, either first or last, they should be well grounded in the duties belonging to wifehood and motherhood.[8]

DRAPERY OF CONSERVATORY DOOR, &c.

*54   Drapery for a door, 1887. The obsession for 'dressing' a room lingered until the end
of the century*

HEAVEN HELPS THOSE WHO HELP THEMSELVES.

THE
FAMILY ECONOMIST;

A Penny Monthly Magazine,

DEVOTED TO THE MORAL, PHYSICAL, AND DOMESTIC IMPROVEMENT
OF THE INDUSTRIOUS CLASSES.

VOL. II.

1849.

HE WHO WAITS FOR DEAD MEN'S SHOES MAY GO FOR A LONG TIME BAREFOOT.

HE LIVES WELL WHO LIVES IN PEACE.

The Cottage Homes of England!
  By thousands on her plains,
They are smiling o'er the silvery brook,
  And round the hamlet fanes:
Through glowing orchards forth they peep,
  Each from its nook of leaves;
And fearless there the lowly sleep,
  As the bird beneath their eaves.

The free fair homes of England!
  Long, long in hut and hall
May hearts of native proof be reared
  To guard each hallowed wall.
And green for ever be the groves,
  And bright the flowery sod,
Where first the child's glad spirit loves
  Its country and its God.

LONDON:
GROOMBRIDGE & SONS, PATERNOSTER ROW,

AND SOLD BY ALL BOOKSELLERS.

BEGGARS FEAR NO REBELLION.

55   A domestic magazine aimed at encouraging lower-class thrift and hard work

A few pages further on she itemizes what these duties should achieve.

> A comfortable fire-side, well-cooked food, no disorder, no litter of any kind; keep the home room free from disagreeable reminders as in courting days; let no smell of washing and ironing pervade the home, no talking of Susan's short-comings, or of baby's ailments—baby should be in bed when Mr Hall returns, and then be sure that no basket of stocking-mending or household needlework be introduced to his notice, under the idea that he may see how industrious you are.[9]

The housewife must *be* industrious, but not conspicuously so. She must not attempt to share her responsibility with her husband. On £150 a year it must have taken considerable art, not to say effort, to remove the evidence of housekeeping from the eyes of the husband, but such, according to Mrs Warren, was a requirement of home-making. Again we can see how the ideal was geared to provide satisfaction for the husband. Returning from *his* hard day's work he did not want to be bothered by the evidence of *hers*, nor, which seems more surprising, did he want to see his child.

By this time the connection between physical health and moral well-being was often being explored, and there was more emphasis on the necessity of the home being a healthful environment. Tidyness and the elimination of dirt were seen not only as moral duties, good in themselves, but rather more as necessary adjuncts to the promotion of good health. Fresh air and exercise, the benefits of gymnastics, rational dress—the promotion of less constricting clothing—were all significant in the movement towards eliminating the fragile, fainting image of women. That a woman should have plenty of useful activity was important, and little girls were encouraged to be more energetic in their play. In the anonymous *A Few Suggestions to Mothers*, 1884, the connection between busy-ness and physical and moral health is discussed.

> Inevitably the most cheerful, most contented, and pleasantest people are those who are daily fully engaged. In most cases gloom, depression, sour temper, irritability, lowness of spirits, and all kinds of morbid humours, arise from want of proper occupation, and in some cases it is not so much delicacy of health which renders people miserable as the want of something definite to do which will engage the mind, and so contribute to physical health. Idleness is a fruitful source of unhappiness to young and old, and much misery is often caused by it. Children should be taught to find occupation for themselves.[10]

Here was the reaction against the idle middle-class woman, with servants to perform all the domestic duties, and minimal responsibilities. But the reaction had been building up throughout the Victorian period—in fact the whole idea of home-making was a part of it, for home-making gave a woman something to do that was essentially womanly. Without it it would have been very difficult to write the above, for unless pleas for more active women were coupled with feminist arguments for more occupations to be open to women, there was little scope for the home-centred middle-class wife except in house management. Going for walks and doing exercises were small compensation for feeling useless.

Advertisements and catalogues also contributed towards the education of the young wife, though their aid was rather more dubious. As the period progressed women were less likely to be inclined to shape their home in the image of their parents, for they were inevitably more aware that there were other possibilities open to them. They would see what the magazines and newspapers contained, what their friends' homes contained, what the shops contained, and would form their own ideas about who and what to emulate. It became more difficult to choose, and thus the exercise of a discriminating taste became more important. Furniture stores, like Maple's in Tottenham Court Road, opened and presented an enormous range of items. Manuals of housekeeping were more interested in how the home was run than in how it was set up, but there were authoritative, even authoritarian, views of what the home should contain is very evident. Again, as in Mrs Beeton's lists of kitchen utensils, the rules were tailored to income, as the following advertisement suggests.

> THOSE ABOUT TO MARRY should obtain the improved book of estimates . . . where they will find a four-roomed cottage can be completely furnished for 23 guineas; a six-roomed house completely and neatly for £70; an eight-roomed house, with many elegances and substantialities for £140; and a mansion of fourteen rooms furnished with that style, beauty and durability for which this house has obtained so large a share of public patronage, for 350 guineas. A single room or a single article at the same moderate charge. Smith's warerooms, next door to the Clerkenwell Police Court.[11]

Of course it was to a shop's advantage to be persuasive about what must be bought, but the gradations are nevertheless fascinating. The cottage is 'completely' furnished, the house 'completely and neatly', the larger house with 'elegances and substantialities'. And it is interesting that the word 'style' does not come into it until the mansion is reached. In other words, style cost money.

This kind of advertisement, with its suggestion that the furniture warehouse can not only supply gradations of need but inform an innocent young couple what it ought to be supplying, was part of the response, which in this case might be seen as exploitation, to the proliferation of choice. The machine and mass production were the main cause of this. Certain products became cheaper and more readily available, furniture was less likely to be hand-turned, more likely to be factory-made in large quantities, and the most expensive did not always mean the best. The modern concept of 'good value' had its origins in the Victorian period, but there was not yet the consumer alertness that there is now. So there was some concern, amongst those who cared, that people should be able to discriminate, both in terms of taste and value. And such was the impregnation of most aspects of life with a moral sense, or the feeling that there should be a moral sense, that good taste and good value were almost synonymous. An object that was carelessly made, or badly put together, could not be tasteful. William Morris was to take this even further,

56   A cartoonist takes a satirical look at the hallowed ritual of the family meal

and argue that an object that was not lovingly made could not be beautiful.

Charles Eastlake's authoritarian attitude, in his *Hints on Household Taste*, towards the regulation of taste and design was a positive reaction to the nadir of taste John Gloag describes. The belief that there were clear rights and wrongs, and that only within strictly defined limits could individuality be permitted dominated his aims. He wanted to put some backbone into ideas about interior decoration. Magazine articles on the subject tended to reflect this attitude. Certain colours must go together—if there is blue, there must be yellow—while certain others must never be seen together in the same room. Certain rooms must be predominantly dark, others lighter—drawing rooms should be brighter than dining rooms, insisted Rhoda and Agnes Garrett in *House Decoration* (1876). Certain objects are so desirable as to be necessary, others are sheer ostentation. There is not always any detectable logic or utility behind these views, but there is no question that they were strongly held. There is not always an explanation for the rules that are stipulated; there seems to be no reason for a dining room to be darker than a drawing room. But it is clear that there was a general willingness to be told what to do, that many people were uncertain in their judgments or ignorant of the possibilities, and had no idea how to translate their own vague inclinations into reality.

Charles Eastlake was one of several who were anxious to establish criteria of

57   *A Queen Anne style drawing room of 1895 indicates a move towards more sedate decoration*

taste that were both of practical use to the home-maker and kept in sight the moral principles that the end result involved. Others were concerned to point out that a true home could be a very modest affair—and this emphasis involved playing strongly on the home as a moral environment: what was required was a good home, not an elaborate one. It was obviously helpful to the status quo of the class and social structure that it should be believed that morality and good management did not depend on money, but there were more worthy motives involved in this emphasis. There was a rapidly increasing lower middle class, who were anxious to live decently if not lavishly, and there was also a genuine, and fascinating, confusion amongst many respectable Victorians over their attitude to money. Money played a most conspicuous role in Victorian society, but Victorians were reluctant to acknowledge this, they were reluctant to allow their respect for this commodity to appear too great. Money, cash, was less clean than property. Novelists often tried sublimate their attitude by presenting cash as the reward for good behaviour— Dickens does it in *Our Mutual Friend* by rewarding Bella Wilfer for curing her materialism with, precisely, losts of money. His argument is that money is good if the people who have it are good. The obverse of this argument is that the people who don't have money don't deserve it, and although there were some Victorians who used this argument—Samuel Smiles was the great proponent of the belief that hard work and a good life would win a confortable income—it was very difficult to apply it widely and rigidly. And also undesirable, for if everyone who deserved it was rewarded with cash the social system would disintegrate. It was important to remind people that to win a degree above poverty was itself an achievement.

Thus, there was considerable insistence that the humble abode was also a worthy one, that what one ought to be doing was to be making the best of ones lot through industry and cheerfulness. The *Ladies' Cabinet* of 1844 put it succinctly.

> Enter the humblest dwelling under the prudent management of a discreet and rightly educated female, and observe the simplicity and good taste which pervade it. The wise mistress has nothing gaudy in her dress or furniture, for she is superior to the silly ambition of surpassing her neighbours in show. Her own best ornaments are cheerfulness and contentment; her highest displays, those of comfort and a comely gladness; her house is the abode and token of neatness and thrift; of good order and cleanliness; which makes it, and its various divisions, look better than they really are.[12]

This is a humble home but, I would think, a middle-class one, or perhaps an artisan's—the language is thoroughly middle-class, and it is clearly an encouragement to those who might have had more extravagant ambitions in the arrangement of their homes. The article concludes that the achievement of 'neatness and thrift', 'good order and cleanliness, is a woman's highest function. When Ruskin talked of the sanctity of the home he clearly implied that a disordered household could not be sacred. The Victorians were not able to structure the world as they would have liked; they could not impose the kind of order that indicated efficiency and achievement. But they could structure the home, and the family within it, and we can again see a compensatory process at work there. Four walls and a closed door did not make a home. Lavish surroundings, however well looked after, did not make a home. The ethic of home-making had to be able to include the humble as well as the ambitious, the cottage as well as the mansion, and ultimately it rested on the connection between good order and good feelings. Love could be expressed in the absence of the sewing basket, truth in a well-cooked dinner, purity in a dust-free parlour. That these symbols were any less valid than those we ourselves employ to express what marriage and the home ought to mean is doubtful. And some of our contemporary symbols are not so different. That they were accepted by a large body of the Victorian middle class is clear, but we should perhaps see the repeated emphasis, which at times seems almost obsessive, as the reflection of an ideal to be worked for, rather than a widespread reality.

By the end of the century the education of taste had reached a large proportion of the middle class. A newly married woman would often pride herself on her ability to set up her new home efficiently and tastefully. In H. G. Wells' novel

Marriage (1912) he describes a woman who-does just this, and has very clear ideas about what is necessary for the kind of home she wants. But there was also a reaction against the cosier aspects of the idea of home-making, a reaction against the insistence that this was a woman's chief function and that its neglect was morally damaging. While there had been considerable discussion of the necessity of educating women in the practicalities necessary for home-making, in the 1880s and '90s there were complaints that that kind of education was too restricting. Many believed that though a woman should certainly be equipped for domestic tasks, her education should consist of a great deal more than this. But even the feminists did not suggest that men should take upon themselves any part of domestic responsibilities. Dickens has his memorable picture, in *Dombey and Son*, of the bachelor Captain Cuttle (who is nervous of females) preparing chicken with egg sauce and boiled potatoes, but there would have been very few men who were in the position of having to do their own cooking. Most men would have contrived

58   *Maple & Co advertised reproduction furniture, 1893*

to have a woman perform this function. If they did not marry one, or have a convenient sister or mother, they employed one.

A servant, though, could never be a home-maker in the same way as a wife. The
wifely image, sacred and protected, was an essential element of the home. It was
not just her efficiency and 'comely gladness' that counted, but herself, her identity
as wife. Ruskin is unable to disentangle the image of wife from the image of home-
maker. Dickens is full of substitute wives, pure and devoted sisters and daughters,
who tend the men in their lives, brothers and fathers, and make their homes for
them. It does not matter that they are not wives in fact, for they are in function and
symbolic value, but the relationship has to be close, there has to be a family bond.
In Dickens the women concerned gladly take on these responsibilities. In Dickens'
own household it was his sister-in-law, not his wife, who was the home-maker. He
was critical of his wife's failings, and in his fiction his good women, the women of
which he himself clearly approves, are always good housekeepers. We can only
guess at the numbers of women who had no choice but to be their brother's or
their father's housekeeper, and did so with discontent.

Women's education remained confused and debatable long after public opinion
was accepting that it should be more robust and extensive, and the problem of how
best to equip girls for their domestic role remained unsolved. The new educational
institutions for girls tended to ape the long-established and in many cases outmoded
institutions for boys. It was felt by some of the most vigorous advocates of female
education that girls had to prove themselves on the established terms. The board
schools began to teach domestic economy, but the ladies colleges were more concerned with classics and mathematics. The general feeling was that it was a
mother's responsibility to tutor her daughters in the art of home-making, and
mothers were frequently addressed on the subject. But if they were not good at it
themselves they were unlikely to be successful at instructing their daughters.
Ultimately the achievement of the newly married woman, even with the help of
books and streams of advice, was likely to be largely a matter of trial and error.
How many women were really able to believe, I wonder, that home-making was
their natural function, that they were innately formed if not practically equipped,
to accomplish it? And how many women led wretched lives because they had no
home to make, and were denied the function they were told was theirs?

These discrepancies between women's education, their functions in later life,
and their symbolic value is of the greatest significance, for the Victorians could
never quite make sense out of them and this caused revealing tensions. Most
middle-class women for most of the century were educated so that they could
perform socially and fill in their time in a not totally useless fashion. A woman
without the ability to handle a little music, a little drawing, and lots of needlework,
was considered lacking, as was a woman who was socially gauche. Boredom was a
constant risk—but a bored young woman was usually considered to be a spoilt
young woman. She *ought* to have something useful with which to occupy herself.
And she was expected to perform her tasks and her pastimes with conviction. Out
of such small accomplishments was expected to grow the vital skills of sanctified

59   The tasteful arrangement of 'things' reflect the Victorian's need for, and cultivation of, 'order'

home-making. Most young girls would be regular church-goers and subjected to considerable propaganda on the importance of their future task. At times something near hysteria can be detected in the insistence on both the sanctity and usefulness of women. At other times, often in the fiction of the period, there is the presentation of a bland unreality. Those who criticized women who failed as homemakers, either because they neglected their responsibilities or because they simply did them badly or without interest, did not really know how to deal with the problem. They usually wanted to believe in woman's innate ability to perform this role, but were faced with the practical necessity of sacred womanhood requiring to be taught how to boil a leg of mutton and how to contrive the washing so that the smells would not pervade the house.

Class was part of the problem. The busy little housewife could most readily be seen as a fairly modest personage, but the serene wife and mother had more elevated overtones. Age came into it too. Dickens' Agnes Wickfield's substantial background meant that as a *child* she could be the busy little housewife, but this was much less appropriate for her as an adult. The general attitude is that the lower your class and the younger you are the more beneficial is sheer industry. It was good for you and for the environment. Yet, at the same time, there was a feeling that the industry shouldn't be too much in evidence, as if conspicuous busy-ness, like conspicuous consumption, or conspicuous wealth, was ostentatious and vulgar. (I think one can generalize fairly usefully, and say that men quite liked to see the busy-ness—they tend to describe it fondly—but women felt that only the results should meet the male eye.)

Although class influenced the image, it became more and more necessary for the ideal of the home to accommodate a wider class and economic range. It was seen not only as a stable feature of the social structure, but as a unifying feature. It could bring together a disparate society without disturbing the hierarchy. So it was important to cherish the belief that all wives and mothers were essentially working towards the same end, to provide an environment of comfort and security, a physical and moral refuge, for the men and the children in their care.

The Domestic Ideal

The discussion of home-making may have suggested a rather lifeless environment apart from the actual performance of domestic tasks, and indeed many Victorian photographs, in their grave rigidity, suggest this too. But the image of home was not necessarily consistent, nor did it develop consistently. Only the essential fact that home is and must be different from the world outside is found everywhere. Apart from this, domestic reality had considerable variations, though the dominant ideal, middle-class and confined, is usually detectable.

Life in the home was not always static, or even orderly. Cheerfulness, which itself has a suggestion of energy about it, was important, liveliness often encouraged, especially where there were young children. For all the grave talk of sanctity a moral environment did not have to be either prim or lifeless, and although there is not much evidence to indicate that the surviving notion of Victorian self-entertainment was a widespread fact (there is evidence in particular cases—Elgar's family made a lot of music together), there is plenty to suggest that Victorian homes often contained a rumbustious family life, and that this was enjoyed. The fewer the servants the more likely the parents were to participate in the activities of their children, and so inevitably the picture of the lively and affectionate family tends to belong to the lower middle class, or to the freer atmosphere of rural surroundings. In fact, it becomes increasingly obvious that it is towards this sector of society that the reconciliation of ideals of home and family life tends. It was amongst those who earned, say, under £400 a year, mid-century, that the wife was most likely to be directly involved in the work of running the house and the care of her children. Her home-making talents were most likely to depend on her own participation, and her success with her children on her own patience and ingenuity. The novelists found it much easier to idealize the modest household than the wealthy one, and to see it as expressing a domestic but lively environment of harmony and affection. And it is this image that those who want to remind us of the positive qualities of the Victorian family turn to. Here is an example, a story from the *Ladies' Treasury* of October, 1857, interestingly subtitled 'a Story for Husbands'. It begins with the return of the husband after his day's work.

'You have been sewing too steadily, little wife,' said he; 'I must take you out for a walk after tea. I shall get a seamstress to help you if these children outgrow their clothes so fast.'

Mary laughed a merry little laugh. 'No such thing—I am not tired a bit—at least, not now that you are here; beside, don't you work hard down in that close counting-room, your poor head bothered with figures all day? Do you suppose a wife is to fold her hands idly, that her husband may get gray hairs? No, you and I will grow old together; but that is a long way off yet, you know,' and Mary shook her brown hair about her face. 'Come, now for tea. I have such nice cakes for you; the children have been so good and affectionate; to be sure, they tear their aprons occasionally, and perhaps break a cup or a plate, but what is that, if we are only kind and happy? Oh, it is blessed to be happy!' and Mary would have thrown her arms about her husband's neck, but unfortunately she was too short.

The smoking tea and savoury cakes were set upon the table—followed by the children, bouncing and rosy—fairly brightening up the room like a gay bouquet. With one on either knee, Henry Hereford listened, well pleased, to tales of soaring kites, and sympathized with disastrous shipwrecks of mimic boats, nor thought his dignity compromised in discussing the question, whether black, blue, or striped marbles were prettiest . . .[1]

The story is addressed to husbands clearly as a plea that they should participate to a greater extent in the lives of their children. There is no suggestion that it is a wife's duty to keep her children out of her husband's way. Obviously the picture of domesticity here is sentimentalized, and Mary with her merry laugh is distinctly offputting, but it is significant that the home is presented as an environment of cooperation, of kindness and happiness, mutual tolerance and assistance. Much of it depends on the unselfish attitude of the wife, who is happy to count her blessings and not complain.

This picture should be taken into account, for the weighty emphasis on the duties of the home-maker and the sanctity of the hearth sometimes obliterates the fact that the home could be a place of cheerful noise and activity as well as of solemnity and protection. The innocent gaiety of family life does quite often emerge as a domestic ideal, and as significant a contrast to the harassment of working life as the emphasis on home as a refuge. But it is not discussed with the same seriousness. The innocence is important. The flying of kites and the selection of marbles are activities untainted by the corruption of commerce. Pretend shipwrecks are an innocent alternative to the realities of wrecked fortunes. Yet these activities are also real, they are a genuine and unrestrained part of a child's growing up. Victorians experienced ineffable relief that domestic occurrences could be both real, of immense importance in human terms, and yet contained within a world protected from the harsher kind of realities.

We return to the word protection. An Englishman's home is his castle—his ultimate defence against an intrusive world and against the lives of those he prefers not to be involved with. In *Great Expectations* (1861) Wemmick literally has a drawbridge separating his home from the world of work. When work is over and he can safely retreat the drawbridge is raised. Within the home, ideally, and according to the more enlightened thinkers on the subject, men and women were free, free to do what they wanted, free from external worries, free to pursue their modest and innocent pleasures. But the pleasures had to be modest and innocent, playing with the children, cheery conversation, tea around the fire, for anything else would be an invitation to the enemy to enter the refuge. This affected attitudes to sexuality. It was assumed that domestic sex was not the same experience as illicit sex, and that the domestic partner should not behave sexually in the same way as the bought woman. The home should be a lively and affectionate place, but it should not be a place of excess of any kind. This meant inevitably, at times, the curtailment of spontaneity, discipline and self-control, and preferably an instinctive appreciation of what the limits were.

The fact of Victorian anxiety was pervasively influential. The most consistent feature of the domestic ideal was that the home should contain certainty, reliable values, and unchangeable solidity. To do this it had also to be isolated. I have quoted the passage from Disraeli's *Sybil* which presents the idea of the home as hostile to the idea of community, and perhaps one of the Victorians' most consequential failings was their difficulty in coming to terms with the idea of community. Certainly the isolation of the home mitigated against it. Carlyle, in a famous passage from *Past and Present* (1843), thundered against the fragmentation of society, and although he did not suggest that the emphasis of the sanctity of the home contributed to this, it is interesting to read the passage in the light of the domestic ideal.

> We call it a Society; and go about professing openly the totallest separation, isolation. Our life is not a mutual helpfulness; but rather, cloaked under due laws-of-war, named 'fair competition' and so forth, it is a mutual hostility. We have profoundly forgotten everywhere that *Cash-payment* is not the sole relation of human beings . . .[2]

It was the 'laws-of-war' from which the home was intended as a refuge. Yet, the ideal of the home was, precisely, 'the totallest separation'. By shutting out the laws of war and the realities of the cash nexus a family was also shutting out fellow beings. The most significant 'relation of human beings' appeared to be that which took place within the family and the home. Yet, as we shall see, many Victorians, men and women, found this limitation dismayingly hard to live with.

The domestic ideal clearly had to be as positive and as active as possible, which is one reason why the rather soulful image of femininity that Ruskin expressed couldn't survive the century. The angel in the house had to be more active, a more distinct personality, than Ruskin was happy to allow. For the home to be tolerable at all there had to be the suggestion that there was an authentic and constructive life going on within it. Again, we come back to the emphasis on female busy-ness: the bringing up of children, the sewing of their clothes, the provision of meals, and so on had to be seen as real life, had to be given their due weight as essential activities. But, as so often, the Victorians were torn. Should women refrain from recounting to their returned husbands the details of petty domestic problems, or

60   A decorous provincial wedding—'The Health of the Bride' by Stanhope A. Forbes, 1869

were petty domestic problems not petty at all, but significant aspects of real life that needed to be faced and discussed and solved like any other difficulty? Was domesticity, the activities it involved, important in itself or were the functions of women simply insignificant? There were contradictions here that were never resolved. That there was a confrontation between home and the world was accepted, but the implications of seeing it as a confrontation, or at least a separation, were never faced, and rarely explored.

The married couple, preferably with children, was seen as the ideal unit of society, easy to control and ready to conform, in its own interests. There was little thought, until a few daring voices were raised towards the end of the century, that marriage could be anything other than the well-established institution that the Victorian middle class seemed to want it to be. Of course individual failures in marriage were sometimes conspicuous, and the motives for marriage were not always admirable. Husbands and wives did separate and divorce, families were broken up. Men and women often married for money, or for convenience, or for

numerous reasons other than loving commitment. Young women wanted establishments as much as husbands, but only through the latter could they acquire the
former, and young men, or not so very young as they tended to marry late, wanted
domestic care and the symbolic value of a wife and home. The pros and cons of
marrying for love or for money were hotly argued. Marie Corelli attacked what she
called 'the modern marriage market', the selling-off of daughters to the highest
bidder, while others argued that marriage for love was a lot of romantic nonsense.
And if we look at marriage in the context of the domestic ideal we can see the
problems involved in expecting the home to survive by love alone. Here, from the
Fortnightly Review of October, 1872, is one version of the idealization of marriage,
an inflation of its moral strength.

> It is a marvellous instrument of education. It develops the sense of moral
> responsibility, and, therefore, the mainspring of right action, more completely
> than any other determinant of our lives. It imparts strength to the weaker
> nature and softness and moral beauty to the stronger, blessing at once both him
> that takes and her that gives. The sweet companionship of well-matched
> minds, whose most potent bond of union lies in the very fact of their difference,
> is in itself almost a Religion, for it quickens the spiritual instincts, and enlarges
> the social sympathies.[3]

Yet all this quickening and enlarging was for the benefit of a subservient wife—'her
that gives'—and a dominant husband—'him that takes'—within the four walls of
their home. It is the woman who gains morally, by giving—or at least that is the
suggestion here. The moral marriage was in some incalculable way meant to
influence society for the better at the same time as maintaining a refuge from the
pernicious influences of society itself. The true home was meant to be an example
to others less fortunate, yet its nature was to construct barriers against prying eyes.
The example was through knowing that the ideal home existed, or should exist,
rather than through direct experience.

To some extent this contradiction was overcome by attributing to women a
kind of porous quality of influence whereby simply the existence of the female
improved the world. If the woman herself was protected from noxious influences
she could radiate her own good influence to the benefit of all who might come into
contact with her and even to all who simply knew she was there. In fact, in some
ways, minimal contact and exposure were preferable. The best sort of woman,
Ruskin said, 'can only be divined, not discerned, by the stranger', because the best
sort of woman does not express her personality or her talents. Her isolation was her
asset. Marriage, though, was an essential part of social cohesion, not because it
brought people, other than husband and wife, together, but because it fixed them
in identifiable units within which they could be expected to behave in an identifiable
way, and which influenced the way they behaved in society. It was much easier to
cope with people in labelled units than with individuals who had no closed context.
The fact that a major impulse of marriage was to imitate the pattern already
established clearly helped to regulate the structure of society: marriage was, as an

institution, self-perpetuating. That this imitation was often pointless and material-
istic, and sometimes destructive of individuals, did not matter. The results were
the same as if it were constructive and generous. The continuity of behaviour and
aspiration, and therefore of society, was maintained.

Not only were all discussions of the home centred on the duties of women, but
almost all discussions of women were centred on marriage and the home. But many
women did not marry, and the inevitable effect of seeing women primarily as homemakers was to disparage the usefulness of those who never had the opportunity.
There was some reaction against this, but the stereotype of the sterile and useless
old maid was general. Part of the stereotype is the belief that she could only save
herself from sourness if she could find someone or something to which to dedicate
her life. There was a great anxiety amongst most women to get married, and a
tendency to believe that those who were lucky enough to marry should not complain if marriage turned out to be less than they had hoped. Men, of course, were
liable to take advantage of this anxiety, and to contribute energetically to reinforc-
ing the idea of marriage as a privilege for women, a privilege they should repay in
terms of service and the devoted fulfilment of duty. Women were destined for
service—Charlotte Brontë complains against this assumption bitterly in her novels
Jane Eyre (1847) and *Shirley* (1849)—but the attitude remained strong throughout
the period. Women were lucky if they had the opportunity of giving service, and
unfulfilled if they did not, and obviously the most important environment for the
giving of service was the home.

61   *A musical evening, 1870*

The ideal of service was of course a religious one, and the home was often seen as a place of worship. This passage from an article by Elizabeth Lynn Linton on 'Womanliness' in the *Saturday Review* indicates the duality of the saintly home-maker, both worshipped and worshipper.

> She is womanly when she asserts her own dignity, womanly when her highest pride is the sweetest humility, the tenderest self-suppression; womanly when she protects the weaker, womanly when she submits to the stronger; to bear in silence and to act with vigour, to come to the front on some occasions, to efface herself on others, are alike the characteristics of true womanliness; as is also the power to be at once practical and aesthetic, the careful worker out of minute details, and the upholder of a sublime idealism, the house-mistress dispensing bread, and the priestess serving in the temple.

This was written in 1870, a time when a number of women were beginning to question the morality of the idealism indicated here. The writer goes on to be more specific about how a woman should fulfil the domestic ideal.

> She thinks it no degradation that she should take pains to please, to soothe, to comfort the man who all day long has been doing irksome work that her home may be beautiful and her life at ease . . . her womanliness inclines her to loving forbearance, to patience under difficulties, to unwearied cheerfulness under such portion of the inevitable burden as may have been laid on her . . . she understands that she too must take the rough with the smooth; but that, as her husband's way in life is rougher than hers, his trials greater, his burden heavier, it is her duty—and her privilege—to help him all she can with her tenderness and her love.[4]

Clearly the article was written with the growing female discontent in mind, but there is nothing here that had not been said by others before. It might well have been reassuring to those who had perhaps begun to wonder whether the domestic role really was the noblest function of women, but it would hardly have convinced those who were already casting around for a very different kind of perspective. The priestess serving at the temple of the home: some would have represented her as being sacrificed on the altar. If the wife is priestess then the husband is god, as this passage clearly indicates. He is both the source of power and the major beneficiary.

It was in the Victorian period that the now standard middle-class pattern of marriage, man at work, woman at home, emerged, and the man's absence from home contributed as much to the cult as the woman's presence. The contradictory Victorian attitudes to work and wage-earning contribute significantly to the domestic ideal. Within the home the housewife can work industriously in the unshaken faith that everything she accomplishes is praiseworthy, and as a reminder that hard work *can* be enclosed, intimate, family-centred, safe. Neither the cash nexus nor the dishonesties of competition will infect her. (But it is interesting to reflect on the implications of financial ruin, a favourite Victorian subject, on the

62   The morning after the party. Drudgery and poverty haunt the ideal of conviviality and plenty

domestic ideal. It forces economic realities cruelly within the home.) Within the home bourgeois ideals could be enthusiastically encouraged without risk of their being flavoured by exploitation, or ruthlessness, or unfairness. The bourgeois domestic ideal was a tame and comforting supplement to the Protestant ethic, and only within the comprehensible unit of the home could a woman be expected to carry the weight of this ideal, both in practice and in symbolic value.

Part of the domestic ideal required that not only should a man not be plagued by the details of petty domestic problems on his return home, but he should not be expected to perform any kind of morale boosting role. There was a terrible failure to admit that the home could be a breeding place of discontent.

> All that excess of flattering and petting of which women are so fond becomes a bore to a man if required as part of the daily habit of life. Out in the world as he is, harassed by anxieties of which one knows nothing, home is emphatically his place of rest, where his wife is his friend who knows his mind, where he may be himself without fear of offending, and relax the strain that must be kept up out of doors: where he may feel himself safe, understood, and at ease.[5]

Home is where a man can be himself, but where a woman should repress herself for his benefit—in fact, the suggestion often is that without a woman's repression a man *cannot* be himself. Women were constantly being told that they should disguise their feelings if they were other than warm and affectionate, and make light of their problems, for the home should not be allowed to become a place of strain or worry. It is the theme of many novels and stories. The happy home is where the heroic housewife disguises all difficulties and uncertainties. We can see how, implicitly at least if not directly, that there was an alarming tendency to see the family not as a unit of cooperation and sharing, but of division and duplicity—for whatever noble motive.

Inevitably there is a suggestion of hypocrisy. There is often the doubt lurking behind the image of the home that the whole thing is not founded on a genuine sense of shared interests (there were plenty of Victorians who were straightforwardly prepared to leave love out of it) but on pretence and pretension. Dickens' grotesque Lammles may have been exaggerations, but they were symptomatic. We will probably never know how sincerely the domestic image was conformed to, or what sacrifices were required in the process, although some novelists and commentators are full of hints. What is clear is that, at whatever cost to their own personalities and talents, women were expected both to create the soothing atmosphere of the home, to sustain it, and to symbolize it. And there were many who believed that not only were women essential to the preservation of the home but the home was essential to the preservation of the essential characteristics of the female.

> . . . if our women, whom hitherto we have regarded in a certain sense sacred to the home life, come swaggering out into the streets like noisy brawlers in a rude crowd, they must forego their privileges of respect and protection for that liberty which includes self-assertive competition, rough words, and rougher shouldering aside; as must needs be among people struggling for peace and precedence. What constituted the old sacredness of women? For one thing her very confession of weakness; but mainly her unobtrusive life of help and love, the holiness of her function as mother, the sweetness of her office as wife.[6]

From this we can get a very good idea of what it was that the home was intended to protect women from. For the anti-feminists the woman who ventured 'into the streets' was always characterized as aggressive and unfeminine. Home and femininity were dependent on each other—and the woman who was neither wife nor mother, through choice or through misfortune, was seen as less feminine than her domesticated counterpart.

The qualities of both home and wife were enlarged by motherhood. 'Woman, as the mother, represents the most sacred idea in life' (this remark appeared in the *Saturday Review* as late as 1895) was a typical comment. That children could be a cause of friction and competition within the family was rarely considered: it was, as we shall see in a later chapter, felt that they should be firmly contained within the domestic ideal, and attitudes to children and their personalities were shaped by this. Maternity, of course, brought to mind the madonna aspect of womanhood, and again we can detect an element of over-compensation. Pregnancy and childbirth were risky and painful, the first year of an infant's life still highly vulnerable,

63   *Knitting on the bookshelf, toys on the floor enhance the 'naturalness' of this scene of family happiness, 'Mama's Birthday', 1871*

and just as death itself was wrapped in layers of sentiment to make it tolerable, so was motherhood. Tolstoy, in his disturbing story 'The Kreutzer Sonata', which he wrote towards the end of his career, writes desperately about the agonies of parenthood, the continual fears and worries, the devastation of the loss of children through illness and accident. The compensatory effect of a calm and radiant image of mother and child, a natural and elevated welding, is clear. The mother, like the housewife, had to be seen not only as essential to the fabric of society, but also as essential to social morality.

> The strong instinct of maternity which is an essential part of woman's character has helped to keep the lives of women pure and clean; and the welfare of the home, with its varied interests, is secured by the mother's influence, which is the real bond of family life.[7]

Of course it was often pointed out that there were good mothers and bad mothers. But what is confused in this passage is the distinction between instinct and responsibility. A strongly developed maternal instinct, even assuming that most women shared it (and even a woman whose maternal instinct was strong could hardly be blamed if it was not still thriving after the seventh or eighth child) did not automatically produce a dedicated and efficient home-maker, 'the real bond of family life'. When talking of motherhood the practical tendency, gaining

64 'Domestic bliss' by John Leech, 1842. A tongue-in-cheek portrayal of the 'stern' father

solidity through the nineteenth century, becomes dimmed by images of sanctity. The 'something special' about motherhood was liable to divert attention from practical domestic tasks, as well as enhance their nature.

For those who perhaps most needed a refuge, although they would hardly be helped by the idea of female sanctification, the domestic ideal was, inevitably, virtually irrelevant. The daily realities of the working-class housewife usually entailed an effort for survival that allowed no room for the luxuries of middle-class domestic sentimentality. The defeat of dirt and the provision of meals of some kind were a triumph in themselves for many women, and the home could only mean a refuge in the most elemental sense, a refuge from wind and weather. The domestic squalor of many of the working class was, in fact, yet another of the troubling realities of the world that the middle class tried to shut out. And although good management and hard work were urged on the working class, it was hard to see how the most committed newspaper article or the, generally sporadic, assistance of charitable organizations, could make much impression on this kind of typical situation.

> . . . the woman is obliged to remain constantly in the close court or neglected narrow alley where she lives, surrounded by all the evils adverted to; dirty child-ren, domestic brawls, and drunken disputes meet her on every side and every hour. Under such circumstances, the appropriate employments of a tidy housewife in brushing, washing, or cleansing, seem vain and useless efforts, and she soon abandons them.[8]

Octavia Hill, who worked to improve housing conditions in London in the 1860s and '70s, found that the only way she could make an impression was by involving herself intimately in the lives of those she was trying to help. Octavia Hill was a remarkable woman. Most of those who were most insistent about the value of the bourgeois domestic ideal were not inclined to go the lengths she did to bring some real improvement to working-class family life, though they were often ready to detect and denounce the ills thereof. There was a genuine and deep fear that the conditions of living and working amongst the poor would seriously damage society. Shaftesbury was afraid that 'domestic life and domestic discipline must soon be at an end; society will consist of individuals no longer grouped in families; so early is the separation of husband and wife, of parents and children'.[9] Yet how were the demands of work and wage earning to be lessened? The only answer to the threat to the family seemed to be that women should stay at home.

The sentimentalization of the domestic scene and the domestic role was encouraged by the belief that the home should be an environment for the expres-sion of the softer virtues and feelings, qualities that were deemed incompatible with the outside world, a belief that has been responsible for a whole syndrome of sexual type-casting. It seemed scarcely possible to be sentimental or romantic about making money, although some tried and Dickens succeeded, but one could make the fruits of money-making more acceptable by both sentimentalizing and elevating them. The impression is of the man returning jaded from work to soak up the womanly virtues expressed in his home, which renewed him for the contest which had to be joined again the following day. The domestic interior reflected this womanliness, as many have noted. Not only in its rounded shapes and curves and ornamentation, but in its warmth and its neatness, suggesting as they did love, security and efficiency. Domestic objects were reassuring. They didn't change. They were totally in the control of their owners, they were familiar and reliable, a kind of domestic gold standard. They helped both men and women to be sure of their values and beliefs; they could relax in the legitimate enjoyment of life's embellishments.

Within such an environment it was assumed that the best features of humanity could operate. Yet the contradictions shriek for attention. We have looked at some of them. The much-praised Smilesian ethic of hard work, the work that will bring rewards in cash and social mobility, must take place outside the home. And if the money-earning work does not require the functioning of the best qualities of mankind, how doubly contaminating it is, and how doubly necessary to be de-contaminated by the gentle influences of home. Yet the traditionally masculine qualities that the Smilesian ethic demanded were usually represented as splendid, even heroic. And indeed there is something of an imitation of the chivalric pattern, the knight wielding his sword amidst dangers for the sake of a woman who loves and solaces him. But the contradiction of which we are now perhaps most readily aware is the assumption that the best in humanity could grow and be expressed within so closed an environment. It is hard for us now to see the closed environment fostered to provide for the best in humanity; we notice instead the best in humanity forced to conform to its restrictions. The predominant attitudes to both women and children emphasize this.

That the Victorians wanted to make the world a better place is undeniable. That they usually had to settle for making the home a better place, according to their own lights, is fairly evident, and in doing so they tended to see the home as a substitute for the world, or as an alternative. As long as the home could be seen to be good, and the world to be bad, this could be acceptable. But sometimes the home patently was not good, and sometimes there were opportunities for making the world rather less bad than it had been. It was this kind of thing that gave rise to tensions both inside and outside the home, that made feminism, for instance, so difficult for the Victorians to cope with, for it seemed so much more of a threat than a right. If women left the home, what could society fall back on to convince them that life wasn't continually on the brink of anarchy and immorality? The angel in the house was at the root of multitudes of Victorian assumptions and ideas, and Victorian rationalizations and ideals.

What kind of life within the home did the domestic ideal provide for? There are two lasting images, one of the calm, quiet family busy with their separate tasks around the fire in parlour or drawing room, their activities reflecting their accept-ance of their status, the other of the family united in a single entertainment, at the piano perhaps, or listening to a novel read aloud. But the possibilities of shared entertainment were not very extensive. People often lament the fact that television,

65 Restoration of mutual confidence between Mr and Mrs Micawber . From David
Copperfield, *1850*

for instance, has encouraged the idea of self-entertainment to die away, but one
wonders how extensive it really was. The evidence of novels and memoirs suggests
that the most uniting shared activity of many families was family prayers, and
many would have considered that this was as it should be. The shared experience of
children could bring pleasure and unity, and that there was sometimes jollity and
spontaneous activity I have tried to show. But there is also a great deal to suggest
that the family, like society, was often fragmented, the husband's life separate
from the wife's, the children's separate from their parents. The family of Charles
Booth the social investigator saw little of him: he worked with dedication and
commitment, his wife looked after their many children. Yet she was an uncon-
ventional and sharply intelligent woman who familiarized herself with his work
and interests, shared his principles and his sense of commitment. Both were the
kind of thoughtful and progressive people who might have turned their attention
to the quality of their own family life. She was uncomplaining about his lack of
participation. Their children were conscious of their father's unfamiliarity.

Did the wife spend evening after evening soothing the husband's brow, as some
of the passages I have quoted would suggest? It seems unlikely. There may have
been extensive conversations, card playing, newspaper and magazine reading. But

66   *The women deal with fractious children, the husband maintains a determined aloofness*

I would guess that there was a great deal of boredom, and that boredom rather than frustration might well have accounted for the middle-aged frequenters of prostitutes, and that boredom almost certainly accounted for the flourishing state of gentlemen's clubs. And that boredom was probably responsible for female nervous disorders. And that boredom certainly stoked the fires of feminism. The overriding impression is that entertainment was something that went on outside the home, at the theatre, the music hall, the pleasure gardens, all of which were dubious localities for the respectable married woman and her daughters. There is an unspoken assumption that entertainment, other than that of the dinner party or the 'At Home' or the ball, is either a lower-class or a masculine need. Only with the rise of the cinema does entertainment outside the home transcend the barriers of sex and class. The lack of amusement at home helps to explain the rapidly growing readership of novels and of books of all kinds. It was not just the idle females of a cossetted middle and upper class who read to fill in the time, or a newly literate working class seeking escapism, but the busy housewife in need of some relaxation and amusement in the evenings. Many may have read only the Bible and evangelical tracts, but that reading was one of the most appropriate activities within the Victorian home is certain.

Visitors provided some diversion, though the etiquette involved may well have not allowed much in the way of relaxation. But visitors were important, for if the main motivation of home-making was for the sustenance of the husband, a subsidiary was for the delectation of friends. They, perhaps more than the husband, were the ones who judged the success or failure of the home-maker. The strain of visits, though, and of the expectation of visits, could be considerable, especially for the new and inexperienced housewife, for visitors meant exposure, they meant letting something of the outside world in, even if it was only the echo of one's own, and they might mean criticism. The business of visiting could be an ordeal. But the Victorian household was certainly geared for visiting of an accepted kind, at recognized hours, and within a recognized context.

The structure of the Victorian home, with its emphasis on the compartmentalization of activities, with its fragmentation, and the demands of the domestic ideal, the necessity of order and organization, clearly mitigated against spontaneity. It wasn't just the paternalistic structure of the family, with its expression of authority often unresponsive to the family's needs, that restricted human activity within the home, but the very aims of home-making. In Edwardian children's books there is often a striking sense of adventure and exploration, of anarchy even, expressed through children discovering life on their own account, independent of adults, and sometimes solving problems that defeat the grown-ups. In this, I feel, we can see a significant revelation of the restricted nature of the domestic ideal. The need for order and comfort, the need for security and protection, the need to foster the sanctity of womanliness and motherhood, all these things that the Victorians considered both moral and sustaining, overshadowed, if they did not actually cripple, the vital requirement of free activity and expression. When stories begin to be written that are clearly, if indirectly, about the liberation of children, we can see a vivid reaction.

The domestic ideal was inevitably introverted and isolated. It was a comfort to thousands of men and women to know that they were doing what society expected of them, and that the features of their domesticity were echoed and imitated in thousands of homes recognizably like their own, but it fostered one of the now most widely acknowledged disturbing factors of modern society: the lack of community, the isolating of the family, the problems of cooperation, and a failure in understanding the radical challenge involved in the reconciliation of the true home with the real world.

Trends in housing throughout the Victorian period did nothing to open out the domestic ideal. Victorian-initiated suburbia seems to embody so much of what is obnoxious in this trend for it concentrated on the home within at the expense of the environment without. Improvements in working-class housing most often encouraged the imitation of the limiting middle-class ideal, which meant an imitation of middle-class isolation. It has taken something like three quarters of a century for the idea of community to begin to challenge the idea of privateness. But privateness was what the Victorians thought they wanted, and seemed to want increasingly through the century. They thought it was right and they thought it was necessary. Community became something that was paid for out of the rates. Life, the moral life, was what went on within the home.

The Domestic Prison

The closed door of the Victorian home not only kept the world out, it kept individuals in. By the 1880s there was a growing sense that the home was often a place to be escaped from, and some direct criticism of its nature. But there were intimations in fiction long before this that the home was a place of restriction and sterility. In so much Victorian fiction there are wives and mothers who fade away, and there is the impression that this is because of a terrible negativity, a lack of purpose in their lives, a lack of environment to develop personality. In *Dombey and Son* the first Mrs Dombey dies because 'she would not make an effort'—such is the judgment of Mr Dombey and his sister. But Mr Dombey thought of his wife as merely part of the furniture—'he certainly had a sense within him, that if his wife should sicken and decay, he would be very sorry, and that he would find something gone from among his plate and furniture, and other household possessions, which was well worth the having.'[1] Mr Dombey's home scarcely provided an atmosphere in which his wife, or anyone other than himself, might have flourished; but as she had no importance as a personality this did not matter to him. Mr Helstone's home in Charlotte Brontë's *Shirley*, also a novel of the 1840s, is very different from Dombey's—he is a country curate, not a city merchant—but the fate of Mr Helstone's wife is similar.

> He thought, so long as a woman was silent, nothing ailed her, and she wanted nothing. If she did not complain of solitude, solitude, however continued, could not be irksome to her. If she did not talk and put herself forward, express a partiality for this, an aversion to that, she had no partialities or aversions, and it was useless to consult her tastes. He made no pretense of comprehending women, or comparing them with men: they were a different, probably very inferior order of existence; a wife could not be her husband's companion, much less his confidant, much less his stay. *His* wife, after a year or two, was of no great importance to him in any shape; and when she one day, as he thought, suddenly—for he had scarcely noticed her decline—but as others thought gradually, took her leave of him and of life, there was only a still beautifully-featured mould of clay left, cold and white, in the conjugal couch, he felt his bereavement—who shall say how little?[2]

This chilling account is unalleviated by the fierce wit that Dickens employs, but the home in both novels is quite barren. It can sustain only the male life, and that only because the home, in itself, is of little importance to the men concerned. Children, in these cases daughters, Florence Dombey and Caroline Helstone, grow in spite of, not because of, the environment. Florence grows up to win for herself an ideal—in conventional Victorian terms—domestic setting, and Caroline to be suspicious of the kind of conformity and suppression that such a domestic setting often required.

The significant feature of the two novels, very different in outlook and intention, one by a man who needed domestic comfort, the other by a woman who challenged assumptions about women's duty to supply it, is their uneasiness about the idea of the home. They both contain vivid examples of domestic situations that are destructive. Neither produce convincing alternatives, although Dickens conforms to the dominant bourgeois ideal in his picture of Florence's marriage. That the Victorians were troubled by their version of the home at the same time as they reverenced it there is little doubt. The full impact of this realization did not emerge until towards the end of the century, but it rumbles throughout. We can see in novels examples of the family and the home as repressive institutions, although few, novelists or anyone else, were prepared to say so outright. Later, with, for instance, Samuel Butler, we find a full-blooded condemnation of the paternalistic family and the restrictive home, and the theme is there in Mark Rutherford too. This was nothing to do with feminism, but the male child in rebellion.

When Beatrice Potter, later to be Mrs Sidney Webb, visited the home of her cousin Mary Booth, she was aware of the stuffy air, the darkness and a vaguely oppressive atmosphere. Mary herself seemed always to be pregnant or recovering from childbirth, and although she didn't complain she did wish sometimes that she could be more active, that she could more positively help those, like her sick father, who needed help. This was not a repressed or a sterile household in the sense that Charlotte Brontë and Charles Dickens were concerned with, but it troubled the alert and progressive Beatrice. The home could so easily become a place in which personality could not survive, and every member of the family, man, woman and child, could be in danger. The effort to preserve the home as an ideal environment, the effort to enlarge and insist on its importance socially and morally, was clearly partly a result of a sense of unease that was as much about the home itself as about society. We can see this in Ruskin, who contributed so much to the publicizing of the ideal. He himself had an upbringing of the strictest Calvinist rigidity. It produced not a rebel, but a romanticist. That he was personally unhappy and emotionally inadequate the evidence is clear—his own marriage was never consummated and his idealization of womanhood led him to find perfection only in little girls—yet he sustained a vision of ideal (adult) womanhood, ideal marriage and the ideal home. The cult of the home was partly an effort at compensation. The home was idealized partly as a form of escapism (the development of the two-pronged function of escapism, providing security on the one hand, adventure on the other, is fascinating) and partly because they could hardly fail to see how unsatisfactory the home and the family could very easily be.

The paternalistic structure of the family, which itself reflected the hierarchical

67 and 68   The comforts of The Club always offered a ready bulwark against marriage

structure of society, was bound to appear more stark within the confines of the domestic interior, although at the same time that interior was cushioned and padded as if in an effort to soften it. The authoritarian husband and father may well be an exaggerated figure, but clearly the nature of the home itself assisted in this exaggeration. For if husband and father chose to dictate, there was no escape. Wife and children, and to a certain extent servants who were dependent on employers and good references, had little alternative to staying where they were, however difficult or painful the experience. For most of the century women had virtually no financial independence. Divorce was difficult and expensive, and until 1920 could only be on grounds of cruelty or desertion, not, for women, of adultery, although men could divorce their wives on the grounds of adultery. As Geoffrey Best puts it in *Mid-Victorian Britain*, 'the absolute rule for all sub-affluent marriages was—like it or lump it; and for even affluent marriages the same crude rule might hold, for beyond getting legally free of an obnoxious partner lay the terrible economic problem: how could a woman—let alone a woman with dependent children—make an independent livelihood?'[3] Before 1878, when there was a new Divorce Act, it was extremely difficult for a woman to escape a tyrannous marriage; after 1878 it was still extremely difficult to survive after escape. For children of

What off again? I suppose your going to see the Handsome Landlady! you were talking about in your Sleep last night

No my dear I'm going to the Club.

course escape was even more difficult. Except in specific circumstances of divorce or separation the father was the child's legal guardian. But apart from that middle-class children were discouraged from habits of independence. If they found themselves in an intolerable domestic situation, what could they do, or where could they go? David Copperfield's famous flight was possible because he acquired the habits of the working-class child. He had learned to fend for himself. By and large, though children sometimes ran away from school, they did not run away from home.

Children had little opportunity to question the hierarchy under which they were likely to be brought up, especially when so often servants were more directly responsible for their well-being than their parents. The hierarchical structure helped to sustain the fragmentary nature of family life. Husband and wife had their distinct roles and areas of control, the wife's probably beneath the authority of the husband's. The wealthier a household, the more likely was the life of the children to be separate from that of their parents, and the amount of freedom they had to depend on the whims and principles of nurse and nannie and governess. It would be a mistake to exaggerate the rigidity of the paternalistic structure of family life, but it certainly could be rigid. It allowed opportunities for the tyrant, and imprisoned the tyrant's victims, if husband and father chose to behave thus. Dickens, at the same time as illustrating some of the most treasured aspects of domestic happiness, provided numerous instances of something very different. His novels are full of male tyrants, whose sadistic cruelty is profoundly disturbing, and within his fictional households this kind of cruelty flourishes as often as domestic bliss. And there is not only cruelty. There is sterility. There is domestic confusion. There is boredom. There is lack of communication. Dickens' own household scarcely fulfilled his ideal. Not only did he consider his wife a bad manager, he resented the frequency with which more children appeared without, it seems, accepting that he was equally responsible for their appearance. In fact, although Dickens has for generations been associated with cosiness, the most striking homes in his novels are very far removed from any such thing. The cruelty in Dicken's novels, in the context of the society he is examining, is much more insistent and significant than the kindness.

One of his difficulties, and this was widespread, was the inability to see the home as a fertile environment for a deep sexual relationship. Sex is not absent from the Victorian novel, or Victorian discussion in general, but it is most evident in its least acceptable forms. Victorian fiction is full of elopement, adultery, prostitution. Much of the most memorable social investigation of the period concerns prostitution and sexual delinquency. In the novels plot after plot turns on the possibility of illicit sexual relationships. But marital love as meaning something more than the wife accepting the authority of her husband and the husband providing for his wife in return for her domestic abilities is an elusive quality in Victorian writing. This is partly explained by attitudes to female sexuality; sex was generally thought of as part of what a woman had dutifully to give rather than pleasurably receive. Instances of a warm family life are not rare; hints of a warm, committed sexual relationship are harder to find, and part of the explanation certainly appears to be that the Victorian home itself was not congenial to such an emphasis. The bedroom was not a centre of married life—in spite of the high birth rate. It was often cold and functional. A heated bedroom was a luxury, an indulgence. In the manuals of house decoration by far the greatest attention is paid to the living rooms, the rooms where family life is lived and visitors are received. There is much less space given to bedrooms. And one cannot fail to get the impression from Victorian fiction that eating is much more important than making love.

This is linked with another notable lack in the dominant picture of family life, the lack of a quality of sharing. Clearly, the hierarchical structure militated against this too. We have seen how part of the domestic ideal was the belief that responsibilities should *not* be shared. The dividing lines between different roles and functions scarcely encouraged a sense of sharing between different family members. Mothers were told they should instruct their daughters in domestic skills, but not in a spirit of allowing them to feel they could contribute importantly to the running of the household, and thus, perhaps, usurp the structure. The aim was to equip them for their *future* role. Of course there were exceptions. But this is the general tendency. It was hard for middle-class parents to know how to share their lives with each other, or with their children, for the definition of their functions within the home allowed little opportunity for this. Mothers were told they should spend as much time with their children as they could, but this was less for mutual pleasure, than in the interests of moral welfare.

When most Victorian commentators talk of love, they automatically see it within the paternalistic structure. For the man this involves protectiveness, for the woman service and submission. Even the romanticists, like Marie Corelli, who insisted on the power and importance of romantic love, could not remove it from the straitjacket of prosaic realities. The idea of romantic love may have been an effort at compensation, but it could not be an escape route from the demands of domestic life—which is one of the reasons why some vigorously attacked it. Romantic love was possibly a way of glossing realities, but it was also a weapon against feminism. If it was adventure that the 'new women' wanted, could not romantic love provide it? But it was hard to convince that romance could flourish within the Victorian domestic scene, and where else could it go?

In the 1860s and 70s Mrs Lynn Linton, who had had a good share of toughening experience, wrote a series of essays criticizing the 'advanced' woman, the 'girl of the period' as she called her. She condemned the beginnings of a critical attitude towards marriage and the home.

The emancipated despise marriage as servile submission unbecoming the free-born soul; but they forget that the ideal on which marriage is founded is love, and that no true-hearted woman that ever lived, who loved her husband, desired anything but submission. It is the very life of a woman's love—her pride, her glory, her evidence of self-respect. If she loves, she desires her husband to be greater than herself, and she believes him to be so . . .[4]

69   *Found out. A dramatic moment imagined by Augustus Egg. Women, if comfortably married, could not afford to stray*

This is her version of romantic love, and a common one at the time. Yet it was clear to all but the most obtuse, and it was certainly clear to Mrs Linton, that marriage was far from a perfect institution. Mrs Linton's own marriage was not a success. While insisting that love meant female submission, she also conceded that there should be some escape for women from 'enmity and tyranny', if that should arise. 'The woman, as the weaker, ought to be protected from the possible ill-treatment of her lord, and be in some sense free, though bound.'[5] Mrs Linton's problem of terminology here reflects a more general difficulty. How could a woman be free, though bound? How could she be protected by the home, and protected within the home? The very qualities that helped to preserve the home from outside threats made it that much more difficult to protect any single member of a family from the threats within.

Mrs Linton, a voluble and intelligent writer, is riven with contradictions, but they are rewarding contradictions from our point of view, because so revealing. While insisting that love is the mainstay of marriage she asserts that the wife who 'cannot live happily without being made love to' is more like a mistress than a wife. 'Placing all their happiness in things which cannot continue, they let slip that which lies in their hands; and in their desire to retain the romantic position of lovers lose the sweet security of wives.'[5] Security: that is a key word. Love, romantic love, can't last, but security can, and is preferable, and worth the sacrifice. This of course confirmed female subservience, but it also, more insidiously, helped to perpetuate the 'closed door' attitude to the home. If security is more important to women than anything else, it can only be expected that they will be ready to tolerate, if not to actively welcome, the domestic prison. And this extended not just to wives. Unmarried adult females of any status came into this category. The unmarried aunt, sister or daughter could be expected to pay willingly for the security of a home in terms of the service she could give. The orphan could be expected, in gratitude for a 'good home', to work in payment for its benefits. To be given the shelter of a roof and economic security was bound to be of the greatest importance to women in an age when there were few opportunities for middle-class women to earn their own livings. The law confirmed female dependence, the home relied on it, and the way was open, inevitably, to exploitation.

It was not only women and children who were confined behind the closed door. Home could be a prison for men also. We can only guess for how many of them the evening return home from work was an entry into the prison house rather than the refuge. The fact that the inevitable strains and conflicts of domestic life were not meant to be admitted and openly discussed could result in an atmosphere that was intolerable for husband and wife alike. Many husbands might well have settled for less order and more good nature, for more muddle and less rigidity, but they were told what home should be like, what wives ought to do and be, just as women were, and it was understandable that they should blame women for the home's failings. Men did not necessarily exact submission and domestic perfection because it suited their natures or their personal sense of what life should offer, but perhaps because on every hand they were being told what life ought to offer, what they ought to ask of it. The Victorians could not stop telling each other what life ought to consist of. It would be silly to think that men were less susceptible than women to this kind of pressure.

But there is one significant difference, and that is that it was immeasurably easier for men to escape. Most of the time their presence in the home was neither required nor expected. When they went out to work they escaped, or it could be seen as an escape if home did indeed seem prison-like. There are many stories and novels in which the husband's later and later hour of return from work is a direct reflection of his dissatisfaction with the domestic scene. The moral of these stories almost always is that the wife is failing in her duties. There is one particular story in which the husband finds his wife's inadequacy so hopeless that he goes off to the silver mines of Nevada. The husband's escape wasn't usually so drastic—there were plenty of possibilities nearer at hand. There were numerous places of entertainment at which he could spend his evenings rather than occupying the family hearth. There were easily available sexual alternatives. If he could afford it he could even set up an alternative home, comfortably furnished according to the home's essential requirements, in which a mistress could be installed whose status as kept woman might well make her more sensitive to the needs of her benefactor than his wife. The crucial point is that a man could remove himself from an undesirable domestic situation, and often did, while for a woman it was very difficult, and any attempt to do so might well involve scandal.

The man's escape did not necessarily mean that he sought a sexual alternative. He might choose to spend his evenings in the relatively innocuous surroundings of his club. The fact that women had no comparative alternative to the home, except the home of some other woman in a similar position, was obviously a significant factor of her position. The legacy of this situation remains with us. A woman wasn't expected to need an alternative to the home, neither as escape nor as merely a change of scene. Her entire existence and function was expected to take place within it. Very often the mid-Victorian woman would be content to accept this, perhaps even in a spirit of gratitude that there was a home to accommodate her function. But by the last quarter of the century the rumblings of protest were fairly loud, and inevitably marriage itself, as an institution, was isolated as a source of repression and constriction. Attacks on marriage became explicit, and along with these attacks on the structure of the family and the assumption that part of the essential female function was to bear children. There had always been women who found children an interference with freedom, but Victorian women were continually being told that even when they could afford to buy freedom, by employing others to care for their children, they should not use it. But it was not only marriage as the context of childbearing that was under attack, but marriage as a way of life. Mona Caird was scathingly articulate in her descriptions of a married couple as 'a pair of carriage horses', never allowed a separate existence, and praised the refusal of right-minded women to be mere 'breeding machines'.[6]

Many people were alarmed. Without children, the whole idea of family life and its dependence on a paternalistic structure would be undermined. Without marriage the unity, the very existence, of the home would be damaged, and ultimately the fabric of society would be destroyed. It was impossible for the imagination to see any other way of organizing society other than on the basis of family life taking place within the security of the home. Even those who attacked the institution of marriage, such as Grant Allen, a novelist of some popularity, could not imagine any viable constructive alternative than a fairly conventional home within which a woman cared for her children and a man provided financial support. The man and the woman were not actually married, but the way of life was little different. Even now, more than a hundred years after the beginnings of energetic reaction to Victorian ideas, there has been little exploration of alternative methods of structuring society, and there remains a deep-rooted fear that the end of the family will mean the end of society as we know it.

Certainly there were some social reformers, Marx and Engels most authoritatively, who specifically saw the family as a repressive institution which could be manipulated against class interests. In this sense, also, the home could be seen as a prison, the prison of a class as well as of individuals. The predominant middle-class attitudes to the working-class home, the effort to strengthen working-class home life and to use working-class stability as a means of middle-class security bears this out. The home was seen as a fundament of society, and any effort even to change it, let alone dispense with it, was a threat to society. Yet it became increasingly clear to the Victorians themselves that the Victorian home and Victorian attitudes to domesticity and the family were less than satisfactory. This manifested itself as rebellion, which gained little, but it must have been felt more generally and intimately as anxiety, and anxiety was liable to result in retreat.

Uncertainty about the home and the family certainly contributed towards the growing feminism. There were some who specifically identified the manipulative role of the family and saw the home as an environment of stifled talents. Florence Nightingale wrote in her diary,

> The family uses people, *not* for what they are, nor for what they are intended to be, but for what it wants them for—its own uses. It thinks of them not as what God has made them for, but as the something which it has arranged that they shall be. If it wants someone to sit in the drawing-room, *that* someone is supplied by the family, though that member may be destined for science, or for education or for active superintendence by God, i.e. by the gifts within. This system dooms some minds to incurable infancy, others to silent misery.[7]

Florence Nightingale was clearly thinking mostly of women and her own hard-won road to a career, but the same could be said of the family's male products. Samuel Butler's *The Way of All Flesh* (1903) describes the destruction of a son's personality by a father. Growth, imagination and independence could all be stifled within a closed and rigid home by parents who thought they were acting for the best. The products of such a home might well succeed and feel satisfied as long as there continued to be a similar protected and inflexible structure of support. But we can also see that fascinating character, the Victorian male obsessive eccentric, General Gordon, perhaps, or Edward Lear, to name two who are very different, as the product of the removal of a cushioned environment on growing up. With such emphasis on security and structure the discovery of their absence could be shocking. The home, inevitably, emphasized the potential anarchy without.

Domestic harmony had to be worked for. There was widespread recognition that it was not a natural or spontaneous state, but an understandable reluctance to pursue the implications of its artificiality. Women, in particular, were continually being called upon to resort to artificiality, in striving for effect, in repressing their own natures, in the interests of the 'little community' of the home. 'It is essential to your making home happy that there should be much self-denial, a spirit of forbearance, an occasional surrender, for the sake of peace, of supposed rights, a willingness to forego what you could rightfully claim as your own' wrote one commentator, in a book on *Female Piety, or the Young Woman's Friend and Guide* (1871).[8] In other words, the potential for conflict within the home is immense, unless there is someone always prepared to give way. The same author admits that home can be *seen* as a prison, but for him, and for so many Victorians, dissatisfaction is a question of attitude rather than genuine grievance—for genuine grievance can always be conquered by a moral nature. In order to make the home work, the members of a family must believe that it is the best place to be. There is an act of faith involved. Repeatedly Victorians asked for this act of faith, and cast anxious glances from time to time at the fact that the need of an act of faith implied the disturbing possibility that there were doubts. Here is the author of *Female Piety* again, suggesting, almost, that the home is a state of mind rather than an actual abode of bliss.

> If you would make home happy, you must of course be happy at home. No one can diffuse joy who is not joyful. The passions are infectious, because the heart is sympathetic. Cheerful persons make others like themselves, and so do gloomy persons. . . . A young person whose heart finds its resting-place in the domestic circle, whose sympathies are with household scenes, whose chosen companions are her parents and her brothers and sisters, whose pleasures are the sweet interchange of domestic offices and affections, whose loved employment it is to make her daily contributions to the comfort of the little community within doors, and whose good-humoured disposition radiates from smiling eyes, and speaks with gently curled lips, such an inmate is a blessing to the house in which she dwells. . . . But observe the opposite to all this, the girl that looks upon her home as a prison rather than a paradise, and thinks that to stay at home is a penance rather than a pleasure; and accordingly is anxious to escape from it, and is ever seeking opportunities to effect her purpose. Her gloomy aspect, her sullen disposition, her discontented air, her repulsive taciturnity, her peevish expressions when she breaks her silence, her unsympathising isolation, what a member of the family do they make her! She has at home no associates, no objects of strong affection, nothing to engage and interest her heart, but is ever seeking occasion to slip away, upon any pretence, or for any engagement.[9]

Home requires a full commitment and a cheerful and positive attitude towards it—on the part of the females within it at least. The seeking of interests outside it, or the admission that home might not be able to sustain all the requirements of female personality and interests, cannot be tolerated. Seen like this the home begins to look fragile and precarious. Yet the home was the solid, enduring unit of society, or so it was claimed. The Victorians on the whole found it impossible to admit that the home might be highly vulnerable, but impossible also to concede that it might not depend on the continuous, dedicated involvement and activity of women for its survival. There is still a strong belief that a home is not a real home unless it maintains warmth and food and consolation, particularly for the breadwinner's return but also for the children's return from school, and that the creation of these things is the special province of women. Countless advertisements turn on this deeply rooted feeling. For the Victorians this was the corner-stone of their attitude towards work, marriage, the family and sex. Hence the discreet alternative house-

70 and 71   Sir William Orchardson's sad portrayal of a mariage de convenance. *The Victorians were quite well aware that convention could also bring desolation*

holds in St John's Wood, for in these sex could be wrapped in warmth and food and consolation: it became domestic. Sex could be packaged in domestic wrappings, marriage embellished in the same way, family conflict subdued and work comforted by the same kind of padding. In these four central areas of bourgeois life the domestic scene was fundamental.

John Stewart Mill, writing in 1869, pointed out that men and women had a great deal more to do with each other than in former times—although it may seem to us that in fact they still led very separate lives, and there may be an element here of the way Mill would have liked things to be rather than the way they were. But he clearly approved of the fact that, as he saw it, domesticity had become much more important in the lives of men.

> The association of men with women in daily life is much closer and more complete than it ever was before. Men's life is more domestic. Formerly, their pleasures and chosen occupations were among men, and in men's company: their wives had but a fragment of their lives. At the present time the progress of civilization, and the turn of opinion, against the rough amusements and convivial excesses which formerly occupied most men in their hours of relaxation—together with (it must be said) the improved tone of modern feeling as to the reciprocity of duty which binds the husband towards the wife—have thrown the man very much more upon the home and its inmates, for his personal and social pleasures: while the kind and degree of improvement which has been made in woman's education, has made them in some degree capable of being companions in ideas and mental tastes.[10]

This may have been true of a small intellectual élite. In such a situation Victorian men and women were exceptionally well off in having the time and the opportunity to communicate freely with each other about their lives, their interests and their activities. But it is clear elsewhere that such communication was exceptional, that the weight of convention and the consideration of what was proper were against it. Mill of course was hardly typical in his attitudes: mutual responsiveness was not a part of what the rules required from husband and wife, or parents and children. There were often complaints that it was a bad system that allowed a man and a woman to marry when they scarcely knew each other, and often to live through decades of married life without getting to know each other much better, but no one knew quite what ought to be done to rectify it. Freedom before marriage and freedom after marriage to explore personality seemed equally dangerous and distasteful.

Mill clearly wanted the home to be a place where both men and women could be their real selves, and there were many who believed that that was just what it was. J. A. Froude, another intellectual, for instance—though it should be remembered that his writing here is imbued with a spirit of nostalgia rather than actuality, but equally nostalgia influenced what was expected from the present.

> When we come home, we lay aside our mask and drop our tools, and are no

longer lawyers, sailors, soldiers, statesmen, clergymen, but only men. We fall again into our most human relations, which, after all, are the whole of what belongs to us as we are ourselves, and alone have the key-note of our hearts. There our skill, if skill we have, is exercised with real gladness on home subjects. . . . We cease the struggle in the race of the world, and give our hearts leave and leisure to love.[11]

Froude seems to be assuming that men's real selves are their domestic selves, not their professional or working selves. He accepts the division between working life and home, between working relations and 'human relations'. But many men would have been aware that most of their sense of fulfilment and interest came from their working lives, that their domestic lives represented a recuperative passivity, a necessary rest from the creative activity they pursued in the real world. The division remains. It is still often hard to reconcile the self at work and the self at home.

The anxiety about this situation is most apparent in the debate about feminism, the feeling was so strong that things would fall apart if women did not remain in the home. Not only would the essential qualities of the home disappear, but the essential relationship between men and women would collapse. Many people found it impossible to visualize what the relationship between men and women could be, if women gained the freedom some were clamouring for. An article in *The Queen* of 1873 attempts to confront the issue. It argued that if women began to think of themselves as the equals of men a mutually advantageous relationship would become impossible.

There is a small amount of friendship existing between men and women; underneath the conventional surface of politeness is a deep undercurrent of enmity. The strange fight that has long been going on between the sexes about the various professions to which the latter has laid claim, testifies to the truth of this. When women cease from being lovers, when they shake off the yoke of submission, and range themselves side by side with men as equals they become at once rivals and enemies. This outbreak of women against men has been both strange and pitiful. One great cause is that women do not care to study men so as to understand them and expect too much personal attention from them. They expect their husbands to tolerate all their habits: their costly and incessant change of fashion, their powder and cosmetics, their monstrous erections of dyed and false hair, their padded figures, every rounded line made by milliners and none by nature.[12]

In other words, the message as before: harmony, domestic and social, depends on female submission. Yet often those who attacked women on the grounds mentioned here, who condemned the stridency of the feminists and the artfulness of the new woman, were loudest in their recommendations of a very similar kind of artfulness in the running of the home. A hindsighted diet of this kind of magazine article, of which the quantity is endless, soon irresistably suggests that there was a complex web of artificiality and duplicity woven to encompass the home. The

72   'The Last Day in the Old House', by Robert Martineau, 1862.

indication in the above quotation is that beneath this web there is a battlefield, but there is no suggestion that there might be a degree of immorality involved in advocating disguise.

The battlefield could perhaps be kept in the background, but the tensions could not. They were liable to be present even in those homes which approached the nearest to the domestic ideal and were places of genuine comfort and relaxation. Beatrice Potter visited the Booths in their country house also, and found it, in contrast to the London house, a place of warmth and happiness. But Mary complained furiously that she had to be a 'domestic machine'. The atmosphere of 'satisfied affection' which Beatrice found was not created without frustration and a sense of grievance on Mary's part.[13] Many men and women must have been able to conduct their domestic life with reasonable happiness and a reliable sense of security and without such frustration. Where would society be if the majority were acutely sensitive and incapable of hypocrisy, or at least of sublimation and disguise? But the insistent and religious tone of so many descriptions of the domestic ideal gives us a clue not just to the importance of the home in Victorian society but to the rarity of its perfection. It is no accident that so many Dickens' ideal domestic scenes contain not husband and wife, but father and daughter, or brother and sister, or that where it is husband and wife the husband is in the form of a father figure and the wife of devoted daughter. It is no accident that family happiness is rarely portrayed without a sense of imminent threat, sexual, economic, the threat of disease and death. Family happiness was not something permanent and stable, but fleeting and vulnerable. Revealingly, many Victorians described family scenes with a strong overtone of nostalgia—this is the way I remember my childhood home, this is the way it ought to be. I quote J. A. Froude again, but we have to ask the question, was it ever really like that? Is it not that nostalgia was as important a part of Victorian protection against a troubling world as idealization?

> How beautiful to turn the life page back to those old winter firesides, when the apple hoards were opened, and the best old wine came up out of its sawdust, and the boys came home from school to tell long stories of their fagging labours in the brief month of so dear respite, or still longer of the day's adventures and the hair-breadth escapes of larks and blackbirds. The merry laugh at the evening game; the admiring wonder of the young children woke up from their first sleep to see their elder sisters dressed out in smiles and splendour for the ball at the next town. It may seem strange to say things like these have any character of religion; and yet I sometimes think they are themselves religion itself, forming as they do, the very integral groups in such among our life pictures as have been painted in with colours of real purity. Even of the very things which we must search for in the business of life, we must go back to home to find the healthiest types. The wildest pleasures of after-life are nothing like so sweet as the old game, the old dance, the old Christmas, with its mummers and its mistletoe, and the kitchen saturnalia.[14]

Who would want to escape from this into an adult world of difficulty and responsibility? Yet the 'escape' was enforced. The only redress was for the adult to create his own refuge. But one man's refuge was another's prison, or the same man's prison, or his wife's prison, or his children's prison. However comfortable the environment, once the home was seen as a place from which escape was impossible, however likely it was to be necessary, it was half way towards a prison house. The Victorians struggled with a dim recognition of this fact. But the home of course triumphed. It is beyond the scope of this book to examine its products and its consequences, but it is worth remarking that it is unwise to generalize. If the Victorians were wrong to insist that everyone, everyone from the same class and with similar expectations that is, ought to benefit from the same set of rules, it is quite clear that a great many people did benefit. The need to conform and to accept what is already established is as natural as the urge towards individual expression.

73   *The innocent ideal of childhood depicted on children's wallpaper, 1880*

Children

The Victorians considered parenthood an obligation and motherhood, at least, a blessing. A married couple without children was odd, incomplete, an infertile wife a failure (infertility was rarely thought of as the responsibility of the husband) and a woman who deliberately took measures to prevent conception was, by most people and through most of the period, execrated. But the large Victorian family was a sign not so much of a deep natural need and love for children as of an inability, or a reluctance, to think in terms of producing fewer of them. There was a 'surplus population', there were crowded conditions, there were people who could not find employment or enough to eat, there was a heavy burden for those with a sense of responsibility and money. But it was not for the middle classes to slow down their breeding: the lower classes were encouraged to marry late, to emigrate, to beware of sexual excess within marriage, and the high infant mortality could be regarded as a more or less natural way of controlling the size of the population. Until around the 1870s the middle-class mother was regarded as having a duty to produce more, the working-class mother to produce less. The change came when it had to be admitted that the economic strain on the middle-class family with numerous children could be considerable, especially for those families on the fringes of the middle class, who were especially anxious for the future of their children, and who had to make a small income purchase a significant amount of respectability. The physical strain also, of repeated confinements on women became less likely to be considered as inevitable. The middle-class family began to get smaller.

Yet children were important for just the same reason that they were a burden, socially and economically important, that is. They would be the next generation who would carry on the struggle to 'do better' and to 'get on'. The bourgeois ethic of improvement was very much at the heart of sections of the lower middle class, and the parents' efforts were to be carried on by the children. Thus the parents had to do the best they could for their children to set them on their way, buy them a good education, get them started in a job with prospects, or groom their daughters as candidates for marriage to a man with prospects. Hopes and expectations would be geared to status. The Napoleonic dream of rising to great heights from obscurity might have encouraged some individuals but it did not establish a widespread pattern. Families were ambitious for their children, but modestly so: security was the important thing.

For parents who aimed their children at the professions expenses could be very high. There were school fees and university fees, plus the money a young man of good family could be expected to spend while enjoying the privileges of these institutions—think of all the Victorian novels which feature young men and their debts. Whatever the choice of profession the initial expenses were likely to be high—commissions in the army had to be bought, or medical practices, and it cost Betsy Trotwood £1,000 to set up David Copperfield in his law career. And during periods of training or apprenticeship parents would be expected to finance their children. Upper middle-class children were not likely to be financially independent until they were well into their 20s and were not likely to be in a position to marry until approaching 30. Upper-class children would probably not consider it desirable to be financially independent so long as there were parents or relatives prepared to keep them in funds. Independence meant responsibility.

On a more modest level it could be a financial strain simply to allow a child to benefit from, after 1870, a free education, and of course many working-class parents were in no position to allow their children to spend time at school which could be spent earning. This was particularly true in rural areas where the exigencies of the agricultural year depended on seasonal child labour, and in areas of specialized cottage industries, such as straw plaiting or lace making, where very young children could be taught a basic money-making skill which they could pursue under the eye of their parents. For most of the working class the idea of 'getting on' was irrelevant. The important thing was the wage, survival from day to day, and it was difficult to visualize a situation in which even the ability to read and write would make any significant difference to the future of the next generation. This is one of the reasons why the working-class attitude to change has tended to be suspicious; change was seen as a threat to basic needs rather than an improvement to prospects. For the subsistence wage earner the slightest alteration could make all the difference between survival and starvation. But there were those who pinned all their hopes on the value of education, drove themselves and their children hard to acquire it, and were sometimes bitterly disappointed at what it brought. There were others whom learning encouraged to be rebellious, which was just what the middle classes feared.

The vast gulf between the 'two Englands' is nowhere so strikingly seen as in the children, and in attitudes to children. Working-class children were regarded from their birth as potential wage earners or as contributors to the material welfare of the household. Although there was legislation to restrict child labour in mills, factories and mines—the 1834 Factory Act was the first—there were ways around it, and other ways in which children could make their contribution. Children were often working at glove making or lace making or similar cottage industries which could be worked at in the home or in small groups before the age of five, though they were paid miserably for their labour. Lucy Luck, born in 1848, went to work in the silk mills at Tring before she was nine.

I was too little to reach my work, and so had to have what was called a wooden horse to stand on. At that time children under eleven years of age were only supposed to work half-day, and go to school the other half. But I did not get many half-days at school, as Mr D- [with whom she lived] was a tailor by trade, so I had to stop at home in the afternoon to help him with the work. But I have never been sorry for that, for I learned a lot by it. Neither was I eleven when I had to work all day at the mill.[1]

Lucy earned 2/6 a week at the mill, and did five yards of straw plaiting every evening to add to her earnings. She was 'on the parish', without a home in the middle-class sense, paying her wage over for her keep in the homes of others. But compared with many of the harrowing tales of child workers Lucy did not have a bad time. Even after the Ten Hours Bill, limiting the hours of factory work, thousands of undernourished children worked on their feet all day, often driven by the whip, and staggered home half asleep, often too exhausted even to eat before they collapsed into whatever passed for a bed in their home. Home life for many working-class children had little meaning. Home was the place where they slept, probably sharing a makeshift bed with brothers and sisters. For those who were not out at work home was, from a very early age, the place where they worked. George Sims described, in *How the Poor Live* (1881), a four-year-old London slum dweller left in charge of a baby sibling. 'There she sat, in the bare, squalid room, perched on the sack, erect, motionless, expressionless, on duty . . . left to guard a baby that lay asleep on the bare boards behind her, its head on its arm, the ragged remains of what had been a shawl flung over its legs.'[2] For urban slum dwellers who had the chance for play there was little space. Crowded streets, filthy courts and passages were the usual playground.

Working-class children had responsibility thrust upon them. Yet they, like middle-class children, had no rights, and their toil earned them no respect. The fact that they often rapidly learned to look after themselves, and that this involved a cunning, a quickness and a knowledge of the world that seemed unchildlike meant that they were distrusted by the respectable. Education might have been seen as a way of taming the working-class child, but it could not be expected to change dramatically the working-class attitude to children. To allow a child to remain childlike was a luxury most working-class families could not afford. The middle-class family, on the contrary, was likely to insist that the child remain childlike long after the acquisition of adult habits of responsibility and independence might have been expected. There was no way of protecting the underprivileged child; they were a constant reminder to the middle class of what lack of protection could mean.

The middle-class child's shield was the home. If a primary function of the home was to provide an environment of comfort and protection for adults, no less important was the provision of discipline and protection for children. It was not the discipline of real life and experience, where qualities of independence and resource were an asset, but the discipline of an authoritarian order which essentially taught children that the best human qualities involved obeying rules rather than adapting to circumstances. It was family-centred, and exclusive, and there was throughout the century a jealous protection of the rights of the family, which meant the father, and a profound reluctance to allow any interference by the State with the family.

74   Music was a necessary accomplishment, 1872

The middle-class family was, almost paradoxically, a symbol of individual power.
This is the way Ivy Pinchbeck and Margaret Hewitt put it, in their essential book,
Children in English Society.

> Traditionally both the legal and the social structure of the family in England
> expressed the principle of paternal domination which religious sanctions had
> long supported. To propose that the State should restrict the exercise of
> parental authority was thus not merely to propose a restriction of parental
> rights which had long been established at law, but to propose a modification of
> a family pattern which had been held to be the will of God. Together, tradi-
> tional interpretations of the significance of both the laws of man and the laws
> of God for the maintenance of social order proved powerful obstacles in the
> path of those who wished to legislate for the independent rights of the child.[3]

Gradually there was legislation to protect the child at work, but very little to
protect the child at home. Parents had no legal obligations towards their children
and children had no means of redress against their parents. Clearly parents had
certain moral responsibilities, but if they deliberately undernourished or mal-
treated their children there was no way the law could interfere. Their children

were their property. Like the wife, the child was expected to be protected within the home from possible threats without. There were no means of protection from the threats within.

Thus the stereotype image of the cruel paternal figure, like Murdstone in *David Copperfield*, has considerable meaning, as does David's helpless mother, for, although she was David's natural mother, and Murdstone his stepfather, she had no right to challenge his authority. Most Victorian fathers were probably not physically cruel, at least not comparable with Murdstone although corporal punishment was extensive, but if they were there was nothing that could be done about it. Legislation to improve the position of children was very slow to come, and did not bite significantly until into the twentieth century. The State would not interfere to protect the individual if it meant that the family unit might be weakened. And the family unit was considered to be, in a sense, the individual's protection from the State. Any idea of a *Welfare* State, a State whose business it was to care for its citizens, was abhorrent. And this was partly so because of a profound unease at the thought of usurping the authority of the head of the household: the authority of husband and father was a crucial feature of his identity, and he was the representative figure of the family. Children were not, individually, of great importance. Again Pinchbeck and Hewitt.

> Children had never been of much account in England. All too many died before they reached maturity. Those who survived were hurried early into the ranks of adult society. Useful, in so far as they could be exploited; valued, perhaps, where their marriage might add to the family fortune; but not the focus of attention when the family was thought more important than the individual, and when the urgent business of maintaining or advancing family fortune absorbed the energies and interests of adults.[4]

Yet, if the middle-class child was in some respects 'hurried' into the adult world, expected to behave like a little adult in adult society, expected to sit quietly in his party clothes while waiting for the guests to arrive, and if not to be tied to his chair, in many others, as we have seen, the child was held back from adult life. A son might well not gain independence from his father until he himself became a husband and could imitate his father's authority. A daughter moved from filial subservience to wifely subservience. In the latter case, and often in the former, there was no interim in which a young adult might have been expected to discover other ways of doing things, or new vistas of authority. Dickens' novels are full of childlike adults, as well as adult children. Many Victorian writers inclined towards a belief that childlike innocence was the best of all possible states—remember Froude's nostalgia for his childhood home. Again, we can detect a need for compensation. The father is the ultimate authority within the family, the authoritarian structure confirms the state of childhood, and so childhood itself must be seen as something very special, like femininity a potent though protected force in society. And there was also the belief that innocence was its own protection: those who did not know could not be sullied.

75 *Happy children, a gay Christmas scene with a grandfather of Pickwickian*

benevolence looking on, 1858

There was in the nineteenth century until the '70s a steady increase in the birth rate. There were simply more children, although so many died as infants or when very young. In even the most casual reading about the Victorian period we are more aware of the existence of children than in any previous age. This is partly because children were increasingly seen as separate from adult life, there are children's books, children's games, children's activities which are distinguished from those of adults in a way that had not been so evident before. But it is also because there were simply more children, middle-class families were larger and the presence of children was inevitably more insistently felt. Working-class children were conspicuous on the streets. Children's labour was depended on in the mills and factories, as it cost so little and there were always jobs that small fingers could do better than large. In the nineteenth century we become aware of children as a commodity, but we also become aware of them as a burden. A working-class child was valuable if he worked, just another mouth to feed if he didn't, a burden on his family, and ultimately on society. Middle-class Victorians were never quite sure what working-class children were for, if not to work. They began to realize that it was a bad thing to have small children down the mines or amongst the mill machinery, but if they weren't being useful what were they but 'surplus population'?

Even humanitarian views of children in poverty tended to be tempered by thoughts of their use: they could be put to a good trade, or taught to sew, or put into service. A good child was a useful child. But it was harder for the middle classes to apply this attitude to themselves. They had their own large families to cope with—and of course the larger the family the more difficult it was to compartmentalize children off out of earshot and eyesight. Even the most spacious household could hardly disguise the existence of nine or ten children. There is in Thackeray's *The Newcomes* (1851) a description of Clive Newcome working in his studio with his young son happily occupied with his own drawing in a corner. But how harmonious a scene would this be with ten, or six, or even two young children sharing the studio? Inevitably the larger the number of children in any one household the more difficult it was to absorb them into adult life, and the dictum that children should be seen and not heard makes increasing sense. How else to make life tolerable? And there was a space problem. Even a fairly opulent Victorian terrace house or villa might contain only two rooms for children, and the idea of children sharing the living space of the adults to the extent of pursuing their own amusements and untidy activities in drawing room or parlour was clearly unacceptable. As more and more people crept into the ranks of the middle class and more and more 'respectable' housing was required, the Victorian middle class could expect less space to live in. The rooms in late Victorian semi-detached villas are often small, and space for children to indulge in any kind of expansive play at a premium. The correlation between economics and space and size of family first becomes evident in the last quarter or so of the nineteenth century. By that time the Victorian home could not sustain a large family and at the same time maintain the standards that were regarded as necessary. And by that time many Victorian

76   Brickmakers'-children receive their wages at the end of the week, c. 1870

women had gained in knowledge and independence to the extent that they were able to make use of methods of limiting their families. The increasing use of birth control methods, which were being publicized as early as the 1820s, was as much the result of a bourgeois instinct for survival as of feminist insistence on female liberty.

The middle-class mother was given a great deal of advice about how to bring up her children, and the parent who consigned her children to the care of others without retaining an intimate involvement was likely to be criticized. Mrs Ellis's *Mothers of England* was one of the earlier volumes of advice, and it insisted on the necessity of mothers engaging fully in the upbringing and the training of their children. Mrs Ellis was quite clear that the end products were largely the mother's responsibility. But of course most middle-class mothers had help of some kind, however great an interest they took in their children. Only the wealthy were likely to have the full array of nurses, nannies and governesses, but the modest household would have a nursemaid, and the blessings of motherhood could be dwelt on without continual reminders of the chores. The sheer business of keeping a Victorian infant and its vast quantities of garments clean was considerable. A nursemaid could not remove the daily worry about its health, but she could handle

THE EQUESTRIAN.

77   *Childhood innocence idealized by M. K. Brown in 'The Equestrian', 1851*

a large amount of the hard work, and above all she meant that the Victorian middle-class mother was not housebound.

The exaggeration and the enhancement of the mother/child relationship was inevitable. The difficulties of pregnancy and childbirth, the vulnerability of infants and young children to disease and ignorance in their care, meant that the young child was particularly precious. Religious connotations came strongly into play too. Few Victorian writers can resist the temptation to hint at the Virgin and Child when mentioning motherhood. Added to this was the religious sense of motherhood as a supremely noble vocation.

> If she be a mother, still higher, nobler is her mission. If to the weak hands is entrusted the task of rearing the young immortals, for service here, and glory hereafter; if the gem be given to her to polish which shall one day sparkle in the crown of the Saviour, let her walk softly, for angels might envy her high vocation, and the Almighty looks to see how she is nursing the child for Him.[5]

This particular passage was addressed to working women, but it expressed middle-class attitudes (a way of the middle classes giving the working-class child an identity) and a middle-class attempt at rationalizing early death which seems, now, highly distasteful. The important thing is that motherhood was considered to be very special, and its enhancement was partly religious, partly sentimental, partly self-defence, and partly the result of a hard-headed attitude to the next generation. The child was, or could be, a valuable piece of property, an ensurance of a family's continuity, a guarantee of inheritance. Thus, this kind of sentimentalization of motherhood can be seen as a fairly thin disguise of a much more prosaic attitude.

> Oh! wonderful sensation of motherhood, when the weakest woman self-constitutes herself the guardian of a weaker than herself. Then, in those first hours of anxiety and pain, the woman's soul seems to undergo a renovation. On awakening she emerges strong in the power of her love, the perfect woman, because at last, the law of nature is fulfilled. There are tender sympathies called forth in the existence of her child; there are depths of devotion, of love, which are never aroused till maternal affection bids them live and put forth their roots.[6]

Birth itself is seen as a religious process, renewing the soul, the law of nature related much more closely to the spiritual than the physical, as might be expected. This passage is from an example of third-rate popular fiction, but reflects an attitude widely absorbed by the reading public.

The child was seen as having special qualities of innocence and redemption which clearly influenced the way in which the maternal relationship was represented. (The paternal relationship was rarely one of tenderness, except with daughters, and then only when they were past the infant stage.) This is one half of a disturbing duality. For the evangelical view was that the child was a vessel of sin and required continual correction and chastisement to save its soul. And Victorian children themselves, especially in fiction and especially in Dickens, seem to be full of guilt, full of a sense that they have done wrong, but without knowing how or why. The tone of much of the literature directed at children is evangelical in a way that is sometimes savage. There is a view, which lingers in Calvinist Scotland, that the child is naturally a beast and only severe discipline, including beating, will enable him to become human. It sees children as a hostile and disruptive force. Yet at the same time a dominant view of childhood was of innocence, and the reluctance to allow children to grow up was an effort to prolong that innocence. Clearly, attitudes to sexuality were important in this reluctance—there are times when innocence seems to mean only an absence of sexual knowledge—but there was much more involved in this attitude than that, and it was closely linked with the idea of the home. The Victorians knew what a dirty business life was, and that the central ethic of 'getting on' inevitably dominated on entering a far from innocent world. They wanted their children at the same time to get on and remain unsullied. To preserve the protective nature of the home seemed to be the only way.

They were never able to reconcile these opposing attitudes. The guilt and innocence of children (look at Charlotte Brontë, George Eliot, Dickens, Mark Rutherford, many memoirs and biographies) infects every aspect of feelings about the family. The orphan is a particularly poignant focus of this, or the child who, like Maggie Tulliver in George Eliot's *Mill on the Floss* (1860), does not feel fully a part of her own family. The orphan has no reliable context in which to grow up, cannot assume that duty will be tempered by love. The orphan is a major figure in Victorian mythology, the outcast without home, without family, without an anchor to society. Interestingly, in fiction the orphan very often has a more positive identity and a more positive will than the child who is carefully wrapped in home and family. But the orphan's poignancy arises not just from the fact that there are no parents (there are often unpleasant surrogate parents) but from Victorian adults' doubts about what children really were, how they should be defined. They found it hard to think of children as individual personalities, as varied in their natures and their attributes as adults. The rigidity of rules and patterns of training and education allowed little room for individuality to flourish. Wilfulness is a cardinal sin. The child who made too much impression on the scene around him was dangerous.

At times children seemed to be regarded as pieces of property, their worth dependent on their cash value and their marriage prospects—Dickens satirizes this attitude in *Our Mutual Friend* when he describes the attempted 'deal' in Georgiana Podsnap. There was obviously an engrained fear that children might challenge parental authority and disrupt the calm security of the home. In other words children were, potentially at least, an internal threat. Discipline was the weapon against this, its severity again a good indication of anxiety. Towards the end of the century there was a tendency, with the emergence of an interest in eugenics, to regard the child as a specimen—the important thing was to breed and rear 'good quality' children, so the unfit, morally and physically, should not be allowed to breed, and the mother's special responsibility was to ensure that her children were pure and beautiful additions to the human race.

78   *Dolls' clothes and dolls, c. 1860*

This kind of confusion and duality clearly heightened the importance of the many books and articles printed which gave advice on how children should be brought up. It was widely agreed that discipline was the crux of the matter and obedience a child's duty, but there were many who advocated that discipline should be exacted by example, not by force. Parents should be firm but kind. But where punishment was necessary its administration should not be shirked, for correction was for the child's good. Frances Power Cobbe defined the kinds of obedience that could be expected from a child.

> 1st. The obedience which must be exacted from a child for its own physical, intellectual, and moral welfare.
> 2nd. The obedience which the parent may exact for his (the parent's) welfare or convenience.
> 3rd. The obedience which parent and child alike owe to the moral law, and which it is the parent's duty to teach the child to pay.[7]

While Charlotte Yonge addressed herself to the children, or rather the daughters, of the house.

> Reverence your parents. Do not let your father be looked on merely as purse-bearer, from whom money and consent are to be forced, or your mother as the slave of all your whims, the household drudge, who bears all the cares, makes the contrivances, does what no one else likes, and endures to be domineered over; while you fancy yourself devout, intellectual, or charitable, or gay. Unless you bear your part with them, and make their happiness and good pleasure your prime earthly object so long as you are daughters at home, all the rest is utter hollowness.[8]

Daughters in particular were continually being reminded of their duty to their parents, and in the second half of the century the emphasis in books of this kind—Charlotte Yonge's was published in 1876—was on the preparation of daughters for this filial role rather than the marital one. For the numbers of women who would never marry were increasing, and the cure for a dissatisfied spinsterhood was devotion to the care of others.

Yet one wonders, when reading the many books of advice and instruction addressed to parents and children (almost always daughters rather than sons: there is a marked absence of advice to sons) how great were the feelings of frustration and inadequacy they induced. For many the ideal contained within them must have been so far from the reality of experience. In the *Englishwoman's Domestic Magazine* of 1868 there was a long-lasting debate on the question of 'ought we to whip our daughters'—a clear sign of the failure of the gentle persuasion advocated in most of these books. It was argued that corporal punishment, which we can take for granted as being an accepted method in raising boys, was necessary to 'convert a wicked and stubborn nature into a sweet and loving disposition'; 'unless a Mother uses her authority in this way she loses all hold over her children, and when fear and reverence cease then good-bye to all affection.'[10] The belief that fear was an essential component of love may seem to us amazing, yet it was an exact reflection of what Christians were enjoined to feel towards God—God and parents, particularly fathers, were to be feared and loved. And in fact, of course, we still find the same argument used now, though put somewhat differently: force, and only force, produces respect, and without respect for the older on the part of the younger, the structure of both family and society collapses. The debate in the *Englishwoman's Magazine* ranged over the most suitable method of corporal punishment—strap, slipper or birch—with a strong feeling that the most painful, the birch, was the best for the child's moral welfare. It was a short step from this kind of moral justification of brutality to the kind of reign of terror which did indeed, if only rarely, exist within the Victorian home. Here is a letter from another magazine, of 1871.

> I have borne for twenty-two years with all humility and gentleness of spirit all the insults of a coarse nature. I have been a devoted slave to the man I swore to

love and obey: I have borne insults and hard work and words without a mur-
mur, but my blood boils when I see my gentle innocent girls tremble at the
sound of their father's voice.[11]

The magazine's response to this complaint was to advise that 'as he is the breadwinner you must bear it with a meek and quiet spirit' which neatly sums up the
economic status of women and its effects. A mother could not protect her children
against a tyrannous father, and had to share their fate as, for most of the period,
she shared their status, and there was little point in popular literature advocating
rebellion. The chances were that it would only bring more unhappiness to the
victim.

The problem of discipline was an enduring one. The structure of the home, and
the fragmentation of life within as well as of life in society as a whole, meant that
any degree of anarchy could amount to the most radical rebellion. Defiance of a
parent on a tiny matter could be momentous. The attitude to punishment was very
often not that it should be geared to the nature of the offence, but that *any* offence
was evidence of wickedness, and therefore required drastic punishment. This
inability to discriminate was characteristic of Victorian authoritarianism: we can
see it in the family, in the schools, in the punishment of crime. There was no such

*79   'Children in the Temple Gardens', 1883. Artisan's children enjoy the summer
evening. Much of their entertainment was likely to be outdoors*

thing as mitigating circumstances. When this authoritarianism was enacted by parent substitutes—nurse or nanny or schoolteacher—the situation was complicated. In some ways it was preferable that relationships with parents should not be sullied by the necessity of punishment—though in cases where nannies administered the punishment rather than parents this relationship was likely to be tenuous. In other ways it was appalling that the parent substitute should have the right to enact this kind of brutality. Jonathan Gathorne-Hardy in his book *The Rise and Fall of the British Nanny* quotes Lord Curzon on the subject of his tyrannous parent substitute.

> She persecuted and beat us in the most cruel way and established over us a system of terrorism so complete that not one of us ever mustered up the courage to walk upstairs and tell our father or mother. She spanked us with the sole of her slipper on the bare back, beat us with her brushes, tied us for long hours to chairs in uncomfortable positions with our hands holding a pole or blackboard behind our backs, shut us up in darkness.[12]

Often, though, parents were regarded from a distance with considerable awe while children's relationships with nannies were warm and affectionate. Nannies and nurses could often be less exacting than parents, simply because they were not overloaded with a sense of moral responsibility.

Sadder, sometimes, than the discipline and the savage punishment is the picture of quiet repression that frequently emerges. The rigidity of time-tables and regulations was often institutional in its dimensions, and contrary to any sense of warmth and relaxation in the home, and the larger the household the more likely it was to depend on system in its running. Noel Streatfeild's *The Day Before Yesterday* (1956) contains the reminiscences of a children's nurse of the early twentieth century who remembers predominantly the rigid timetabling of her day and the uneventful lives of the children—they 'led such quiet lives, and had so little time to themselves', she reflects. 'When they had time to play the nursery was always tidy, for it was a general rule only two toys out of the cupboard at a time, if another toy was wanted one of the others had to be put back.'[13] The children saw little of their parents, a brief visit in the evening for which they were dressed up and specially prepared, and during which anything less than best behaviour was intolerable. 'The greatest treat, and it was a very rare one, was when Daddy came up to the nursery for a romp, or to read to the children. Very excited the children got, quite above themselves really, when that happened.[14]

The kind of organization and orderliness that was expected in this household would have been impossible without quantities of servants. In this house, near Doncaster, there was a staff of 22. To look after two small children there was a head nurse, an under nurse and a nursery maid, plus the assistance of other servants who made up the fires, fetched and carried, and did some of the cooking. Hemmed in by adults, there was little chance even of high spirits.

Everything had to happen to the minute. At ten sharp we were out with the

80   On holiday at the seaside the father can relax with the children

prams, and pushed them until half-past twelve. Luncheon was one o'clock. Then from two until half-past three another walk with the prams. This was followed by tea at four o'clock. Then there was dressing up the children before they went downstairs, and they were taken into the drawing-room to the minute, and brought up again to the minute. Then there were their baths to get ready, all the water had to be carried. Then bed. I was supposed to be in bed myself at 9.30, but that was something which could not always happen to the minute, for with the washing, ironing, and running in of ribbons I couldn't get done in time.[15]

When adults outnumbered children this kind of regimentation was probably fairly representative of nineteenth-century country house living, although it shouldn't be allowed to disguise the sheer quantity of work that was involved even in the care of only two children, and the fact that the larger the house and the more ostentatious the life style the greater the work. For the middle-class mother coping with four or five children even with the help of a nursemaid and a cook was likely to be hard and continuous work. So in some respects we must see regimentation as an attempt simply to manage, to keep things under control. A lack of discipline in a large family could mean chaos, a practical misery as well as morally undesirable.

Even with regimentation and repression the vitality of childhood breaks through to the surface with all the charm and attractiveness that most of us like to associate with children. Nowhere is this so apparent than in the toys that children played with, which were numerous and ingenious. In general the Victorian attitude to playthings was that where possible they should be instructive. T. W. Erle's *Science in the Nursery*, published in 1884, was a detailed expression of this view. But this attitude, if anything, encouraged ingenuity and imagination in the production of toys that were educational at the same time as appealing. All kinds of mechanical toys, balancing, levering and moving toys, came on the scene in the Victorian period, to join the dolls houses and the hobby horses and hoops and spinning tops that we think of as being peculiarly Victorian. The literature of childhood suggests that escape into a world of imagination was important to the child, at least to the sensitive middle-class child who was lucky enough to have the opportunity, and toys, dolls or model soldiers or miniature steam engines, could assist this escape. Model theatres and puppets were important aids to self-expression, and books, although children's reading was mostly heavily supervized, a vitally important way in which children could have legitimate time to themselves. The sheer quantity and variety of children's toys indicate that in spite of the quiet lives described above playing was an activity that took up a considerable amount of most middle-class children's time, and although toys did tend to indicate an imitation of the adult world, dolls houses, for instance, meticulous in the miniature detail of a bourgeois household, this was and is a highly important feature of children's play.

It is impossible to escape the distorted images of childhood that the Victorian period throws up, the child weighed down by adult responsibility, the child entrapped as a wage earner in the cash nexus, the child laden with guilt, or sentimentalized beyond recognition, the child unnaturally silent and still. At the same time some Victorians some of the time enjoyed their children, and many children survived their upbringing remarkably well. The image of severity was deliberately cultivated, and there were parents who clearly felt that to take pleasure in their own children was an indulgence that was dangerous both for themselves and for their children. But the sentimentalization of children was a sure sign that the Victorians wanted to relax in their attitudes, wanted to be able to see their offspring as charming and innocent and beguiling creatures. That they could smile at them one moment and beat them the next is not so much an impossible incongruity as a sign of the characteristic Victorian malaise, their dismaying tendency to see everything in absolute terms, and to make compromise and reconciliation as difficult as possible for themselves. But in fact, in the more knockabout environment of the not very well-off middle-class home there had to be compromise in order to survive: it is one of the first lessons of family life. That sentimentalized version of parents and children I quoted in a previous chapter, with its lively but essentially well-behaved children, is not so misleading as an indication of one aspect of reality. If the parents often felt that they should not allow natural affection to outweigh their sense of moral responsibility it does not mean that the natural affection was not there. They felt that their duty was to prepare children for survival in a world that would be essentially the same as, though hopefully better than, their own. Although most Victorians wanted society improved, they were also fearful of change, and to prepare their children to encounter change, or to be ready to adapt to change, was beyond them—and probably beyond us. The repetition of an established structured pattern was important. But there was a variety of ways in which this could be done. Paternalism could be benevolent, a genuine belief in domestic harmony could afford a degree of relaxation, and the vast spectrum of individual response could have all kinds of influences.

The middle-class family became smaller. There was less pressure on parents. Attitudes to women and of women were changing, and with increasing opportunities for education the daughter's submissive centrality in the home was eroded. Even without direct challenge parental authority was inevitably modified as a younger generation became aware of the uses of independence. The most striking Edwardian children's stories, as I have pointed out, are very often about children, middle-class children, who find themselves without the traditional structure of authority, without the reliable security of the Victorian home. The moral of the stories of E. Nesbitt, for instance, is that children can cope, they are adaptable, they can rise to an occasion, they are resourceful, they are tough—tougher, in fact, than the adult who has for long been dependent on a traditional way of doing things. In the Victorian period fictional children only emerge as independent

81 'The Christmas Pudding' by Kenny Meadows, 1849. A slightly jaundiced view of happy youngsters at a Christmas feast

personalities when they *have* to fend for themselves, like David Copperfield, or when their imaginations can allow them to escape from the adult world, like Maggie Tulliver—but, significantly, these children appear in books written for adults. The development of the children's adventure story was an important imaginative alternative for the home, school and family bound child. In the Edwardian period the children of fiction emerge in spite of adults and their world. The movement is towards dispensing with adults altogether, the creation of children's worlds in which adults are of minimal importance and cannot interfere with the main business of living, or are enemies, and can be legitimately attacked. That comes after the First World War, in Arthur Ransome, for instance. But it was a movement that had to happen. It was the child's escape from the Victorian home.

Changing Needs in Housing

In the nineteenth century, for the first time, dwelling places were mass produced. The rapidity of urban expansion is one of the most reiterated facts of the Industrial Revolution. There was very little attempt to keep up with the housing needs of that part of the population that contributed most to the growing size of towns and cities. There were a few enlightened employers and philanthropic individuals who thought in terms of rehousing the poor or improving the houses they had. But there was another kind of movement visibly stirring in the Victorian period as well as that in to the cities—a movement upwards. And housing, the type of housing and its situation, was very much a sign of this. Most of the new housing was put up for the benefit of the increasingly wide section of society who were able, or very nearly able, to call themselves middle class.

There is nothing in working-class housing to compare with the acres of respectable suburban building, which was often jerry-built (the term dates from the 1880s) and almost always rootedly conformist, which has irretrievably characterized so many of Britain's towns and cities. Even that housing that came a long time after the death of Victoria tends to have a Victorian flavour, not necessarily in design, but in its reflection of life style. It radiates a life style that is inward, well ordered, or aspiringly well ordered, behind closed doors, conformist, divided from business and trade—and usually at a distance from shops—by gardens and hedges if possible, and by a general air that life depends on the solidity of brick and the quality of curtains. The Victorian middle-class home did not like to be looked in upon. It did not want to expose its interior to uninvited eyes, as if such eyes might detect its reliance on just those things it tried so hard to exclude. There is a guarded look about the windows. There are steps and entrances as an added bulwark.

The dominant assumptions about housing needs are middle-class, even when they are applied to the requirements of the working population. Needs were measured against what the successful and secure felt they, and others, deserved. It seemed perfectly logical to most Victorian minds to insist that the less successful and the lower status needed less, and this wasn't entirely a question of what could be afforded. That there were minimal requirements it was gradually accepted, but always with a reluctance to provide benefits for free. The respectable citizens of Manchester did not want to pay rates which would mostly be used to finance drainage and water supply for those areas of the city which had none and where they themselves did not live. Many people believed that rates were not a responsibility but a kind of imposed charity, and although Victorians believed in charity they also believed in choice. They did not like to be told who were the deserving. And they liked to be seen to be charitable. There was always the question of whether the underprivileged deserved assistance. There seemed to be no human law that indicated that those who had worked hard to gain and maintain individual security should contribute to the security of others who often seemed, self-evidently, to have worked less hard and less deservedly. There was the argument that it was not good for people to get help and hand-outs. It was one of the many things the Victorians worried about. They were never sure whether to regard the poor as victims or profligates. They sought some universal law which would both clarify and justify what appeared to be the inevitable order of things, and they accepted the inevitable by deeming it the natural order of things. It was natural that some should have more than others, natural that some should get to the top and others should stay at the bottom. They were uneasily aware that the getting to the top of one meant the staying at the bottom of many, but there was always the rich man and the needle's eye to make poverty acceptable. A Christian morality might help to salve the conscience, but it could not solve the problem. New thinking in science seemed to confirm the unequal reality—social Darwinism made the 'natural' order intellectually respectable.

And in most parts of the British Isles the unequal reality was there for all to see, in its most basic form, the immediate environment of life. There were a number of investigators who by the last quarter of the century were documenting the facts (and with a lot of argument about the best way of doing this). Charles Booth's *Life and Labour of the People of London*, an amazingly detailed and extensive work put together with the aid of many helpers, not least his wife, appeared in 1889. Benjamin Seebohm Rowntree's *Poverty: a Study of Town Life* (1901) was an investigation of York and the way the poor lived there. There were other more modest works, Octavia Hill's *Homes of the London Poor* (1875) for instance, but these were the two giants. Rowntree estimated that between 25 and 30 per cent of England's urban populations lived in poverty, what we would now call below the poverty line—and he was one of the first to establish how to assess poverty. He worked out exactly what was required to maintain a family of two adults and three children in a state of what he called 'physical efficiency', and worked out that most labourers' families in York, even when the wage seemed just adequate, were living in a state of 'primary poverty', either because there were more than three children or because they were unable to maintain the total discipline over expenditure that was required—'Nothing must be bought but that which is absolutely necessary for the maintenance of physical health, and what is bought must be of the plainest and most economical description.'[1] 'Primary' poverty meant, simply, that there was not enough to eat.

In other words most labouring families would never be able to have any expectation of occupying more than a very low minimum standard of housing, and even if they were working for a benevolent employer, like the Rowntrees themselves, they were dependent on a middle-class definition of their needs. It was the well off,

82   Octavia Hill

not the poor themselves, who decided what poverty was. It was the 'experts', well intentioned as those who took the trouble almost always were, who worked out the minimal needs in food and housing, and how much money should be spent. And even when the facts were laid out with the care and authority of Booth or Rowntree, there was much argument about what, if anything, should be done about them.

There was a profound inability to come to terms with the facts of slum living in the major cities, apart from simply accepting their existence. There were of course attempts to eliminate slums and replace them with housing suitable for the low paid. The earliest were the results of private philanthropy—the move towards municipal responsibility in housing was slow. Most municipalities were more eager to spend money on the erection of splendid town halls than on slum clearance, which was due partly to the fact that very few people seriously considered that anything could be done about them. The town halls served to distract the eye from the squalor. Self-help might enable a few to pull themselves out of the slums, but responsibility for pulling down the slums themselves, and replacing them with adequate houses for the same people, was quite a different business. And when slum clearance was attempted, as Jack London pointed out in his *People of the Abyss* (1903), the housing that replaced them was not for the original slum dwellers but for people, artisans, and better paid labourers, who already had expectations of a decent environment. 'The slum people had simply drifted on to crowd other slums or to form new slums', Jack London wrote.[2]

Slums were regarded as an organic feature of urban existence, and there seemed to be no limit to the quantity of human life they could absorb. That was, in a sense, their great advantage. With an increasing birth rate, urban magnetism, and increasing quantities of immigrants, there was no hope for cities like Manchester, Liverpool, Glasgow or London maintaining the most minimal of standards, even if the will existed. Housing was in the hands of private speculators and private landlords, whose thinking was obviously determined by the money they could make, not by the needs of population. S. G. Checkland, in *The Rise of Industrial Society in England 1815–1885* (1964) describes what tended to happen.

As more persons converged on the towns the supply of housing inevitably failed to increase proportionately. For it was easier, on a step by step basis, simply to divide into smaller and smaller units, with families sometimes

83   New houses, Gascoyne Road, Hackney, c. 1855

occupying merely a portion of a room. With such a premium upon shelter, and with no standards to maintain, it was too tempting to take in a lodger, adding further to the disruption of the family. Those who were commercially interested in town housing found that there were greater gains in a policy of overcrowding than in one of reconstruction. Moreover, in fairness to such landlords, it was too much to ask that they should take such a new and daring initiative. They were essentially men and women of petty, pre-industrial mind, who knew how to make gains where an intense demand for a facility in short supply had arisen, but they were incapable of the initiative necessary to place the matter on a new basis. Slum landlords have never been slum clearers.[3]

Octavia Hill found that the landlords were the problem, willing to exploit their tenants and to condone bad behaviour. As long as money was to be made out of overcrowding there was an enormous barrier to comprehensive attempts to improve the situation. And of course there were no comprehensive attempts. And no one was sure who might legitimately be expected to take on that kind of responsibility. Octavia Hill quite independently undertook to improve housing. Her work was effective, but tiny in proportion to what was needed. We now take it for granted that such a responsibility exists, but the Victorians were in the early stages of thinking about whose business it was to undertake works that had no hope of profit or even of any form of tangible return. S. G. Checkland continues.

> The challenge of an adequate housing programme was very complex. There were all the problems of design: what kind of house would be suitable for such occupants, what kind of facilities? Anything that was more than barely minimal would mean a cost of construction that was prohibitive. Indeed house-owning artisans were sometimes found opposing a sanitation programme for fear of increased local taxation. Pipes and fittings were usually very poor, and buried in the plaster so that water companies had to be very careful when raising the pressure. In some areas the building operatives were charged, and with some justice, with keeping down recruitment through apprenticeship, thus keeping their own wages up, but curtailing the housing supply. Skimping was all too general—in slump to get the cost down in order to sell at all, and in boom to speed completion before prices broke.[4]

There were isolated attempts at improvement and replacement, like Octavia Hill's, but neither imagination nor pragmatism could come to grips with the vast scale of the problem, or with the capacity of human beings to endure and survive the most appalling conditions.

In 1845 the Metropolitan Association for Improving the Dwellings of the Industrious Classes was founded, and in 1849 their first efforts were completed. The Albert Family Dwellings (Prince Albert interested himself in the design of model housing) went up in Deal Street, Stepney. They were five-storey blocks of flats, each of four rooms—kitchen, scullery and two bedrooms—and although there were certain basic amenities, mains water and lavatory, they were not much

84   *Squalor, fun and community spirit mingle in Doré's illustration of a typical*
'court', 1872

more than minimally adequate. But the rents were high, 3/6 to 4/- a week. Such efforts could not possibly help to alleviate overcrowding where it was at its worst, for overcrowding was partly the result of being unable to pay for more than a small amount of living space. The same organization built Albert and Victoria Cottages, only two storeys high, but although rents for these were lower they seemed to many people, the people who helped finance such projects, to be an improvident use of land. Low density urban housing was clearly a luxury philanthropists could not afford. There were other attempts to provide housing for the lower paid. The American George Peabody left money for the putting up of workers' housing in London, and the results are still in existence in areas such as Clerkenwell. To modern eyes they look grim, dark, dirty, any open spaces concreted over. But they were the inevitable Victorian result of a maximum use of land and space, very little choice in siting, and a highly inflexible idea of the requirements of the working man and his family. Octavia Hill's experiments began in the 1860s. Her criticism of the landlords was so strong that she decided to become one herself, to show how it could be done. She began by buying three properties in Marylebone, cleaned them up and did necessary repairs, and then let rooms at fair rents. It was a great success. She always insisted that it was necessary to treat the poor, however improvident they seemed, with courtesy and friendliness, and found that they responded in kind. This is how she described the success of her scheme.

It appears to me then to be proved by practical experience, that when we can induce the rich to undertake the duties of landlord in poor neighbourhoods, and ensure a sufficient amount of the wise, personal supervision of educated and sympathetic people acting as their representatives, we achieve results which are not attainable in any other way. It is true that there are Dewllings' Improvement Societies, and the good these societies do is incalculable; I should be the last to underrate it. But it is almost impossible that any society could do much for such places as the court of which we have spoken, [where the houses she bought were] because it is there not so much a question of dealing with houses alone, as of dealing with houses in connection with their influence on the character and habits of the people who inhabit them. If any society had come there and put those houses into a state of perfect repair at once, it would have been of little use, because its work would have been undone again by the bad habits and carelessness of the people. . . . You cannot deal with the people and their houses separately. The principle on which the whole work rests is, that the inhabitants and their surroundings must be improved together.[5]

Of course there is a strand of paternalism, or maternalism, in this, but Octavia Hill did establish genuine friendly relationships with the people she helped and there is no doubt that individuals and families gained considerably from her work. She was very much concerned with the environment, with open spaces and playgrounds and parks. She saw the importance of recreation to family life.

Inevitably population pressure on the urban centres got worse, as people

became increasingly dependent on what the congested areas could offer them—
nearness to work, a sense of community (this tended to disappear in the worst of
the slums, but in areas that were characterized to a great extent by the nature of
local employment it was much in evidence) and of shared experience. Rents were
high, sometimes half the wages went on rent and the more crowded the area and
therefore the greater the demand for living space and the worse the standards, the
more a family might be expected to pay, though food prices were often lower in the
centres of towns than in the outlying areas. It was important to be as near to work
as possible. Suburban developments which depended on the growing commuter
services were bound to be for the better off. Most labourers could not afford to
pay for transport. Once a man or woman had arrived in the city to live and work,
or just to sink, unemployed and underfed, into the morass of urban humanity, the
chances of ever making the effort to get out again were slight. There was so much
happening in the city, so much varied activity, there was always an illusion of
choice, of expectation, of hope. It seemed worth looking for work, or simply walk-
ing about the streets with some vague hope that something might turn up, when

85   *Interior of Peter Robinson's, 1891. It began as a linen draper's shop in 1833*

there was so obviously a great deal going on. Yet the signs of destitution and the bleakest, grimmest poverty, were a continual reminder of what could happen. In an area like London's East End—though London's poverty was to be found in pockets all over the city—squalor and the degradation of humanity were a generalized situation; only the courageous few dared to individualize it, dared to investigate and isolate poverty in terms of the individual. It was too grim and distasteful an exercise for most people, and intruded too severely on their own images of comfort and security.

The process from individual interest to public responsibility was slow. It was not until 1875, with the Artisans' Dwelling Act which empowered the clearing of slums and the rebuilding of housing, that there was national legislation on the subject of housing. Ten years later the Housing Act extended the scope of the earlier legislation, but these Acts while they made it possible for local authorities to take action, by allowing compulsory purchase for instance, could not compel them. It was not until the last years of the century that the problem of housing began to be confronted seriously as a public responsibility. By that time the problems of high density urban areas were so deeply rooted that they had become, as we can still see, virtually perpetual. Slums could be cleared, but the housing that replaced them *had* to be high density, there was no alternative on valuable urban land, and *had* to be let at economic rents—without, at least, an extent of change in social attitudes that would at the time have amounted to revolution. In the Victorian mind decency involved privacy and separation, and the communal use of amenities was too powerfully redolent of such slum characteristics as the sharing of privies and water taps. Separation, a tendency against the communal use of space, seemed to be the answer to slum squalor which involved the crowding together of many families, no chance to separate the sexes, no chance to be decently private. The attitude to the use of space reflected middle-class compartmentalization, and it was very hard indeed for a family cooking, eating, washing, themselves and their clothes, sleeping, and occupying their leisure hours in two or three rooms, or sometimes in half a room, to imitate the standards of the middle class. The dedication with which some tried indicates the courage and determination with which a section of the working class, inevitably the better off, struggled upwards.

The development of public responsibility, slow though it was, helped this struggle. But it did not help to any significant extent the plight of the habitual slum dweller. For the slum dweller simply could not afford to live decently. And although he was often the victim of unscrupulous and rapacious landlords there was little alternative for him. Hence the confirmed tendency that Jack London comments on, for the cleared slum dweller simply to find another slum. Eyesores and smells and health hazards could be removed, but that did not necessarily improve the situation of the people who festered within them. The basic need for shelter at as low a cost as possible guaranteed the perpetuation of the slum, somewhere or other in the urban mass.

Cooperation helped a little, in some of the industrial areas of the north and

86 *Queen Anne style red brick and terracotta in south-west London, c. 1880*

midlands. Those with the determination to help themselves were sometimes able to combine to their mutual benefit. There were some housing schemes that were the result of artisans' cooperative housing associations, and some that were the result of charity. But it was a long, slow and difficult business, and again did not help those most in need. Some municipalities made attempts to cope with the problem. In 1846 Glasgow Town Council destroyed some of the city's worst tenements and built, solidly and substantially, new ones. In 1866 there was a City of Glasgow Improvement Act which allowed for more slum clearance, an initiative that impressed a number of people concerned with housing. But in spite of these moves in the 1880s 25 per cent of the city's population were living in homes of one apartment, and in spite of the city's wealth only eight per cent enjoyed the spaciousness of houses of five rooms or more. Glasgow had experienced the common trend in the rapidly expanding industrial cities. In the 1840s there had been energetic building—railway stations, banks, churches, a City Hall, a Corn Exchange, and houses for the upper middle class who moved out of the city centre. The homes they vacated were taken over by landlords who let a room to a family. The pattern of overcrowding and deterioration was established, and repeated itself over and over again. As soon as one set of people were in a position to move out to better housing, there were others eager to occupy the vacated space. There were no restrictions imposed on landlords, no standards demanded. Whereas in the 1830s the working environment had begun to be improved, the living environment remained immune until the end of the century. Glasgow's efforts, praiseworthy though they were, did not prevent the city gaining one of the most notorious reputations ever for its slums.

Another hazard was that construction was entirely in the hands of private companies, and the enforcement of building standards was minimal. The energy of speculative builders depended entirely on the returns they could expect. In Glasgow in the 1890s builders revealed a conspicuous lack of interest in putting up housing for rent by the working classes. That wasn't where the profits were. The most evident signs of late Victorian building can be seen in the area, ranging from very modest to almost palatial, of housing for the middle classes. It is in the inner suburbs of now decayed respectability that we cannot fail to notice the trail left by the Victorian builder. In the second half of the century, although there were moves towards slum clearance and replacement, the building of housing for specific categories of workers, for the railwaymen or the millworkers or the miners, slackened. The numbers of workers in the manufacturing industries were, overall, declining, although specific industries were expanding. There was not the need to provide housing for newly set up mills or newly enlarged factories. And agricultural labour was declining too, so the incentive to build model cottages for farm labourers also dwindled. But the population was not declining, and the possibilities for a home worthy of the name were for thousands non-existent.

The expanding section of the population was the lower middle class, and a great deal of the urban building in the second half of the century was for their benefit. Vast tracts of London's suburbs were created for the growing army of clerks who were needed to maintain the running of business and buying and selling. There was a self-conscious need to establish an identity in terms of the outward signs of respectability, a need which, once it could be supplied and underpinned by a sense of security, shaded into complacency. The most memorable example of this is the Grossmiths' Mr Pooter in their *Diary of a Nobody*, a summation of late nineteenth-century inner suburbia. Mr Pooter is the proud new tenant of 'The Laurels, Brickfield Terrace, Holloway', and his eager but complacent immersion in the trivialities of suburban life is both endearing and amusing. Here he is, in the first chapter, describing his new home.

> . . . a nice six-roomed residence, not counting basement, with a front breakfast-parlour. We have a little front garden; and there is a flight of steps up to the front door, which, by-the-by, we keep locked with the chain up. Cummings, Gowing and our other intimate friends always come to the little side entrance, which saves the servant the trouble of going up to the front door, thereby taking her from her work. We have a nice little back garden which runs down to the railway. We were rather afraid of the noise of the trains at first, but the landlord said we should not notice them after a bit, and took £2 off the rent. He was certainly right; and beyond the cracking of the garden wall at the bottom, we have suffered no inconvenience.[6]

Pooter's home is a marvellous indication not only of what was considered desirable —the front breakfast-parlour—but of what was considered acceptable—the railway at the bottom of the garden. The book is a finely detailed indication of a certain level of snobbery, of the symbols of a respectable life. The front door with its flight of steps is not actually used, but it is important. There is great emphasis laid on the duties and activities of the single servant. And one of the most important features of the Pooters' lives is their relationship with trandesmen. They are probably earning no more than their butcher, but they are in no doubt that they are in a different class, and that it is incumbent upon those in trade to treat them with respect if not deference. The preservation of the barrier between trade and its customers was of the greatest importance.

The Pooters have no doubts about the acceptable symbols of respectability; they know what they are and they make them happy. A much more interesting, complex and painful expression of a particular kind of middle-class problem can be found in the novels of George Gissing, where he explores the difficulties of middle-class people who cannot maintain the respectability to which they are accustomed, and of lower-class people who are striving desperately to haul themselves into higher categories of status. In *New Grub Street*, published, like *Diary of a Nobody*, in 1892, Gissing describes the agonies of a young middle-class couple with very little to live on and the need, on the part of the wife at least, to cling to the illusions of middle-class respectability. She cannot cope with the realities of keeping house and caring for a baby and managing economically. She feels that the lack of a servant is a terrible admission of descent. And her husband is fully absorbed in trying to write sellable fiction.

Gissing's couple are living in a small mansion-block flat. By the 1880s and '90s mansion blocks were going up in parts of central London, Bloomsbury, the Baker Street area, for instance, later in St Johns Wood, as middle-class housing. Some of these contained spacious flats which imitated the dimensions of earlier Victorian building, but many of the flats were, like the *New Grub Street* one, very small, with no provision of servant's quarters, containing perhaps three small rooms and a kitchen, adequate for a bachelor perhaps, or a young couple, with a servant coming in daily. If the less well off had waited until they could afford to get married, on a mid-Victorian basis, they would never have married at all, and housing had to be adjusted to the fact that middle-class couples were setting up house together with very little money. Their sense of themselves would not allow them to settle in a working-class area or to occupy artisan housing; thus the proliferation towards the end of the century of smaller flats and smaller houses, in areas of new suburban development, or in central areas where old housing was being replaced. From the builders' point of view more was to be gained from building mansion blocks for the respectable than from tenements for the workers.

In London and the south the class orientation of building was marked, and the finer shades of distinction were easily detectable. In the north this was less the case, not so much because buildings were not raised with particular kinds of people in mind as their occupants, but because there was a greater uniformity of style.

*87   Speculative terrace in Woolwich—a dull uniformity common to many London
suburbs*, C. *1880*

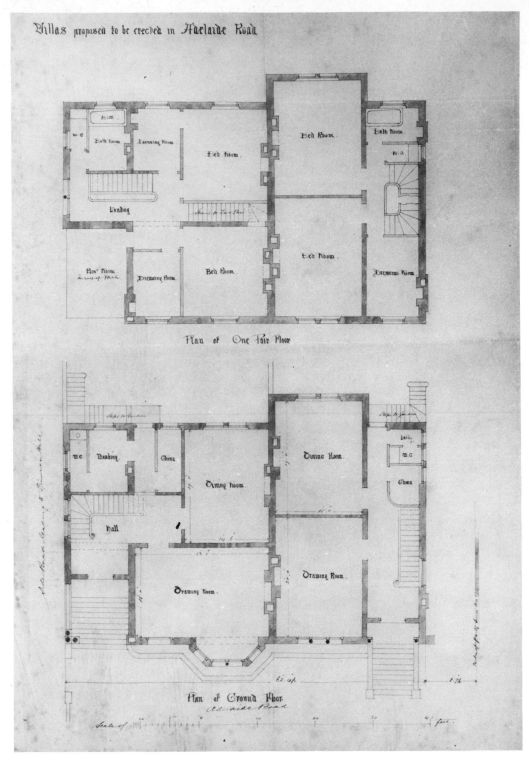

88   *Plans of a spacious villa in Adelaide Road, St John's Wood, London*

Although those who made the profits tried to escape from those who laboured it was, except in a few cases where money could buy a landed gentry style of life, more difficult when profit-making depended on a fairly intimate involvement with the labour. The gradations of middle class are less distinguishable in northern cities. Even in Edinburgh, where sensitivity towards shades of respectability has had a long tradition, fine distinctions in styles of building do not exist, and the extensive use of sandstone for all types of building lends a pleasing air of consistency to the city, broken most startlingly by twentieth-century corporation housing and bungaloid sprawl.

The most significant and extensive building in the second half of the century was, though, in suburban development. Yet it was expensive, often wasteful, and frequently detrimental to just those ideas of home life that the mid-Victorian period had consolidated. Suburbia took the breadwinner further from his home, added a tiring journey to his day's work, and could not but make the prison-like aspects of the home more evident. At the same time the suburban home accentuated many of the treasured but damaging characteristics of the Victorian home. The wife was likely to be more isolated, more dependent on house-bound activities. Most suburbs were developed without much attention paid to the amenities of shops and entertainment. The negative and introverted character of many suburbs is partly due to this, for the combination of the closed door and the lack of civic life left very little outward signs of human activity. The kind of personality and atmosphere that a particular suburb acquired was almost always dependent on class, for where a family lived reflected their status unequivocally. H. J. Dyos in his book on the development of Camberwell, *Victorian Suburb* (1961), discusses this at some length.

What did the suburbs offer? They offered more space for less money, and a greater opportunity for certain significant symbols of upward mobility, as we have seen in *Diary of a Nobody*. A step up from the Pooters could bring a larger garden and no railway. They offered less dirt and less evidence of the lower classes; they offered an atmosphere of containment and pleasant safety. A sense of separateness combined with a sense of belonging to a community of like people—one might not know one's neighbours, but one could be more sure that they were like oneself. In the teeming city centre it was much more difficult to know who or what people were. The suburbs offered a piece of property and a piece of land that was distinctively one's own, and undistinctively like everyone else's. The front door could be closed with more security, with the comforting knowledge that everyone else in the street was doing the same. But there were contradictions: they cannot be forgotten for long. The front door could be shut, but there were the hazards of the daily journey, and the journeys that had to be taken, if only occasionally, by wife and children. For they could not be entirely confined. There was shopping to be done, and women could not be expected to find all they needed in the locality. The children had to go to school, and when they were older the sons might well be commuting to jobs, and the daughters too by the end of the century. Home life was simultaneously consolidated and disrupted. And the more the reality of shut-in

89   A Glasgow slum of 1868. Note the open drain or 'gulley'

comfort and security was disturbed the stronger the urge to cling to the symbols, and from this much of the equivocal attitude to suburban life has arisen.

For the suburbs from the very beginning contained at least the germ of mockery. There always seemed to be something sterile and ridiculous about suburbia, there was always an awareness of the contradictions involved. They were the ultimate expression of the Victorian need for escape, and the ultimate denial of the richness of life which, in spite of all the other tendencies, flavours so much of what is Victorian. Having defined the home, having made themselves sure, as they thought, of the kind of life they wanted to go on within it, the Victorians then did not know how to make it productive. Home life seemed to depend increasingly on economics rather than attitude. Money and the symbols it could buy threatened to take over from moral conviction, and the nakedness of suburbia offered very little to disguise this trend. The bourgeois ethic had depended on the reconciliation of economics and morality. By the end of the century the home seemed to be not so much a place to hide from the facts of life, as a place to shelter from the attacks on this reconciliation that were coming from all quarters, scientific, political, moral, artistic. In the twentieth century the negative nature of suburbia was bound to be more pronounced.

The Grossmiths' mockery is benign. H. G. Wells a few years later was more contemptuous—his *Ann Veronica* (1909) is a good example. But suburbia had established both its existence and its character too fast for changes to be feasible. The Victorians, it might be said, brought it on themselves, but their inheritors have not thought very hard about possible alternatives. The demand for housing was so great, and the desirable lifestyle so much taken for granted, that the urgent need appeared to be the construction of houses that conformed to the apparent wants and the pockets of an unending supply of customers. The nature of middle-class housing in the latter part of the century was the result of a by now complacent, and in some areas already disintegrating, belief in the home combined with pragmatism and the straightforward commercial attitudes of those who built the houses. Clearly there had to be modifications. Clearly the categories of respectability had to be stretched. But certain middle-class essentials had to be upheld. The middle class did not cook and eat in the same room, if it could possibly be avoided. It certainly did not cook and sleep in the same room. The definition of activity within designated space was obviously wasteful, as it still often is. What a waste of space is a bedroom, if it is only used to sleep in, or a dining room, if it is only used to eat in. The middle class wanted to have privacy *within* the family, not just a hearth and home, with which others might be expected to be content, but individual doors that could shut on individual people. Open-plan living was a reaction to this, and many people who experienced it felt it to be ill-considered. For it was difficult for the middle classes to learn to share their lives in the way that those with little space had to. It was difficult to tolerate playing children and busy adults and the consumption of food, and animals too perhaps, always, constantly, within the same four walls with nowhere at all to go for privacy and quiet. And this fact, the separateness and the privacy of the middle-class household, and the

90   A high degree of standardization characterized most London suburbs. Tooting,
c. 1890

enforced communality of the working-class household, has been a highly influential
factor in the lack of class understanding and sympathy.

    The needs of a Victorian household were of course more than certain specifica-
tions and arrangements of space. Suburban development was partly dependent on
a number of basic amenities, and amongst those that were increasingly viewed as
necessities were drainage, water and gas. In spite of Thomas Cubitt's lead in the
1820s the following generation of speculative builders were not particularly concerned to ensure that these were available. But by the 1860s, with work in progress
on London's main drainage and other large cities taking their sewers in hand, and
gas installations extensive, builders had little excuse for failing to make the most of
what was available. In 1860 the Metropolitan Gas Act defined company boundaries
in London, and most inner areas could be supplied with gas. By the end of the
century gas was generally looked on in cities as a cheap and convenient source of
heat and light. It did not take long for it to become a necessity, rather than a convenience. But there were other things too, 'necessities' that people wanted in their
houses, that were increasingly both available and known to be available. As communications became easier and faster the distribution of goods became easier and
faster. Rapid delivery could be made and advertising could publicize what was
available. This helped to counter any sense of isolation, and facilitated both sub-

urban building and suburban living. In the 1870s the rate of suburban development increased. The department store and the growth of chain stores were added lifelines for the suburban housewife. The 'high street' with its Lipton's and its Home and Colonial could provide a focus, an oasis in the suburban desert, and it was worth the tradesmen's while to compete for custom. The housewife was still able to think of them as providing 'services': she used them, they did not use her. And as the housewife became more likely to do her own shopping, rather than depend on ordering and delivery, or to send the servants, this was important.

Needs, of course, are self-perpetuating as well as being defined, very often, by factors other than those of personal requirement. The middle classes, it might be argued, did not have to get out of the city centres. (Now, of course, the trend has been reversed. The well off are coming back in, to the areas once occupied by decayed housing, and the working-class residents are being banished to council estates on the urban peripheries.) They did not have to put as much distance between themselves and the reminders of poverty as practicality allowed. But the cult of the home encouraged this movement. It seemed to be the logical outcome of a belief in the value of protection and the importance of padding. Although by the last quarter of the century ideas were beginning to change and the interior of the home was less preoccupied with darkness, solidity and disguise the buildings were there, and only time or a great deal of money could change their outward aspect or their inward arrangement. New ideas in design could not seriously interfere with the ethos that had shaped the Victorian home. We can see them, in the remaining chapters, as the signs of unease and of reaction, but not of radical change.

91 *William Morris, attributed to C. Fairfax-Murray*

Design After the Deluge

For us now the Great Exhibition is a convenient symbol of Victorian vulgarity and ostentation. There, in large quantities, under one vast roof, was everything that was worst in Victorian design up to that point, drowning, in its overweening weightiness, everything that was best. Most of the exhibits were not a reliable guide to what people had in their homes, or would subsequently have in their homes, but this does not diminish the significance of the fact that many thousands of ordinary people made the journey to London from all parts of the country in order to look at them. These thousands crowding the Crystal Palace looking at the most extraordinary range of goods were in some respects more important than the goods themselves, for they indicated, not so much an interest in design itself, as a fascinated curiosity about objects, ornamentation, developments that could be seen as the symbols of the possibilities of home life. Middle-class people especially were no longer satisfied with what had been considered the traditional necessities of household life. They wanted novelty and, within limits, adventure, and they accepted exaggeration.

People wanted to feel that they were directly sharing in the consciousness of progress, and owning things was a way of doing it. To some extent owning became more important than enjoying. And the development of a rigid moral sense played its highly important part in the justification of ownership. Many of the middle-class visitors to the Great Exhibition were looking for rewards. They wanted to find out what the right things to have in their houses might be. They understood that they were a part of a society that had a great deal of 'things' to offer, and they accepted that part of their function was to possess a suitable quantity of these things. Everything seemed to combine to convince them that they must own, that they must make it evident that they deserved a positive share of what was going.

Mass production both encouraged and reacted to this demand. New techniques which might at first have been sought as a means of improving design and facilitating manufacture, became overwhelmingly geared to rapid and cheap production. Elizabeth Aslin in her book *Nineteenth Century English Furniture* (1962) explains.

During the early part of the Victorian period there was a determined and continuous search for new materials and new methods of manufacture. Once found the discoverers were almost always certain that their new ideas were capable of universal application since it was assumed that new materials must be, in their very nature, better materials. Similarly it was assumed that the main function of the machine was to produce more quickly than by hand 'a great many copies from an exceedingly good pattern'.[1]

Such an attitude assumed that everyone wanted to have the same article in their homes, and indeed the exercise of individual choice and the formulation of individual preference is not notable in the Victorian period. Even when attitudes towards design began to change, they changed not in the direction of encouraging people to shape their homes according to their own needs and requirements but towards the application of a new set of rules. The arbiters of taste may have become more convincing in the way they arrived at their conclusions about what was good and what was bad, but they were no less insistent that there were rules, and that the sensitive, educated and morally alert individual had an obligation to obey them.

The formulation of rules was a major development. Early Victorian elaboration obeyed no distinct principles, but tended to operate on the assumption of the more the better. The burgeoning of elaborate and over-substantial furniture seemed an appropriate reflection of the burgeoning of production in general. But there was something offensive about this. There had to be a reaction. The initial stages were, precisely, an effort to regularize and bring into order what was going on. Labels were required. It had to happen in the case of architecture as well. The jumble of styles, the tendency to mix them in any combination, to overdo and muddle up, needed, if not to be retrained, to be made sense of. The pattern books of house designs that were being published were a move towards this. They were not necessarily suggesting that one design was better than another intrinsically, but they were identifying and labelling what was available and demonstrating what was appropriate. Charles Eastlake's *Hints on Household Taste* was essentially trying to do the same job. The fact that he was trying to evolve rules but was not able to explain them suggests a sense of urgency in the attempt to regularize a highly confused situation.

By the 1870s the reaction against the heavy and elaborate Victorianism of 20 years before was distinct. But it had begun before that, most impressively in the ideas and work of William Morris and his associates. Morris was one of a number of artists and designers who emerged out of the dense clutter of the 1850s to try to create various kinds of individual distinction in exterior and interior design. Amongst the architects Philip Webb and Norman Shaw were the most interesting. They were concerned with providing living space that was also a creative environment. They did not, in fact, get away from the belief in the home as a refuge, but they opened out its possibilities. They had a more imaginative grasp of the scope of life within the home. They reflect what might be called a transition from a moral emphasis to an aesthetic emphasis in design.

Webb's initial notable achievement was the Red House, which he built for William Morris in 1860. The striking quality of the Red House is that it is both straightforward and suggestive of grandeur, homely but spacious. It is in many ways characteristically Victorian, though without heaviness, with its irregularities, its Gothic arches and windows, its high ceilings, its vernacular touches in no way contradictory to the suggestion of a sophisticated life-style. Morris's ideas and inclinations led him to attempt to revive a more genuine medievalism than the crude devices of many mid-Victorian designers, but the distinctive achievement of the Red House is its translation of the principle of designing for individual needs. Here was no case of a family judging its requirements by what others already had, but of an individual thinking out what his particular ideals in life required.

Morris did not react against decoration itself. The straightforward quality of the Red House is the simplicity of frankness of purpose, not of neutrality. Decoration was of integral importance. The walls were covered with tapestries and frescoes, done by Morris and his friends, on themes that directly reflected their interests and ideals. Lady Burne-Jones, a close friend, described a visit to the house.

> The dining-room was not yet finished, and the drawing-room upstairs whose beautiful ceiling had been painted by Mr and Mrs Morris, was being decorated in different ways, so Morris's studio, which was on the same floor, was used for living in, and a most cheerful place it was, with windows looking three ways and a little horizontal slip of a window over the door, giving upon the red-tiled roof of the house where we could see birds hopping about all unconscious of our gaze.[2]

The activities of the Morris family and their friends and colleagues within Morris's various homes, drawing together as they do hard work, high jinks, conviviality, quarrels and love affairs, take us a long way from the conventional image of Victorian family life. The Morris family life may not have matched up either to their own ideals or more traditional ones, and clearly was often not happy, but there is a refreshing sense that there was room for domestic life and artistic work and human friendship all within the same context. The light, space and colour of the Red House reflect a very different attitude to life from that of the dark and enclosed and well-covered conventional mid-Victorian interior.

This different kind of attitude is echoed to some extent in other designs by Webb, less geared to individual need, and those of Norman Shaw. Shaw's Bedford Park development (1876) is one of the most memorable manifestations of a more enlightened and refreshing attitude to housing that the century produced. He put up houses that had a consistency but not a uniformity of design, were interesting to look at, and were pleasantly open in their aspect and their interiors. Shaw was concerned with environment in a much less restricted way than the usual suburban development reveals. He considered the importance of greenery, of gardens and trees, as well as of amenities, shops and pubs as well as the more prosaic needs. The result was an area of housing that has retained its pleasing character and its sense of containing a less restrained and narrowly encompassed style of life than the usual suburban outcrop.

It was a later architect, C. F. A. Voysey, whose career began towards the end of the century, who articulated a more precise awareness of what was required of

92 *John Ruskin by T. B. Wingman*

the home environment. Like the earlier Victorians he wanted the home as a place of quiet protection. But he also wanted warmth and cheerfulness, an absence of elaboration, and ease of upkeep. The servant problem had become something to take into account. A house, he felt, should harmonize with both its exterior surroundings, and with the lives of those who lived in it. The following passage suggests some idea of how he viewed the interior.

Try the effect of a well-proportioned room, with white-washed walls, plain carpet and simple oak furniture, and nothing in it but necessary articles of use, and one pure ornament in the form of a simple vase of flowers—not a cosmopolitan crowd of all sorts, but one or two sprays of one kind—and you will then find reflections begin to dance in your brain; each object will be received on the retina and understood, classified and dismissed from the mind, and you will be as free as a bird to wander in the sunshine or storm of your own thoughts.[3]

There is a degree of severity in this kind of attempt to liberate the individual from his surroundings, to prevent the intrusion of things on human life. The home as suggested here is not a reflection of individual interests but a framework to them. Its features must not compel our lasting attention. But we can understand the reaction, the impulse away from density and clutter, the need for plain white walls and restrained ornamentation, the need to allow the individual consciousness space and freedom.

In the '70s we can detect a need developing to find the right things, the right designs, the right styles to reflect and harmonize with human life and thought. Always the most sensitive Victorians seemed to be casting about for a style that was definite and assertive, but not crude or vulgar, a style that could reflect positive values but suggest the intimacy of the home, a style that contained warmth and solidity, but was open to life. Webb and Shaw came closest to this kind of achievement, although most people did not understand what they were after. The need probably expressed itself most often as an urge for something different for its own sake, rather than as a positive and thoughtful experiment with changing attitudes to home life.

One of the single most impressive sources of energy in art and thought in the second half of the century was William Morris. Morris tried to face squarely the contradictions of Victorian society of which most of his thinking contemporaries were uneasily and reluctantly aware. Ruskin in his famous essay on 'The Nature of Gothic' in *The Stones of Venice* (1851–53) had said,

> The great cry that rises from all our manufacturing cities, louder than the furnace blast, is all in very deed for this,—that we manufacture everything except men; we blanch cotton, and strengthen steel, and refine sugar, and shape pottery; but to brighten, to strengthen, to refine, or to form a single living spirit, never enters into our estimate of advantages.[4]

Morris wanted to form all men and women into individual living spirits, and his attitudes towards painting and towards design, towards workmanship and towards politics, all reflected this. He did not try to take design out of the realm of morality, he tried to make it more meaningful and more genuine within that context. But it wasn't the stultified morality of the comfortable middle class, with its rationalizations of inequality and its own rewards, but an emphasis of the necessity of individual fulfilment. While Marx defined alienation and suggested a political remedy for the disease of Capital, Morris tried to work out a means of ensuring a rich and creative relationship between life and labour.

In 1861 Morris helped to found the company of Morris, Marshall, Faulkner and Co. as a first move towards this. The idea was to produce genuine designs and artefacts, things that were individually conceived, lovingly manufactured, and of special meaning to the recipient. But there was an immediate and radical problem which he was never able to solve. Individual craftsmanship had to be expensive. The time, skill and care that went into hand craftsmanship could not come cheap— and as soon as it did come cheap it was undermining the dignity and worth of the labourer. 'Have nothing in your house that you do not know to be useful or believe to be beautiful', Morris said.[5] But such an opinion was bound to be élitist. Only the privileged and the moneyed could afford to be as discriminating as Morris would have liked.

Yet he was right to see the overwrought products of the mid-Victorian period as the result of alienation in design. Walter Crane wrote of this period,

> . . . the furniture is afflicted with curvature of the spine, and dreary lumps of bronze and ormulu repose on marble slabs at every opportunity, where monstrosities of every kind are encouraged under glass shades, while every species of design-debauchery is indulged upon carpets, curtains, chintzes and wallpapers, and where the antimacassar is made to cover a multitude of sins. When such ideas of decoration prevailed, having their origins and prototypes, in the vapid splendours of imperial saloons, and had to be reduced to the scale of the ordinary citizen's house and pocket, the things became absurd as well as hideous.[6]

Crane's image here of a gluttonous debauchery of design is a long way from what the mid-Victorians *thought* they were up to, but it was just what offended Morris, morally as well as aesthetically. For him the only way in which the alienation of mass production could be overcome was for both maker and receiver to be truly committed to the product, the maker through his craftsmanship and understanding of what he was doing, the receiver through *his* understanding that what he had in his home was the result of individual expression and skilled and caring work. Morris stressed this over and over again. There had to be this kind of active relationship between craftsman and possessor. But to operate against the grain of social and economic influences was profoundly difficult. It was just not possible to conquer mass production, or to offer a viable alternative, and increasingly Morris began to see that what was necessary was a political movement rather than, or as well as, an artistic one.

His concern for genuineness included not only the involvement of the craftsman but the nature of the materials. He insisted on authentic materials and he detested the efforts at masquerade that so many Victorian manufacturers went in for.

> I have tried to produce goods which should be genuine so far as their mere substances are concerned, and should have on that account the primary beauty in them which belongs to naturally treated substances; have tried for instance to make woollen substances as woollen as possible, cotton as cotton as possible, and so on; have used only the dyes which are natural and simple, because they produce beauty almost without the intervention of art; all this quite apart from the design in the stuffs or what not.[7]

The effort to reconcile quality with domestic and social reality made great demands

93   A lady's sitting room in the 'modern' style, 1881

on Morris, and although he did not, could not, accomplish the revolution he would have wished for, the impact he made was deeply felt by a minority, and has been long-lasting. The ideal he was struggling for was a romantic one, and based to a great extent on an unrealistic grasp of the past, yet it was worthwhile, and as a focus of attack on Victorian complacency, selfishness and crudity was full of vitality and achievement.

Morris based his vision of craftsmanship on what he believed to be the intimacy of life and work in the Middle Ages. The meticulous and unhurried devotion to detail of the medieval craftsman seemed to him an indication of loving production. The absence of separation between work and domestic life, between labour and its products, and the unity of values he, and many others, believed to have existed before industrialization deeply attracted him. Yet he completely ignored as we can see in the following passage the dirt, the squalor and the disease which, though less extensive, were insistent features of life then as they were in Victorian Britain. Here is Morris's vision of medieval purity.

Consider London of the fourteenth century: a smallish town, beautiful from one end to the other, streets of low whitewashed houses with a big Gothic church standing in the middle of it; a town surrounded by walls, with a forest of church towers and spires, besides the cathedrals and the abbeys and priories; every one of the houses in it, nay, every shed, bearing in it a certain amount of absolute, definite, distinctive, conscientious art. Think of the difference between that and the London of to-day.[8]

Morris allows his need for 'distinctive, conscientious art' to divert him from what living conditions must have been like. Yet if he based his ideal on a false interpretation of the pre-industrial age this does not devalue his attempt to come to terms with a problem of vast dimensions. He could not bear to accept that work might in fact be, unavoidably and inevitably, dehumanizing and degrading. Everywhere he wanted to simplify. He wanted to simplify economic relations (which he did not really understand), he wanted to simplify daily life, he wanted to simplify the structure of work which seemed to him to act against the quality of life and to be unnecessarily complicated and embellished.

94   *A severely 'modern' dining room, 1892*

Only let the arts which we are talking of beautify our labour, and be widely spread, intelligent, well understood both by the maker and the user, let them grow in one word *popular*, and there will be pretty much an end of dull work and its wearing slavery; and no man will any longer have an excuse for talking about the curse of labour, no man will any longer have an excuse for evading the blessing of labour. I believe there is nothing that will aid the world's progress so much as the attainment of this, wrapped up, as I am sure it is, with changes political and social, that in one way or another we all desire.[9]

Beauty, for Morris, was not a question of decorative adjuncts, still less of symbols of status, but the result of a deep need for expression as well as of appreciation that he considered potential in everyone. To return to a society in which this expression could be allowed its natural development, and he was sure it had existed once, was what he was after.

In the times when art was abundant and healthy, all men were more or less artists; that is to say, the instinct for beauty which is inborn in every complete man had such force that the whole body of craftsmen habitually and without conscious effort made beautiful things, and the audience for the authors of intellectual art was nothing short of the whole people. And so they had each an assured hope of gaining that genuine praise and sympathy which all men who exercise their imagination in expression most certainly and naturally crave. . . . But in these days . . . the whole people is careless and ignorant of art; the inborn instinct for beauty is checked and thwarted at every turn; and the result on the less intellectual or decorative art is that as a spontaneous and popular expression of the instinct for beauty it does not exist at all.[10]

It matters less that this was probably never true, and that he ignores the massive influences of religion in medieval society, than that Morris felt it to be true. Vulgarity, ostentation, bad taste, were the result of wrong thinking, wrong living and a wrong way of working, and art had a fundamental part to play in rectifying this situation. The relationship of the craftsman to his work was crucial. Mass production cheapened not only the aesthetic value of a piece of furniture, say, but also the moral value. A chair carefully put together by a loving craftsman could indicate a right and moral way of integrating life and work, an attitude to work that was embedded in a larger attitude to life. Many of the Morris designs seem no less distinctively Victorian than cruder products, in the sense that they embody characteristic cultural responses. Take the medievalism, for instance: it informed the immensely popular poetry of Tennyson as well as the more dubiously received poetry and paintings of the Pre-Raphaelites with whom Morris was closely associated, and who decorated some of his furniture and interiors. The response to the age of chivalry was a trend that ran right through the Victorian period. That Morris's wife Jane should wear gowns suggestively medieval, and that he should decorate cabinets and settles with scenes depicting St George, King Arthur and tales from Chaucer was consistent with a general interest in a romanticized version of the past. At the

95   *Drawing room and conservatory, 1890*

same time, it was distinctively Morris, for everything was carried out with a conviction, a dedication and an enthusiasm which was conspicuously lacking elsewhere.
Specifically the kinds of ornamentation are not drastically different. Morris believed in ornament, in carving and painting; he hated a blank space; his wallpaper
designs contain the same imitation of natural lines that earlier in the century was
insisted on; he did not eliminate the curve, although he kept it to the decoration
rather than the basic shape. His fabric and wallpaper designs are often dense, even
cluttered. Yet Morris's designs are unmistakable, and their influence on design in
general was vigorous and liberating.

Morris never solved the problem of how to popularize an art and an attitude to
art that only the privileged and the wealthy could afford. He could never quite
confront the problem of the craftsman, performing with love perhaps, but knowing
that the result would be displayed in a house of a kind he was unlikely to set foot
in himself. Morris and his friends were, of course, themselves an élite, and the fact
that they made things with their own hands did not make them less so. It was good
for them, and enriched their own lives, but what could it do for those vast numbers
who suffered more seriously from cultural starvation, and whose home lives were
inevitably deprived? The sheer energy of Morris's convictions could not help him,

but at least he was able to identify a most radical problem of his age.

Morris influenced an important, though not very extensive or longlasting, movement in 'Arts and Crafts' which in turn made its mark on design in general and on the kinds of things people had in their homes. In 1882 the Century Guild was founded by A. H. Mackmurdo, its aim being to elevate the status of traditional skills, such as masonry, woodcarving, potting and metal-working. In 1884 the Art Workers Guild was formed, and in 1888 the Guild and School of Handcraft and W. R. Lethaby's Cotswold School. The emphasis was on simplicity and good craftsmanship. The underlying attitude was that the absence of utility amounted to an absence of beauty: ornamentation for its own sake was condemned. But although the Arts and Crafts movement made an impression it never became popular—by its very nature it scarcely could—and in some quarters it was roundly condemned. The established trades did not like it very much, as an issue of *The Builder* in 1899 indicated.

> In the reaction which is taking place against display and over-lavish ornamentation, the new school of designers appears to be losing the sense of style and of the dignity of design which accompanies it, altogether. The object now seems to be to make a thing as square, as plain, as devoid of any beauty of line as is possible and to call this art.[11]

It was hard for the Victorians to learn to enjoy simplicity when for half a century they had been tutored in the elaborate, and in the belief that it contained qualities that were of the greatest significance in their self-image. The stolid centre of the middle class was unresponsive to such as Morris and Lethaby. It was more likely to follow the advice of the domestic magazines, where ideas changed with almost imperceptible slowness. And of course there were vested interests in slowing down change.

Yet the middle-class interior was changing. Here H. S. Goodhart-Rendel imagines an interior of the last quarter of the century, a home that would probably have been occupied by a professional middle-class family.

> The front door, not oak-grained as it would have been formerly, is painted sage-green or white with a shining brass handle. Inside it no cast-iron hall-stand receives our hat and stick; instead we find an oriental china tube for umbrellas . . . and a row of pegs and hooks behind a curtain of Liberty cretonne. In the hall hangs a simple Benson oil lamp of copper and opalescent glass; the staircase has a dado of Indian matting, and over the dining- and drawing-room doors railed shelves support some jugs and vases of Royal Doulton stoneware. In the drawing room we find one or two chairs and a cabinet, all of ebonized wood but of light design. They may very well be the Anglo-Japanese ones designed by the architect of the house, Edward Godwin. Above a dado of blue paper geometrically patterned, a paper of paler blue covers the remainder of the walls, its pattern consisting of an open arrangement of bamboo leafage. The window curtains are of gold corduroy. The colour of the woodwork generally is

that of the ground of the wall-paper except that on the door panels are painted birds and apple blossom in their natural colours on a gold ground. On the overmantel are displayed a great many pieces of blue-and-white china, and over the door in this room are blue-and-white plate. To the brass-lever bell handles on either side of the fire-place are attached painted Japanese fans. Hanging on the walls are etchings, china plates and *kakemonos*.[12]

We can see at once that taste has changed, and we can identify the main features. There has been a general lightening of the interior; gold and pale blue now, instead of dark stained wood and deep colours. There is a suggestion of fussiness rather than clutter, and there is a strong Eastern flavour. The Eastern influence became very widespread, and on it was begun and built the reputation and success of Liberty's, which became a kind of symbol of middle-class interest in design.

In the Great International Exhibition of 1862, in which a number of the more interesting new designers had exhibited, among them Morris, and which was altogether aesthetically more interesting than its predecessor 11 years earlier, there was a Japanese section. Arthur Lazenby Liberty visited the Exhibition at the age of 18, and was so impressed by what he saw that he dedicated himself to the bringing of oriental products to the Western world. At that time he worked for the retailers Farmer and Rogers, and his first step was to persuade them to open an oriental department. (There already existed a great liking for goods from India; Indian shawls had been much prized for some time.) It was rapidly evident that there was a market for oriental goods. In 1875 Liberty opened his own shop in Regent Street, and it was so successful that in less than 12 months he had to expand. Many of the most important artists and designers and cultural figures patronized Liberty's, including Morris and his circle, and Carlyle and Ruskin. The soft fabrics and the oriental designs generated a whole new approach to dress and drapery, which became softer, more fluid and less constricting. The Aesthetic Movement was largely shaped by what Arthur Liberty had begun and others taken up, and 'Aesthetic' dress, more natural and less bulky than most Victorian fashions, became acceptable beyond the Bohemian circle of the Pre-Raphaelites, where the women had been wearing loose 'medieval' robes long before the beginning of Liberty's.

Although Morris commended the oriental influence, and it is readily detectable in many of his own designs, Liberty himself did not share Morris's views on hand craftsmanship, and in fact his most significant contribution to design lay in his insistence that his fabrics could be successfully machine printed. He did revive some ancient techniques of weaving and dyeing that were appropriate for the materials he was working with, but only to adapt them to machine use. He could never have built his success on painstaking individual craftsmanship. He needed quantity as well as quality, and he needed reasonable prices.

Many people found the Aesthetic Movement outrageous and many found it ridiculous. It was satirized by George Du Maurier and by Gilbert and Sullivan, and criticized by fashion writers in magazines, but Liberty's certainly survived

96   Morris's 'Acanthus' wallpaper

this, as did many of the Movement's effects. The interior typified by bamboo and coconut matting and blue and white china, or by 'Morris papers on the walls, Burne-Jones' photographs, old china, old carvings, Indian silks everywhere'[13] could be found in the homes of the modish in the last phase of the century. And though it was in reality only a small proportion of the middle and upper classes who responded enthusiastically to these influences there was a more courageous attitude towards experiment. The oriental touch seemed just the thing to bring a little daring, a little lightness and brightness to a sombre interior. In 1882 Liberty's had to expand again. In 1888 and 1891 Arthur Liberty organized exhibitions of silk, and a studio was set up for the study of Eastern architecture and interior decoration. An Islamic influence emerged: there was a craze for mosques and minarets, tiles and courtyards with fountains. The Aesthetic Movement shaded into Art Nouveau, and by the end of the century Liberty's was taking its share of that market also. And, in spite of the initial condemnation, the solid opinion of the magazines succumbed eventually to the oriental influence, and women were advised, positively instructed, to place a Japanese vase or two at strategic points in the drawing room.

But there were still fears that it would all get out of hand, still a strong feeling that there had to be rules. There seemed a danger that people would rush into the latest fad in oriental imitation without understanding what design was about. Christopher Dresser continued to write extensively and promulgated his concern with what he himself called the 'laws' of design—'The decoration of a room is as much bound by laws and by knowledge as the treatment of a disease', he wrote.[14] It was all very well to insist on a fine artistic sense as an expression of moral understanding, Dresser's theme was, but it had to be realized that an artistic sense could only be acquired through considerable application.

> It may be taken as an invariable truth that knowledge, and knowledge alone, can enable us to form an accurate judgement respecting the beauty or want of beauty of an object, and he who has the greater knowledge of art can judge best of the ornamental qualities of an object. . . . Let him who judges of beauty apply himself, then, to earnest study.[15]

By the 1870s design had become a part of Victorian high seriousness. The point is made again and again—'good decorations of any character have qualities which appeal to the educated, but are silent to the ignorant'. But above all decoration itself, and good design in particular, is important—and Dresser shares Morris's view here—because it is a significant reflection, or should be, of the right attitude to life. It *is* a question of morality in the end and even the Aesthetic Movement and Art Nouveau, with their suggestions of escape from morality, can't entirely get away from it. 'Those who ignore decoration cast aside a source of refinement, and deprive themselves of what may induce their elevation in virtue and morals.'[16] To be interested in the way things look and are arranged can in itself be at least potentially elevating. Like Morris, Dresser condemned imitation and unnaturalness and insists on the beauty of functionalism. He looks for qualities of grace, nobility and

97   *Philip Webb, by C. Fairfax-Murray, 1873*

vigour 'harmoniously arranged'. And he sees oriental design, which he advises
people to study, as containing much of the best and most satisfying marriages of
form and colour.

In Dresser, as in Morris, there is a tone of urgent seriousness in the laying down
of principles which is quite different from the bland authoritarianism that is
habitual in writers who treat taste as an accomplishment rather than an art. But
there is a sharing of attitudes too, in, for instance, the belief that different rooms

98   'Taste and harmony', 1880

should be endowed with different characteristics to express their different functions. There is a general belief that interiors should be soothing, and even at the end of the century that the excitement of certain kinds of exotic objects must be controlled. Dresser's opinion is that drawing rooms should be light and dining rooms dark; we have come across this before. In 1876 Rhoda and Agnes Garrett were explaining why.

> The drawing-room is the part of the house which is devoted to the lighter occupations of life: to the reception of visitors and to the enjoyment of those moments of post-prandial leisure in which we have mainly to consider the amusement of ourselves, our families, and our friends. The general aspect of the room should be rather gay than grave, and hence it comes that custom has prescribed the use of lighter and more delicate forms and colours than are admissable elsewhere.[17]

But H. J. Cooper, in *The Art of Furnishing on Rational and Aesthetic Principles*, published in the same year as the Garretts' book, does not insist on darkness in the dining room.

> There should be a warmth and quiet cheerfulness, an air of sprightliness and yet repose, and, above all, an absence of monotony. And here we do not think the end can be better answered than by the judicious employment of some of the really decorative papers that are being produced just now under the influence of a few leading minds. [Probably Morris and Dresser] In some of these there is a variety of outline and a blending of subtle tints, which, while forming a comparative monotone against which pictures and objects may stand out, afford, in their absence, a singularly fascinating study for the eye, without being wearisome or over-engrossing.[18]

All three writers join in the condemnation of vulgarity, but the idea of what vulgarity consists of has by this time changed. Whereas earlier it was tasteless over-ostentation that was being condemned as a sign of nouveaux riches now it is the overstuffing and the heavy drapery and the stolidity, just those features mid-Victorian housewives were being urged to include, that come under attack. Such things are vulgar, unnecessary and unhealthy. The movement is distinctly towards opening out the home, towards the admission of light and fresh air, and towards the restoration of human priorities in home life. Decoration should be soothing, and should suggest repose, but it should not be seen any longer as a means of enfolding, protecting and even incarcerating the human beings within.

> The order of arrangement in furnishing must be this. The living beings in a room should be most attractive and conspicuous, and the dress of man should be of such a character as to secure this. Ladies can now employ any amount of colour in their attire, but poor man, however noble, cannot by his dress be distinguished from his butler; and, worst of all, both are dressed in an unbecoming and inartistic manner. Next come the furniture and draperies—the

99   *The elegance of cane, 1898*

one or the other having prominence according to circumstances; then come the wall and floor, both of which are to serve as backgrounds to all that stands in front of them. In decorating walls, or in judging of the merit or suitability of wall decorations, this must always be taken into consideration, that they are but enriched backgrounds; and it should also be remembered that the nature of the enrichment applied is determined, to a great extent, by the character of the architecture of the building of which the wall forms a part.[19]

This is Christopher Dresser, seeking to restore human priorities in the home, to rescue humanity from the burdens of the domestic interior.

This trend away from the density of the mid-Victorian home environment is revealing. The opening out of the home indicates that the need was being recognized for more scope, not just for activity in the home, but psychological and mental scope too. Individuals should no longer be overshadowed by their furniture or the objects that their rooms contained or the heavy colours painted on the walls. That most of the little upsurges in activity in design did not last very long—the Aesthetic Movement soon dwindled, as did Art Nouveau—is not so important as the fact that there were attempts to counteract Victorian heaviness, and that these reflected the almost unconsciously changing attitudes towards what home life ought to be like. The striking fact was that trends in furnishing and decoration, like trends in dress, in art and in literature, were towards a more liberating, less confined, expression. It was all becoming more rational, more concerned with individual need. If the genuineness that Morris called for was elusive and expensive, and the sham that Dresser condemned persisted, and if taste still had more to do with class than with anything else, it had freed itself a little from the heavy hand of conformist and introverted respectability.

What the Victorians could never escape from was the belief that the home was the most important feature of the social environment and that the way it was furnished and decorated was a very serious business. Taste had been to a certain extent freed from the weight of an unimaginative morality, but it was still firmly within the realm of ethics. It still had everything to do with the value of peoples' ideas and their way of life. It was still the case that there were things that could be done to the home, or not done to the home, that could affect one's value in the eyes of society. A family was still judged and categorized by the nature of its home. That particular lesson was a major inheritance of twentieth-century domestic life.

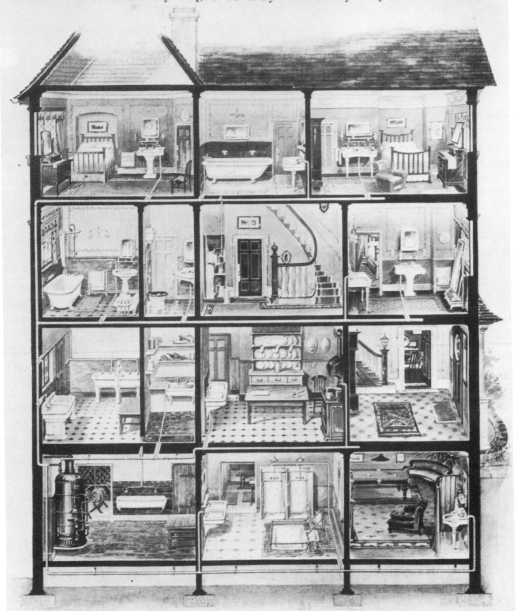

EWART'S
"B" PATTERN "CALIFONT"
Hot Water Instantly Night or Day—At every Tap in the House

The illustration shows the "Califont" fixed in the basement of a house with hot water services to the various rooms.
The "Califont" may, if preferred, be fixed in any other convenient position.
For prices and other particulars see pages 14 and 15.
EWART'S "CALIFONT"—Just Turn the Tap

100   *The 'Califont' hot water system, c. 1890*

Taste and Status

Change is always more noticeable than the lack of it, and although the Pre-Raphaelites and the Aesthetic Movement and Art Nouveau received a lot of attention at the time, and are a focus of interest now, their effects on the average middle-class home were less in evidence. There were modifications in ornament. The Eastern interest manifested itself in the shape of a vase or a Japanese print. The wallpaper might change, the fresh coat of paint might be in a more modern colour; this could be seen as a response to novelty rather than an indication of a radically changed attitude to life. The reactions of the less secure sections of the middle class to the evidence of change tended to be a tighter closing in. In some ways the Aesthetic Movement, for instance, with its association with rather dubious Bohemian characters, the outrageous Swinburne for instance, was seen as a threat against which it was important to maintain a solid front. Traditional religion was being challenged by science, and traditional morality was being challenged by art, and the response of many was simply to cut the challenge out of their lives. The middle class had gone through a period of post-Industrial Revolution consolidation, and most were unable to see that something had been lost through this as well as gained. Neither the solid core of the bourgeoisie nor those uneasily on the fringes were likely to hasten to give up the cherished symbols of their achievement and their security.

On the other hand the nature of those symbols was changing. As always we can see contradictory influences. The bourgeoisie couldn't resist the temptation of new and supposedly better things—a belief in progress had to entail some sort of commitment to novelty—but it was nervous of the encroachment of new ideas. Advertising, the growth of shops, the department store, the ostentatious availability, all combined to encourage the acquisitive instinct, but there was no point in simply amassing more and more of the same thing. Men and women were seriously trying to educate popular taste, but they couldn't keep up with the attractions of acquisition. Liberty's succeeded not so much because there was a vast potential market in 'good taste', but because there was a vast potential market for something new. Department stores, well established by the 1860s, thrived on the same market. With so much available educators felt it even more important to get across their message about what constituted good taste, and why it was important. Inevitably their message was received by those who perhaps needed it least, by the well off and those with artistic inclinations. Those who were rooted in their own absolutism, who felt the need to be, were less responsive.

Only a minority of those who did respond to the appeal for an enlightened and educated attitude towards design, which meant towards home-making too, were genuinely alert to the problems of a closed household within a closed society. Most were prepared to take the best of what was offered and to use it as a symbol not of a genuine openness of attitude, not of a genuine liberation from the more negative features of the Victorian cult of the home, but of, simply, good taste. For this is the way the lesson was absorbed. Good taste was the manifestation of artistry and good breeding and cleverness. The intimate relationship between life and work called for by Morris, the ethical value of a harmonious environment emphasized by Dresser, these were nothing like as important in the minds of the tasteful as the symbolic value of self-reflection through the arrangement of their homes.

Yet this represented a significant transition. By the end of the century there were people who saw the home in terms of self-reflection rather than self-protection. The home was seen more as a personal environment, created by the individual as an expression of the individual. Only for the most daring did this mean an actual rejection of conformity, but it did mean for a greater number of people a little relaxation of the view of the family functioning strictly as a crucial unit of society, guarding its integrity, and suspicious of individuality. Inevitably the growth of feminism damaged the idea of the family as a passive and private and acquiescent unit that supported the social structure by its very lack of action, for Victorian family unity depended so much on paternalism. It had needed a figurehead and an image to which to shape itself. The venturing forth of women beyond the home and the admission of active outside influences had to disrupt this cohesion which, though not without certain positive qualities, had shown itself a threat to the individual. What we can detect at the end of the century is an urge towards giving the individual more leeway, but without breaking the traditional environment.

A writer who explores just this territory is H. G. Wells, who published several novels during the early years of the twentieth century that dealt with middle-class life and marriage. *Ann Veronica* is about a girl who breaks away from her suburban background but is by the end of the book respectably married and running an orthodox professional middle-class household. On the final pages we see husband and wife standing 'side by side upon an old Persian carpet that did duty as a hearthrug in the dining-room of their flat' expecting guests and surveying 'a shining dinner-table set for four people, lit by skillfully-shaded electric lights, brightened by frequent gleams of silver, and carefully and simply adorned with sweet-pea blossom.'[1] For a more specific illustration of a certain kind of middle-class marriage, which would certainly at the time have considered itself thoroughly liberated from Victorian limitations, Wells' *Marriage* (1912) offers an excellent example. There he describes a young, newly married couple setting up house. Marjorie's husband allows her to spend £300 to furnish and adorn their 'old and rather small' house in London. She sets about the task with enthusiasm.

It was an immense excitement, shopping to make a home. There was in her composition a strain of constructive artistry with such concrete things, a strain that had hitherto famished. She was making a beautiful secure little home for Trafford, for herself, for possibilities—remote perhaps, but already touching her imagination with the anticipation of warm, new, wonderful delights. There should be simplicity indeed in this home, but no bareness, no harshness, never an ugliness nor a discord. She had always loved colour in the skies, in the land-scape, in the texture of stuffs and garments; now out if the chaotic skein of countless shops she could choose and pick and mingle her threads in a glow of feminine self-expression.[2]

What are the qualities that Marjorie wants her home to express? Beauty, security, simplicity, harmony, all of which the Victorians would have approved, though they would not have expressed them in the same way as Marjorie seeks to. The mid-Victorian idea of simplicity—remember the continual counsel against ostenta-tion and vulgarity—was not the late Victorian, where there was evidence of a determined effort to abolish clutter and clarify shape. The approach to colour had changed. The idea of what 'harmony' and 'beauty' consisted of had changed. But 'harmony' and 'beauty' were still important, and a sense of security was still what home was about.

Significantly it is assumed that home-making is still a feminine occupation. The attitude expressed here is not only that it is the *duty* of the wife to create a pleasing environment, it is a privilege that is very specially hers (echoing Frances Power Cobbe 30 odd years earlier) and gives her scope for 'feminine self-expression'. Marjorie expresses herself, but she creates for her husband—to Trafford's study she gives 'the very best of her attention'. Woman is still a home-maker, but she is also an artist, and this is where the particular class expression is important. The Traffords do not belong to the solid defensive core of the middle class but to its self-conscious upper layer. They don't have the money to be 'upper middle class' but they distinctly have the inclination to avoid being 'middle middle class'. It is necessary to avoid that typification in the interior of their home. Marjorie feels that her artistic sense can make up for the absence of money—she is beyond, she thinks, the vulgarity of conspicuous spending. But in fact she finds that in order to acquire the right objects for her self-expression she has to spend a considerable amount of money. By the time she is finished she has spent a great deal more than the alloted £300.

Marjorie has certain important aims in mind.
The house she had to deal with was . . . old and rather small; it was partly to its lack of bedroom accommodation, but much more to the invasion of the street by the back premises of Messrs. Siddons and Thrale, the great Chelsea out-fitters, that was due the lowness of the rent which brought it within the means of Trafford. Marjorie knew very clearly that her father would say her husband had taken her to live in a noisy slum, and that made her all the keener to ensure that every good point in the interior told to its utmost, and that whatever was to be accessible to her family should glow with a refined but warm prosperity. The room downstairs was shapely, and in ripping off the papered canvas of the

101   The 'Salamander' portable charcoal-burning immersion heater

previous occupier, some very dilapidated but admirably proportioned panelling
was brought to light. The dining-room and study door on the ground floor, by
a happy accident, were of mahogany, with really very beautiful brass furnishings; and the dining-room window upon the minute but by no means offensive
paved garden behind, was curved and had a little shallow balcony of ironwork,
half covered by a devitalized but leafy grape-vine. Moreover, the previous
occupier had equipped the place with electric light and a bathroom of almost
American splendour on the landing, glass-shelved, white-tiled, and white
painted, so that it was a delight to go into.[3]

This is what Marjorie has to work on. She is after a 'clean brightness of colour
throughout'. Clutter must be out of sight. Every object must be gracefully and
purposefully noticeable. She is unflagging in her efforts after a preconceived effect,
tireless in her search for just the right object to be placed in exactly the right spot.
She dedicates herself to the creation of an environment which expresses her own
good taste, her sense of fitness, her cleverness, but has not obviously involved
spending a lot of money. But she does spend a lot of money. She can't avoid it, but
she tries to make it seem as if her expensive Bokhara hangings were bargains that

her ingenuity and indefatigable efforts had turned up. And having created the environment she then proceeds to live the sort of life that such an environment ought to contain. The subtle workings of snobbery prevent her from seeing that for the kind of genuineness that Morris, for instance, was after, the life must be allowed to shape the environment to be lived in, not the other way round. Marjorie is the victim of her own pretensions.

Wells details what she does, and buys, and puts together. All the time there is a tension between *her* conviction that she is with ingenious economy creating a home for the natural expression of her life with Trafford, and *our* growing understanding that she is using her creation as a way of demonstrating her cleverness and artistry, and that the result reflects the life to which she aspires.

> Her dining-room was difficult for some time. She had equipped that with a dark oak Welsh dresser made very bright with a dessert service that was, in view of its extremely decorative quality, remarkably cheap, and with some very pretty silver-topped glass bottles and flasks. This dresser and a number of simple but shapely facsimiles of old chairs, stood out against a nearly primrose paper, very faintly patterned, and a dark blue carpet with a margin of dead black stained wood. Over the mantel was a German colour-print of waves full of sunlight breaking under cliffs, and between this and the window were dark bookshelves, and a few bright-coloured books. On the wall, black-framed, were four very good Japanese prints, rich in greenish-blues and blueish-greys that answered the floor, and the window curtains took up some of the colours of the German print.[4]

Nothing here is mentioned for its function. It is all there for effect. Even the books are simply bright colours enframed by the dark book case, decorative rather than readable. The important thing is to impress all those who might enter her home and set eyes on her achievement. And a sense of possessiveness pervades the whole. After her first series of visitors Wells comments 'hardly anybody failed to appreciate the charm and decision of Marjorie's use of those Bokhara embroideries'.[5] It was that kind of commendation that she had done it all for.

Home-making had graduated, as Marjorie herself had done. As a product of Oxbridge, she considered herself liberated, artistic, refined, and a reliable judge of the fitness of things. Home-making had become, for people like her (and of course there were not very many people like her) an art, a fulfilment of superior qualities. It had become a very special kind of activity, which involved not just a sense of responsibility as a wife with her husband's welfare at heart, but sensitive and creative talents. The whole business, its activities and its results, was altogether superior, a work of art worthy of admiration. Marjorie has assembled and arranged the appropriate emblems of what she believes life should offer herself and her husband. She has, like most Victorian middle-class couples, preconceived ideas and standards of what married life should be, and an important aspect of this is that she and Trafford should be *seen* to be living a certain kind of life—hence the necessity of emblems. It is ostentation in its most radical sense. The home has become a kind of gallery of objects that are pointers to the status, the achievement and the expectations of the people who live within it, and therefore indicates that status and the symbols of achievement are more important than the nature, the quality, of life itself.

Marjorie thinks in terms of 'feminine self-expression', but the way she expresses herself is determined by the way she thinks other people will respond. She is not 'doing her own thing': she is playing a clever game of one-upmanship. Yet Wells makes it quite clear that she does, indeed, have good taste and considerable skill. She works hard and does well what she sets out to do, and reveals a number of praiseworthy qualities in the process. What Wells does not indicate is whether he himself was aware of how important this must have been for a woman in Marjorie's position at the turn of the century. She is educated, she is sensitive, but she is not very practical and has a romantic inclination. For her to be able to nourish and fulfil this idealized view of self-expression through the home is very important. It became more, not less, important for women to be able to believe that home-making was an activity of value and significance. Marjorie does not consider it morally necessary to create a home, but it is essential for her self-esteem. She is proving herself. She has no job or occupation outside the home, no other role than that of wife, so the only way she can prove herself is as home-maker and hostess.

Thus, the importance of having and expressing good taste did not slacken with its separation from moral values. And the importance of the home as a place of security and repose did not slacken. In some respects the more widely the door was opened to outside influences the more enduring the symbols of these things were required to be. One had to be sure of oneself, and sure of one's objective-correlatives, if one was going to take the risk of dismantling the barricades. Marjorie's convictions are not strong enough to protect her from all kinds of problems that emerge when she begins to discover that one cannot live by emblems alone. To set up the environment for an artistically harmonious marriage and home life does not mean that these things will follow.

It can be said that taste in its reflected emphasis moved away from morality and towards status, but the tone of most writers on design does not allow us to forget the ethical context of taste, and suggests that there is only a limited degree of choice within that context. There are certain proportions and groupings that are 'best', certain combinations of shapes and colours which are not just most effective, but 'right'. But one late Victorian writer at least moved away from this. Mrs Haweis published her *Art of Decoration* in 1881, and her argument is unequivocally that the arrangement of the home should be an expression of individual personality. She is contemptuous of those who simply follow what is fashionable, or generally acceptable. Her feeling is that in general taste has improved, but that people are not always ready to learn from past mistakes. Her language is so colourful she is worth quoting at length.

How long since did the clogged wheels begin to yield to individual efforts? Who was the first hero who pulled up and burnt his 'cheerful' patterned

102 George du Maurier's satirical look at 'Aesthetic' attitudes. The caption reads: 'The Six-Mark Teapot'. Aesthetic Bridegroom: 'It is quite consummate is it not?' Intense Bride: 'It is indeed! Oh, Algernon, let us live up to it!'

103   'My first dinner party', 1890

Brussels, in scarlet and sour green? Who first sold his drawing room 'suite'—
his velvet sofa backed with cotton—his six small chairs with torturing backs,
two arm-chairs, vile marquetry table, and gilt console? The orthodox 'chiffon-
ier' of unmeaning shape, with mirror-back that reflected our frightful bodies
in one focus, and mirror-doors that made fun of our detached legs in another:
and all the floriated false curves and flourishes ground (not carved) in mahogany
and glued wherever they were likeliest to be knocked off—all the false 'embossed mouldings' (also glued on), recalling nothing, in their vacant miscon-
struction of classic types, but human teeth, or emblems of disease ingeniously
connected: where are these horrors now?[5]

She concludes that 'these horrors' have been banished to the seaside lodging house,
but that the things that have replaced them are not necessarily an improvement,
that the newest in design is sometimes 'quite as ugly . . . with stiff patterns instead
of flowing ones, morbid colours instead of gay ones, but equally ill-proportioned,
vulgar, and machine-begotten, perhaps *more* depressing'.[6]

  Mrs Haweis is against the domination of taste by any single particular fashion
or school, and her writing, with its vitality, its emphasis of the importance of
individuality, and her urge toward liberation from restrictions and rules is refresh-
ingly without the solemnity of some other writers on the same subject. If she

appears to be tending towards an 'art for art's sake' dictum she does not confine it to any particular style: 'every age has its particular wants and its particular expression, but no age which truly loves beauty will confine its art to very narrow limits; the more it studies beauty the more elastic it finds it.'[7] The very fact that the late Victorians were still able to talk frankly about beauty as being a necessary feature of the home environment is itself interesting. Mrs Haweis does not hedge her beauty in with moral rationalizations; she needs neither to apologize for nor rationalize her use of the word. Beauty is a part of free expression, and free expression is an individual right. Mrs Haweis is reminiscent in tone of some of those heroines of Meredith's novels who with clarity and courage liberate their own personalities.

The Victorians were not able to liberate the home and family life in the way that some felt to be desirable. There was something of a rebellion against both, but this involved a condemnation of the institution itself, rather than a concern with making it less repressive. The liberation of the home would have necessitated two things that could not happen, first the relaxation of the defensive instinct, so that the home could become more receptive to the influence of the outside world, could become, perhaps, community-oriented rather than status-oriented, and second the evolution of an atmosphere that allowed genuine individual expression. Both moves seemed too risky. The outside world was still something to be feared, the integral aggressions of the family still something to be repressed. In general the middle class, which had consolidated its position so carefully through the century, believed that its strength depended on its resistance to disturbing ideas of free expression and free movement. Feminism, aestheticism, socialism, could all be seen as part of the same threatening displacement. The closing of ranks was instinctive. The more people like Mrs Haweis urged individual expression the more a great many others were inclined to follow the rules they were sure they could depend on.

The anti-Victorian reaction is befogged to a great extent by the First World War. The '20s eruption is exaggerated in its anti-restrictiveness because the monstrous battlefields of the War lay between the 1920s and the reign of Victoria. Just as the immediate post-Victorians were beginning to relax the War came to interfere with what *might* just have been a gradual and natural humanizing of the home. But of course the nature of the home had to depend ultimately on the nature of marriage, on attitudes towards women and towards children, and the flexibility of society as well as of the individual. For the most part pre-war anti-Victorianism is élitist, the response of the privileged, the intellectual, those who could afford to be independently-minded. And most of these men and women concerned themselves not with the immediate realities of the home but with art, literature and ideas.

Morris tried to concern himself with the quality of life and turned his attention to the underprivileged, but who other than a man of privilege could formulate his ideas through a belief in the necessity of beautiful artefacts? Mrs Haweis says 'art is for the people' and echoes the call to educate popular taste, but who other than one who had no more pressing concerns could involve herself so enthusiastically

with the canons of good taste? For, essentially, there is no designer or writer on
design in the nineteenth century, no one who thought about the question (and
probably no one who thinks about the subject now) who was able to contradict the
overwhelming impression that 'good taste' involved the expenditure of time and
money. Morris tried to remind people of the beauty of utility and the satisfactions
of craftsmanship, but himself made furniture that only a few could afford to buy.
His wallpapers hung in the homes of the well off. He did not, could not, go into the
homes of the factory workers and say, I will show you how to make your home more
comfortable and pleasing just by rearranging these things that you have here. He
wanted to free 'taste' from its class restrictions, but the very concept of taste has
tended to belong to the middle class.

The reasons are not hard to discover. At the beginning of the century there was
a great deal of sensitivity about class definitions. Novelists like Jane Austen record
it, and mock the hypocrisy that went with it. With a rapidly growing middle class
and a fluid situation it became increasingly important to know who and what
people were. Where people lived, how people lived, and the things they had in their
houses were the main guides. The aristocracy did not need to worry so much about
these things, because they had their titles and most of them had their land, and
many of them had splendid houses that needed little embellishment to convince
people of their worth. But the newly rich especially did need to worry, because
everyone else was poised to categorize their social status according to the way they
conducted themselves. 'Good taste' became a means of distinguishing the deservedly middle class from the vulgar, those who were sensitive about their responsibilities
from those who simply had a lot of money to throw around. It was a means of
underlining a sense of worth and privilege, and of confirming the divisions between
oneself and others who were less worthy and less privileged. Victorian fiction is full
of characters who betray their lowly origins or their undeserved status by their bad
taste, and are consequently mocked by those who know better. Good taste was, in
fact, an integral part of the middle-class system of self-protection. The fact that it
was embedded in morality did not disguise its function.

To return to Marjorie, the aim of her home-making activities is to define the
status of herself and her husband as a married couple, a unit within a certain social
context. The people she most wants to impress are people with money or titles or
both. She needs to demonstrate that she and Trafford, who have no title and not
much money, are just as good as they are. This is of the greatest importance to her,
as part of her establishment of identity. Taste has always had a great deal to do with
the need to silently demonstrate one's 'quality' to others. The front parlour, the
best dinner service, the best silver, that are only used when there are visitors, the
chairs that are shrouded in dust covers except when there is a party, are part of a
very profound feeling that people want themselves and their symbols to be seen
only at their best. This is particularly true of the housewife, or whoever is responsible for running the home, for she sees the situation within the home as a direct
reflection of herself. What will people think if they find the house in a mess when
they visit? It is a profound instinct deep in the hearts and minds of most women

104 'Improved bathroom fittings', 1890

who run a home. Tidiness, cleanliness, the arrangement of objects, the objects themselves, the pattern on the wallpaper, the quality of the carpet, the machinery and even the food are not only seen as expressions of the female self, but as tests. By these will the home and the home-maker be judged. And although the art of decoration was separating itself from morality by the end of the century, the art of home-making has never quite done that.

We have seen how through most of the nineteenth century women were required to suppress any part of their personalities that might have disrupted household harmony. If it was admitted at all that this involved any kind of sacrifice, it was emphasized that this was thoroughly worthwhile, even holy. The object was the preservation of the sanctity and inviolability of the home. Thus the main tendency through most of the Victorian period was inevitably against flexibility. There was neither the will nor the ability to tolerate emotional or psychological or physical needs that did not conform with a harmony that it is difficult for us to see now as anything but artificially induced and maintained. That there were many, many families that were reasonably content under this kind of discipline I think we must accept. We must not make the mistake of seeing the bourgeois Victorian world as a seething mass of repression and unhappiness, however clear it is that

105   The love of display, an interior of 1895

both could be intense, nor of judging their needs by our own. Needs, like taste, are much influenced by fashion. But we can see an increasing irritation, an increasing fretting, an increasing awareness that there might be other possibilities, and that the alternatives might incorporate daily existence as well as art and literature.

The message of Mrs Haweis was, do not be afraid to have in your home what pleases you, regardless of whether your neighbour has it, or fashion approves, or some self-styled arbiter of taste demands it.

> There are people who love light—large windows which open easily, small carpets which are easily shaken, gay colours. Let them have them. There are others who like darkness, and prefer the smallest panes and most difficult bolts and hinges: give them their way, in no other wise can we get the individual element, *originality*, in a room.[8]

Mrs Haweis wants to free decoration from the restrictions of artificiality and fashion. She suggests that people very often allow their natural good taste to be overwhelmed by what they are told is right. 'It is not quiet tones, nor vivid tones, which make or mar a beautiful room. . . . It is the thought and the skill which can use all things fitly and well, and make them subserve an intelligible purpose. It is the delicate, practised perception . . . which *feels* how to craftily mingle richness with paucity of colour, so as not to tire the senses by either—how to avoid both pomposity and barrenness.'[9] But she makes it clear that originality needs thought, sensitivity. There needs to be conviction, a sense of purpose.

The shift in emphasis is interesting and revealing. Christopher Dresser wants to construct an appropriate environment for a worthwhile life. He insists that there *are* rules. Mrs Haweis feels that rules weigh against originality. For her, decoration is self-expression—'let our homes . . . reflect our warmest and most sympathizing moods',[10] she says. She sees the home as an integral part of an individual's nature and personality; it needs to be above all a human environment, it must suggest life. If everyone followed the same set of rules, however enlightened, there would still be conformity, even if a more tasteful conformity. But people are not the same, and sharing the same economic and class status does not necessarily make them the same. The Victorians wanted to categorize themselves through status. By the end of the century there were those who made self-conscious attempts to detach themselves from the bourgeois image, but the web of status was subtle, and much more difficult to escape.

For many the bourgeois image was still something to strive for. With smaller houses and less living space, with more hard work and less dependence on servants, with a vulnerability that could never quite be forgotten, there remained a vast section of the middle class that felt it could not relax its vigilance. Mark Girouard in his book on the Victorian country house describes succinctly what was happening at one end of the spectrum.

> . . . architects and society were changing together, and creating the society of late Victorian England in which heightened visual awareness was one aspect of a new feeling for the pleasures as well as the duties of life. Moral earnestness

began to seem a little absurd, and it was becoming more fashionable to be beautiful, clever or rich than to be good. The increasing and increasingly educated middle class provided the main recruiting ground for that typical phenomenon of the 1870s and 1880s, the lady of artistic tastes. But the change affected all ranks of society, and in the circles that pivoted round Rossetti, Burne-Jones and others of the Pre-Raphaelites, the old and the new rich mixed freely with artists in a *camaraderie* of beauty lovers . . .[11]

The impact of this glows brightly as we look back on the more colourful events and impressions of the century. But though the Pre-Raphaelites and their successors may have provided excitement for countless conformist citizens who read about them at a safe distance, the camaraderie of beauty lovers was a tiny fragment of society. Neither the complacent nor the vulnerable sections of the middle class were much concerned with that kind of artistry, however adept they were at identifying the symbols of status.

The belief that good taste was the product of the educated and the cultivated could not be seriously shaken. Even Mrs Haweis with her encouragement of the instinctive and the spontaneous and the original is speaking to those who could afford such luxuries. We have looked at William Morris and seen how he couldn't find a way of fitting his functionally simple ideas into a complex, status-ridden society. He himself, in his effort to solve this problem, became aware that society itself would have to be changed, before the kinds of authentic relationships he was after could come into being. Morris felt that economic pressures, the cash nexus, status sensitivity, exploitation, all got in the way of the artist or art lover that every individual potentially contained. There were others who were clearly troubled by the class orientation of good taste, who recognized that there was a predicament, but did not know how to get out of it. There were yet others who felt that the most important thing was to rescue the middle class from stultification. Whatever the preoccupation, neither rules nor the setting aside of rules, neither morality nor self-expression, seemed to offer any hope of severing the bonds between taste, class and money.

H. J. Cooper, a writer whom I have already quoted, has an interesting paragraph. He says,

If . . . the possession of a refined taste is coincident with the higher culture of our intellect and our emotional nature, and especially of the latter, it should clearly be accompanied by a wide-spread sympathy and a breadth of charity for all that, in the truest and noblest sense, claims the one or demands the other. That narrowness of spirit and concentration of self-interest which is satisfied with the mere contemplation of forms and emblems in themselves abstractly beautiful, is, we have no hesitation in saying, no mark of taste. . . . Taste, whatever else it may be, is the embodiment of qualities which the world cannot do without—qualities whose first practical action is rather to cultivate mercy than to foster sentiment; to provide homes for the homeless than to deck the costly mansion, and so down through the cycles of industry.[12]

There is something moving about this lone voice attempting to redefine and humanize the term 'taste'. The redefinition has never been accomplished. Almost all Victorian discussions of 'good taste', and many subsequently, fall into the trap that Cooper draws attention to here—'the mere contemplation of forms and emblems in themselves abstractly beautiful'. It is the quality of life, not a phrase the Victorians used, that matters. An exclusive, inward, private attitude towards decoration, and towards the home itself, is not, Cooper suggests, the right way. Nor is an artificial, outward, status-conscious attitude. It is shelter that matters, not embellishment. Above all we are struck by that phrase, 'the narrowness of life and the concentration of self-interest'. It is fair to say that the Victorians demonstrated in their attitudes towards the home, its physical reality and its symbolic value, the life of the family within it, and the restrictions imposed on the relations with the world outside it, a powerful movement towards narrowing life and concentrating self-interest. The late Victorians were not able to extricate themselves from this, though there were individuals who tried and sometimes succeeded. The question remains to what extent has the twentieth century been able to cope with what it inherited. Perhaps the intrinsic nature of home is that it should reflect the narrowness of life and a concentration of self-interest. Perhaps we all need somewhere where we can define ourselves within distinct and widely acceptable limits. But perhaps also we should take care to recognize that, although the Victorian home may seem alien, even monstrous, many of our assumptions about the home, home-making and family life are still being shaped by attitudes we have inherited from that flourishing, insistent Victorian bourgeois world.

Notes

Publication dates refer to the editions quoted from. Dates of original publication are in the text. Chapter references are used in the case of fiction, where the dates refer to first editions.

Chapter One: The Place of Peace
1 John Ruskin *Sesame and Lilies* 1897 pp 108–09
2 Anthony Trollope *The Small House at Allington* 1862 Chapter 40

Chapter Two: Order, Harmony and Comfort
1 Eliza Cook 'Three Hundred Pounds a Year' quoted in J. E. C. Harrison *The Early Victorians 1832–51* 1971 pp 11–12
2 Mrs Beeton *Book of Household Management* 1906 p 17
3 Sarah Stickney Ellis *The Mothers of England* 1843 p 296

Chapter Three: In the Country and in the Provinces
1 Gilbert Scott *Secular and Domestic Architecture* 1857 quoted in Mark Girouard *The Victorian Country House* 1971 p 2
2 Girouard op. cit. p 10
3 Robert Kerr *The Gentleman's House* 1864 p 74
4 Ibid p 97
5 Ruskin Lecture 'Modern Manufacture and Design' 1859 *Collected Works* 1903–12 Vol. XVI pp 338–39
6 Benjamin Disraeli *Sybil, or the Two Nations* 1845 Book 1, Chapter 3
7 quoted in S. H. Brooks *City, Town and Country Architecture* 1847 p 38
8 Flora Thompson *Lark Rise to Candleford* 1973 p 49
9 Brooks op. cit. introduction p iii
10 Ibid p 15
11 Ibid p 37

Chapter Four: Working Class Houses
1 Elizabeth Gaskell *Mary Barton* 1848 Chapter 6
2 Geoffrey Best *Shaftesbury* 1964 pp 107–08
3 quoted in Margaret Hewitt *Wives and Mothers in Victorian Industry* 1958 p 22
4 Ibid
5 quoted ibid p 10
6 August Bebel *Woman Under Socialism* 1904 p 180
7 Thomas Wright *Some Habits and Customs of the Working Class* 1867 in E. Royston Pike *Human Documents of the Victorian Golden Age* 1967 p 265
8 *The British Workwoman* January 1, 1864
9 Ibid March 1, 1864

10 O. R. McGregor *Divorce in England* 1957 pp 96–7
11 Gaskell op. cit. Chapter 2
12 Brooks op. cit. p 34
13 Disraeli op. cit. Book 3 Chapter 9

Chapter Five: Inside the House
1 Ruskin *Lectures on Architecture and Painting* 1907 no. 2
2 Christopher Dresser *Studies in Design* 1879 p 9
3 Arnold Bennett *The Old Wive's Tale* 1911 Chapter 3
4 John Gloag *Victorian Comfort* 1961 introduction p xv
5 Charles Eastlake *Hints on Household Taste* 1868 p 7
6 Ibid p 17
7 Ibid p 81
8 Ibid p 110
9 S. E. Finer *The Life and Times of Sir Edwin Chadwick* 1970 p 392
10 Anne Bronte *The Tenant of Wildfell Hall* 1848 Chapter 1

Chapter Six: Home-making
1 Frances Power Cobbe *The Duties of Women* 1881 p 139
2 quoted in McGregor op. cit. p 61
3 Mrs Haweis 'What to do with Our Daughters?' *The Ladies Realm* November, 1897
4 quoted in Duncan Crow *The Victorian Woman* 1971 p 200
5 Mrs Elton *Below the Surface* 1857 Vol. II Chapter 1
6 Charlotte Riddell *Austin Friars* 1870 Vol. I Chapter 9
7 quoted in E. R. Hayes *The Dangerous Sex* 1966 p 14
8 Eliza Warren *A Young Wife's Perplexities* 1886 p 30
9 Ibid p 35
10 Anon. *A Few Suggestions to Mothers* 1884 p 26
11 quoted in Janet Dunbar *The Early Victorian Woman* 1953 p40–41
12 'Education of Woman' *The Ladies' Cabinet of Fashion, Music and Romance* Vol. I, 1844

Chapter Seven: The Domestic Ideal
1 'A Business Man's Home' *The Ladies' Treasury* October, 1857
2 Thomas Carlyle *Past and Present* 1843 Book III, Chapter 2
3 Montague Cookson 'The Morality of Married Life' *Fortnightly Review* October 1, 1872
4 'Womanliness' *Saturday Review* August 6, 1870
5 'Sweets of Married Life' ibid October 8, 1870
6 'The Sacred Sex' ibid May 13, 1871
7 'The Maternal Instinct' ibid 8 June, 1895
8 R. A. Stanley *State of Large Towns Second Report* 1845 in E. Royston Pike *Human Documents of the Industrial Revolution* 1966 p 242
9 quoted in Ivy Pinchbeck *Women Workers and the Industrial Revolution* 1930 p 297

Chapter Eight: The Domestic Prison
1 Charles Dickens *Dombey and Son* 1848 Chapter 1
2 Charlotte Brontë *Shirley* 1849 Chapter 4
3 Geoffrey Best *Mid-Victorian Britain* 1971 p 280
4 Mrs Lynn Linton *Ourselves: A series of Essays on Women* 1870 p 50

5   Mrs Lynn Linton   *The Girl of the Period and other Social Essays*   1883   p 133
6   Mona Caird   'Marriage'   *Westminster Review*   August, 1888
7   quoted in Crow   op. cit.   p 43
8   John Angell James   *Female Piety, or the Young Woman's Friend and Guide*   1871
    p 188
9   Ibid   p 185
10 John Stewart Mill   *The Subjection of Women*   1869   Chapter 4
11 J. A. Froude   *The Nemesis of Faith*   1849   pp 112–13
12 quoted in C. W. Cunnington   *Feminine Attitudes in the Nineteenth Century*   1935
    p 208
13 Belinda Norman-Butler   *Victorian Aspirations*   1972   Chapter Six
14 J. A. Froude   op. cit.   pp 103–04

Chapter Nine: Children

1   'Lucy Luck, straw-plait worker' in *Useful Toil* ed. John Burnett   1975   p 69
2   George R. Sims   'The Dark Side of Life'   *Into Unknown England 1866–1913*
    ed. Peter Keating   1976   p 72
3   Ivy Pinchbeck and Margaret Hewitt   *Children in English Society*   Vol. II   1973
    pp 359–60
4   *British Workwoman*   November 1, 1863
6   Mrs Egerton   *The Countess's Cross*   1868
7   Frances Power Cobbe   op. cit. p 80
8   Charlotte Yonge   *Womankind*   1876   p 135
9   quoted in C. W. Cunnington   op.cit. p 185
10 quoted ibid   p 186
11 quoted ibid   p 207
    quoted in Jonathan Gathorne-Hardy   *The Rise and Fall of the British Nanny*
12 1973   p 67
    Sarah Sedgwick   'Other People's Children'   *The Day Before Yesterday* ed. Noel
13 Streatfeild   1956   p 18
14 Ibid   p 20
15 Ibid   p 15

Chapter Ten: Changing Needs in Housing

1   B. S. Rowntree   *Poverty: a Study of Town Life*   1901   p 134
2   Jack London   *The People of the Abyss*   1903   p 58
3   S. G. Checkland   *The Rise of Industrial Society in England 1815–1885*   1964
    pp 239–40
4   Ibid   pp 240–41
5   Octavia Hill   *Homes of the London Poor*   1875   p 51
6   G. and W. Grossmith   *Diary of a Nobody*   1892   Chapter 1

Chapter Eleven: Design after the Deluge

1   Elizabeth Aslin   *Nineteenth Century English Furniture*   1962   p 42
2   Georgiana Burne-Jones   *Memorials*   1904   Vol. I   pp 210–11
3   quoted in John Brandon-Jones   'C. F. A. Voysey'   *Victorian Architecture* ed.
    Peter Ferriday   1963   p 274
4   Ruskin   'The Nature of Gothic'   *The Stones of Venice*   Complete Works Vol. X
    p 194
5   William Morris   'The Beauty of Life'   Lecture to the Birmingham Society of
    Arts and School of Design   February 19, 1879 in *On Art and Socialism* ed.
    Holbrook Johnson   1947   p 79

6   quoted in E. P. Thompson *William Morris* 1955   p 124
7   Interview *The Clarion* November 19, 1892
8   quoted in E. P. Thompson op. cit. p 271
9   William Morris 'The Lesser Arts' Lecture December 4, 1877 in Holbrook op. cit. p 19
10 William Morris 'Art Under Plutocracy. Lecture November 14, 1883 ibid pp 135–36
11 quoted in Aslin op. cit. p 72
12 H. S. Goodhart-Rendel 'The Victorian Home' Ferriday op. cit. p 81
13 'Letter to her Sister' March 6, 1880 Mary Reed Bobbitt *With Dearest Love to All: The Life and Letters of Lady Jebb* 1960 p 156
14 Dresser op. cit. p 39
15 Dresser *Principles of Decorative Design* 1873 p 2
16 Ibid p 15
17 Rhoda and Agnes Garrett *Suggestions for House Decoration* 1876 p 56
18 H. J. Cooper *The Art of Furnishing on Rational and Aesthetic Principles* 1876 p 8
19 Dresser op. cit. 2 p 90

Chapter Twelve: Taste and Status

1   H. G. Wells *Ann Veronica* 1909 Chapter 17
2   H. G. Wells *Marriage* 1912 Book 2, Chapter 1
3   Ibid
4   Ibid
5   Mrs Haweis *The Art of Decoration* 1881 Chapter 1
6   Ibid
7   Ibid
8   Ibid Chapter 9
9   Ibid
10 Ibid
11 Girouard op. cit. p 43
12 H. J. Cooper op. cit. pp 115–16

Further Reading

The following books have been essential to my study, and those interested in pursuing the subject will find them useful and illuminating. The list is not intended as a comprehensive bibliography.

Studies of Victorian architecture, planning and design.
John Ruskin and William Morris are key figures, and their writings, vastly extensive especially in the case of Ruskin, should certainly be looked at. Best to apply, initially at least, to selections: for Ruskin, *Selections*, ed. K. Clark, 1964, and for Morris, Selected *Writings and Designs*, ed. Asa Briggs, 1963. Christopher Dresser wrote extensively on design. Two of his books are *Principles of Decorative Design*, 1873, and *Studies in Design*, 1879. Robert Kerr's *The Gentleman's House*, 1864, and C. J. Richardson's *The Englishman's House*, 1871, are specifically on domestic architecture, while S. H. Brooks' *City, Town and Country Architecture*, 1847 tackles some general principles of planning. In the latter part of the century there were many books on house decoration. Some of these are, Charles Eastlake's *Hints on Household Taste*, 1868; Rhoda and Agnes Garrett's *Suggestions for House Decoration*, 1876; H. J. Cooper's *The Art of Furnishing on Rational and Aesthetic Principles*, 1876; Mrs Haweis's *The Art of Decoration*, 1881; Rosamu d Marriott Watson's *The Art of the House*, 1897. Twentieth century studies of Victorian architecture include Robert Furneaux Jordan's survey *Victorian Architecture*, 1966; John Summerson's commentary *Victorian Architecture: Four Studies in Revaluation*, 1970; and a collection of essays on *Victorian Architecture* edited by Peter Ferriday, 1963. A. J. Youngson's *The Making of Classical Edinburgh*, and Hermione Hobhouse's *Bhomas Cubitt: Master Builder*, 1971, are important for the understanding of pre-Victorian expansion. Mark Girouard's *The Victorian Country House*, 1971, is another major study. John Gloag's *Victorian Comfort*, 1961, and *Victorian Taste*, 1962, are immensely helpful guides, as is Elizabeth Aslin's *Nineteenth Century English Furniture*, 1962. H. J. Dyos's *Victorian Suburb*, 1961, details the genesis and expansion of the suburb of Camberwell and illuminates rhe whole question of suburban development.

The family, the home and social responsibility.
I refer readers again to Ruskin. Studies of some of the great reformers are essential. Geoffrey Best's *Shaftesbury*, 1966, and S. E. Finer's *The Life and Times of Edwin Chadwick*, 1970 are two central ones. Asa Briggs' *Victorian Cities*, 1963, illuminates the problems of municipal responsibility. There have been a number of studies of aspects of life in the Victorian home. Marion Lochead's *The Victorian Household*, 1964, is useful. More recently, Patricia Branca's *Silent Sisterhood; Middle Class Women in the Home*, 1975; Pamela Horn's *The Rise and Fall of the Domestic Servant*, .975; and Jonathan Gathorne-Hardy's *The Rise and Fall of the British Nanny*, 1973, are all helpful. There are so many Victorian books on home-making, the household and the role of women that it is difficult to make a selection. For the earlier part of the century Sarah Stickney Ellis's

books, *Mothers of England, Daughters of England* etc., are typical. Mrs Beeton's *Book of Household Management*, 1861, is a never-ending source of information and attitudes. Look at anything by Eliza Warren for attitudes in the second half of the period. For a more feminist outlook Frances Power Cobbe's *The Duties of Women*, 1881, is reformist but not revolutionary. Specifically on children, Ivy Pinchbeck's and Margaret Hewitt's *Children in English Society*, vol. II, 1973, is invaluable. On working-class housing and home life, Peter Keating's *Into Unknown England 1866–1913*, 1976 is a useful edited selection from contemporary observers, while Octavia Hill's *Homes of the London Poor*, an account of a method of slum improvement, was reprinted in 1970.

This is a highly selective list. For books on specific aspects, look at the Notes.

Index